P9-CEN-509

The Health Risks of Imprisonment

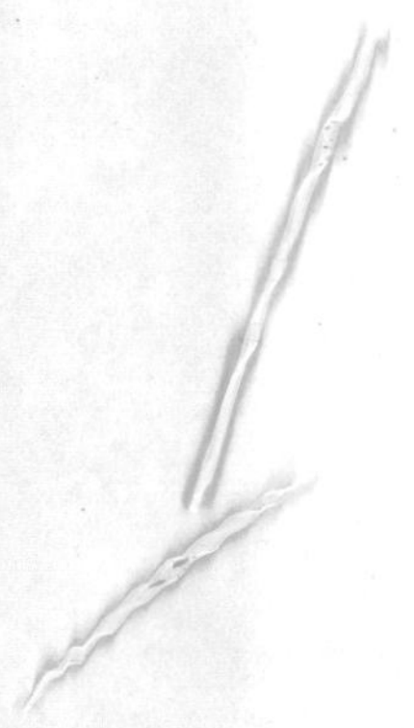

The Health Risks of Imprisonment

David A. Jones
Georgetown University Law Center

Lexington Books
D.C. Heath and Company
Lexington, Massachusetts
Toronto

Library of Congress Cataloging in Publication Data

Jones, David Arthur, 1946-
The health risks of imprisonment.

Bibliography: p.
Includes index.
1. Prisoners–Health and hygiene–United States. 2. Prisoners–Medical care–United States. I. Title.
HV8833.J65 365'.66 76-5620
ISBN 0-669-00651-3

Copyright © 1976 by D.C. Heath and Company.

All rights reserved. No part of this publication may be reproduced or transmitted in any form or by any means, electronic or mechanical, including photocopy, recording, or any information storage or retrieval system, without permission in writing from the publisher.

Published simultaneously in Canada.

Printed in the United States of America.

International Standard Book Number: 0-669-00651-3

Library of Congress Catalog Card Number: 76-5620

Contents

List of Tables

Foreword

The Health Risks of Imprisonment is the outgrowth of a pilot study which investigated a relatively unexplored area. Although considerable effort has been devoted to analysis of prison architecture, management, social structure and treatment plans, very little inquiry has been made into the health of prisoners. Such a gap has been unfortunate since, as this book demonstrates, prison is detrimental to the physical and mental health of many inmates.

In this systematic empirical study, the health of prisoners confined at Tennessee State Penitentiary during 1972-73 is compared with that of adult male criminal offenders who were on probation and parole in the same state during the same period. Medical records were coded and interviews were conducted with representative samples of all three populations. Acute physical morbidity conditions, chronic digestive conditions and selected indicators of psychological distress were reported by prisoners and these data were compared with exactly similar data for the non-incarcerated offenders who were studied, controlling for a variety of demographic variables. In addition, age-specific mortality and homicide rates were constructed and evaluated for prisoners, as were trends relating to attempted suicide and self-mutilation.

The Health Risks of Imprisonment does not propose to explain the causes of health problems among prisoners. It is primarily a descriptive study, which may be utilized as a data source by subsequent research workers and administrators. No attempt is made to assess the quality of health care delivery to prisoners; this is quite a separate matter. Data are, however, presented on the availability of medical consultations, diagnosis, and treatment of prisoners, compared with access to minimum health care by non-incarcerated offenders. The book submits that while prisoners seem to enjoy a somewhat greater access to health care than do parolees or probationers, prisoners seem to suffer from a far greater number and frequency of medical complaints.

This study has generated a realization of the likelihood that imprisonment itself may be dangerous to the health of inmates, apart, that is, from the additional dangers inherent in exposure of inmates to planned events such as medical experiments. The evidence contained in this book should serve as a warning to criminal justice professionals and to the public that a prison sentence may result in collateral consequences beyond civil disability and social incapacitation. Furthermore, this study indicates that the prison condition may be more dangerous for some inmates than for others, and that this relative dangerousness may become manifest in different ways and at different time intervals. The physical or the emotional health of one prisoner may deteriorate more within a few months of confinement, for example, than may another inmate's health after many years.

One clear implication emerges. The trend in the philosophy of the treatment of offenders away from the rehabilitation model towards the concept of "just deserts" as evidenced in the recent publication *Doing Justice*[a] on the one hand and the call for statutory fixed penalties on the other will not in fact result in the equalization of the impact of imprisonment upon different persons who have been convicted of similar crimes. There is, of course, the problem of differential deprivation, or, as it has been termed, "the problem of doing justice in an unjust society."[b] However, as this work reveals there is the further factor of differential risks to health of persons who are serving similar penalties. It is not possible to solve these problems by research methods since science cannot prove values, and different value choices can clearly be involved in the ways in which offenders are dealt with. For example, some might argue that differential deprivation is not relevant, since greater opportunities carry greater responsibilities. The "same" crime is not the same when committed by persons with different backgrounds, but rather mitigating factors might apply where the offenders' opportunities of choice were restricted.

The results of the work reported in this book do not solve these kinds of problems, rather they indicate that the solution may be more complex than might have been thought. At least, this book provides further data that needs to be considered in relation to discussions of the meaning of imprisonment in relation to any of the philosophies of treatment or punishment which might be favored at any time.

Those who have spent time in prison—whether voluntarily as staff or involuntarily as inmates—should not be surprised to learn from this study that many prisoners receive medical treatment that would be unavailable to them outside of prison. Whether the treatment objective is to remove a tumor or revise a scar by means of plastic surgery, health care delivery in prison may be of immense benefit to some prisoners. As this book relates, prisons may be most dangerous to new inmates, for those who have been confined for long periods, and for those for whom the prospect of release is uncertain.

From the research described in *The Health Risks of Imprisonment* it seems undeniable that prisoners and prison records including medical records may be studied by ethical investigators without compromising individual rights of privacy or disrupting prison routines. The author of this book sets forth a number of recommendations, some of which if implemented would facilitate social science research inside of prison and in turn should encourage greater public awareness of the prison environment.

The research design and the methodology that are shown in this book to be useful and workable should be seen more as a beginning than as an end. The health of persons who are confined at each separate institution needs to be scrutinized at periodic intervals just as does each prison's own health care provision and delivery system. Towards such an objective, this is a book which

[a]*Doing Justice*, Andrew von Hirsch, New York: Hill and Wang, 1976.

[b]Ibid.

officials, prison residents, or interested lay persons should not only read but might well cause to be replicated in each state.

Leslie T. Wilkins

Albany, 1976

Acknowledgments

I want to express my gratitude to the Honorable Winfield Dunn, D.D.S., Governor of Tennessee during this study, and to every member of his administration for supporting it, and for trusting me to tell the truth. This study was completed with the authorization and the cooperation of the Honorable Mark W. Luttrell, Commissioner of Correction, State of Tennessee, whose concern for public understanding of penology enabled me to begin my work. Both Governor Dunn, who is a dentist, and Commissioner Luttrell, who has pioneered in prison reform, understood the reasons for my request to examine the health and safety conditions inside a prison environment at a time when officials in several other states refused such permission.

There are several persons who work within the Tennessee Department of Correction to whom I owe specific recognition. Deputy Commissioner E. Ray Farley provided me with open access to all prison records without restriction, and enabled me thereby to use primary data exclusively. Assistant Commissioner Charles B. Bass provided me with open access to all areas of and all personnel within the Tennessee State Penitentiary at Nashville. Frequently, he intervened to countermand the objections to my inquiries that his subordinates raised at points of peak resistance. As a result of Commissioner Bass's personal efforts, I was permitted to remain inside the Tennessee State Penitentiary whenever I desired—day or night, weekdays and weekends—for twelve consecutive months.

Mr. Herbert G. Lee, Director of Probation and Parole, provided me with the willing cooperation of his staff, both at Nashville and within each of his eight regional offices across Tennessee. Mr. Lee supplied me with valuable advice on which I relied heavily in implementing my research design.

Mr. G.F. Rietdorf, Head Statistician, Division of Central Records, facilitated my gathering of data more than anyone else. On many occasions, he worked on his own time to retrieve files that had become scattered, in order to keep me supplied with data on an ongoing basis.

Mr. Robert Childress, Supervisor of Counseling at the Tennessee State Penitentiary, coordinated my movements inside the prison. Because of his steady trust in my integrity as a researcher, I was given access to all prisoners' psychiatric case histories, the most confidential of all medical records. I appreciate the close association I enjoyed with Mr. Rolland H. Cisson, the Supervisor of Classification, and Mr. Evans Fine, the prison psychologist. Mr. Norman Finney, Director of Treatment for the Department of Correction during the early months of my research, helped very much by acquainting me with the inner nuances of a prison system.

Mr. Harley H. Siemer, R.N., Hospital Superintendent, Tennessee State Penitentiary, provided me with unlimited assistance in locating and decoding hundreds of individual inmate medical records, as well as laboratory, x-ray, and hospital admission data. Mr. Don W. Dickinson, Director, Tennessee State Industries, provided me with records containing entries on industrial accidents and lost time among inmate workers.

I express special gratitude to Warden James H. Rose for his indulgence in agreeing to let me finish the research despite his reservations concerning my personal safety. My appreciation is extended to every correctional officer, counselor, and inmate, as well as to the probation and parole officers, probationers, and parolees, who participated in my work. Particularly, I extend my deepest appreciation to one inmate whose name, unfortunately, should not be disclosed at this time.

A number of academics facilitated the development of this study in different ways. Dr. Hans H. Toch was the first person to encourage and support my early ideas for research in criminology. Dr. Stanley B. Williams, Chairman of the Department of Sociology-Anthropology, The University of Tennessee at Martin persuaded Commissioner Luttrell to authorize the initiation of this study. Dean Richard A. Myren, Professor Fred Cohen, Dr. Robert H. Hardt and Dr. Michael J. Hindelang of the School of Criminal Justice, State University of New York at Albany, provided significant input for the formulation and execution of the project. More than to anyone else, however, I am indebted to the efforts of Professor Leslie T. Wilkins; he edited my drafts at several critical stages and guided the work through many byways, but left me total freedom to conduct the study in my own way.

1 Introduction and Background to Health Problems of Prisoners

A. Background

Traditionally prisons have been perceived by the general public as sinister places about which little is known and less understood. A few prisons have become infamous in large measure because of their use in the housing of political "offenders": the French colony at Guyana (part of which includes Devil's Island); the concentration camps of Nazi Germany (such as Auschwitz and Treblinka); Kolyma and the Siberian mines of the Soviet Union (Kara and Nertchinsk Districts) are lurid examples.[1] The prisoner of war camps maintained by the Japanese, North Koreans, and North Vietnamese were notorious, also, as were America's wartime detention camps named Andersonville and Manzanar. By far the vast majority of other prisons throughout the world have remained sequestered from public view, their mysteries well-hidden from public scrutiny.

When the prototype of the fortress-style prison opened at Auburn, New York in the early nineteenth century, public visitation was welcomed by the warden. The prison was built as a labyrinth and it contained a maze of tunnels, from which members of the public could peek at laboring prisoners.[2] From six to eight thousand observers visited Auburn Prison each year, each paying the warden twenty-five cents for the opportunity.[3] In modern times, the general public has been barred from visiting most American prisons. Even close relatives of a prisoner must obtain prior approval from the prison administration as a rule, and even after being approved they are limited to visits on assigned days of the week or the month and within a designated visiting area. Since the revolt at Attica in 1971, some states have permitted civilian volunteers from the general public to work shifts as observers inside various prisons. These experiments have not met with success, and have been abandoned by most of the states that permitted them in the first place; Massachusetts, for example, in 1972 tried, and in a year dropped, the practice.

It is interesting to note that some state officials who have been associated very closely with prisons have chosen not to go behind the prison walls. Federal and state legislators seldom visit prisons apart from an occasional and quick publicity venture; former New York Governor Nelson A. Rockefeller refused to meet the prisoners' demand for a visit to Attica in the 1971 riot. State corrections commissioners customarily have offices at the capitol of the state, far away from its rural prisons. Until quite recently, most wardens of American prisons, following a *kein eingang* (do not enter) policy, chose never to walk behind prison walls for any reason and delegated internal prison management to the deputy warden as "principal keeper."

Because American prisons have followed a kind of *kein eingang* policy throughout most of the twentieth century, the general public has been kept out of touch with the reality of prison environments. Consequently, a variety of rumors have arisen, and some pertain to the health and the safety of prison inmates. Inmates themselves (both during and after imprisonment) have criticized the standards of discipline, nutrition, hygiene, and medical care prevailing in the prisons of different states. The literature is replete with horror stories which, even if only half were true, are appalling in their revelation of prison atrocities.[4]

Prison administrators have denied repeatedly that inside conditions are as bad as some inmate critics have alleged. Unfortunately, neither inmates nor prison staff personnel are qualified to be impartial judges of conditions within their prisons. The public may listen to their testimonies, but then may encounter difficulty in deciding which aspects of the conflicting testimonies to believe. For these reasons, there is an emerging need for prison administrators to abandon the *kein eingang* attitude and permit outsiders to conduct research inside prisons.

Primary evidence on such conditions has not been available for public evaluation for one reason: access to prison records is limited in most states to a select class of individuals who hold public office within some agency of the criminal justice system. Statutes in some states forbid either the verbal or written disclosure of most prison records to anyone except prison officials themselves.[5] Statutes in other states permit some (but not necessarily all) prison records to be shared, but only after censoring.[6] In states where the statutes are not explicit on this point, prison administrators use their general discretion to guard prison records jealously. In addition to the lay public, professionals such as lawyers and physicians of the inmates have been denied access to the prison records pertaining to their clients or patients.[7]

Frequently, prison officials cite each inmate's constitutional right to privacy in support of their denial of prisoner records to outsiders.[8] The extent and the conditions of the privileged status of records—especially prison medical records—involve issues that remain in the process of litigation.[9] Obviously, there are conflicting reasons why such records should or should not be made public. Ultimately the issue of access to prison records may be decided on the basis of the relative benefits or detriments that their publication could cause. Examples of the questions at issue are: What specific prison statistics, if any, should be released to the general public? Should a prison inmate have a right to view and review prison records which pertain to himself? Should this right be extended to an inmate's lawyer or physician, with the inmate's consent? The benefits and the detriments that could be expected from the (limited or unlimited) publication of relevant prison records should be weighed and balanced against the benefits and the detriments of maintaining a standard of absolute privacy for each inmate's prison records. In the final analysis, the health and the safety of all inmates within a given institution must be weighed and balanced against the privacy each individual inmate has a right to enjoy.

In many jurisdictions the state prisoner used to be regarded as the slave of the state,[10] having forfeited, not only his liberty, but also most of his rights as a human being. Slowly but persistently this situation is changing. Enlightened jurisdictions are beginning to make at least the pretense of recognizing the state prisoner's right to retain "all the rights of an ordinary citizen except those expressly, or by necessary implication, taken from him by law."[11] With the recent emergence of widespread concern for prisoners' rights, a number of attempts have been made to draft and to implement minimum standards as well as model legislation for the custody and treatment of prisoners.[12]

Each model bill of rights for prisoners proposes a variety of safeguards. These may range from basic substantive rights that are unconditional and may not be waived (for example rights to a safe environment and to medical care), to contractual rights and duties that may be dependent upon each other. Procedural safeguards may be included to ensure that fundamental due process of law will prevail throughout the confinement stage of the criminal justice system. Nevertheless, issues continually arise regarding the application of many proposed minimum standards within each different prison. Among the most fundamental of these issues is whether the environment inside any given prison is more (or less) dangerous than (or equally as dangerous as) the environment of the outside, free-world community that the prison serves.

In its *Report on Corrections* (1973), the National Advisory Commission on Criminal Justice Standards and Goals argued that prison inmates should live in healthful surroundings (Standard 2.5):

> Each correctional agency should immediately examine and take action to fulfill the right of each person in its custody to a healthful place in which to live.[13]

The National Advisory Commission stated that prison inmates should be protected against personal abuse (Standard 2.4), including:

1. corporal punishment;
2. the use of physical force by correctional staff, except as necessary for self-defense, protection of another person from imminent physical attack, or prevention of riot or escape;
3. solitary or segregated confinement as a disciplinary or punitive measure, except as a last resort and then not exceeding beyond 10 days' duration;
4. any deprivation of clothing, bed and bedding, light, ventilation, heat, exercise, balanced diet, or hygienic necessities;
5. any act or lack of care, whether by willful act or neglect, that injures or significantly impairs the health of any offender;
6. infliction of mental distress, degradation, or humiliation.[14]

Furthermore, the National Advisory Commission specified that each prison should provide its inmates with medical care comparable to that which is obtainable by the general public (Standard 2.6):

Each correctional agency should take immediate steps to fulfill the right of offenders to medical care. This should include services guaranteeing *physical, mental*, and *social* well-being as well as treatment for *specific diseases or infirmities.* Such medical care should be *comparable in quality and availability to that obtainable by the general public. . . .*[15] (Italics added.)

How may these standards be implemented until or unless each indicator of health and safety can be measured or estimated as it exists within any given prison? Does a measurement or an estimate of these health and safety indicators conflict with each inmate's right of privacy? If so, to what extent and under what conditions should one yield to the other? These and other related questions cannot be answered intelligently without first going about the taxing process of obtaining material data in a field setting.

B. Aim and Purpose

The aim of this study is both to propose and to test a methodology for estimating the relative health risks (dangerousness) of (i) life as an inmate within a given prison, compared with (ii) life in the free world outside. The health risks of imprisonment refer to the estimated risk of harm a prisoner may expect to face during a specific period of confinement within a particular prison. Risk means the per capita frequency (rate) at which the occurrence of any kind of harm can be observed, estimated, or predicted among a group of persons over a certain interval of time. Harm includes any impairment of a person's body or mind, whether it is caused by an external source (injury) or an internal source (sickness), and whether it is temporary, permanent, or fatal in its consequence.

This study seeks to determine both systematically and empirically the relationship between the dangerousness of living inside a prison as an inmate and the dangerousness of living outside in the general community. In what ways, if any, may it be more (or less) dangerous for a human being to be confined in prison as an inmate than to remain free in the general community? For example, one might hypothesize that imprisonment protects inmates from automobile injuries, since most inmates do not operate or interact with motor vehicles. On the contrary, one might hypothesize that imprisonment exposes inmates to an accelerated danger of physical assaults, since prisoners interact with other prisoners in a limited environment on a continuous basis, and many of these prisoners are known to become violent and physically aggressive on occasion.

The study is concerned with estimating risk of harm among prison inmates as a class; in this sense, its focus is on the prisoner as victim of sickness or injury.

The cause of the sickness or injury does not matter particularly, nor is the issue to lay blame. Quite obviously, some prisoners become sick or injured as a result of the malice or negligence of others—among them fellow inmates as well as prison staff personnel—or as a result of physical conditions of the institution itself.

Excluded also is the issue of dangers that prison inmates may create for people who are not inmates, including prison staff, visitors, or the public in general. Certainly, prisoners who escape or try to escape may cause injury to others who get in their way. If prisons are unhealthy and therefore dangerous places for inmates to reside, they also may be unhealthy places for staff personnel to work. Both prisons and prisoners may cause harm to a variety of people in addition to inmates. This study separates analytically health risks to non-prisoners caused by prison or by prisoners from health risks to prisoners resulting from any cause during imprisonment. The latter is the concern here, and the inmate as victim is the focal point.

The ultimate purpose is to estimate to the fullest extent possible the overall effect of the prison experience upon any given inmate's health. For example, would the average inmate have remained less healthy, equally healthy, or more healthy had he not been imprisoned or had he been imprisoned for a shorter period of time? Does imprisonment have some positive as well as some negative effects upon the average prisoner's health? The ultimate value to be gained may be the isolation and identification of some specific causes of harm that can be shown to endanger the health or safety of prison inmates. As a result, these dangers—once they become known and realized—may be reduced or eliminated through constructive action.

C. Objectives

The principal objective of the research is to measure or estimate the *per capita* frequency (rate) at which selected indicators of health as well as selected indicators of treatment occur among adult male inmates during an interval of confinement within a state prison.

Selected indicators of health include the following: (1) *mortality*, measured from the frequency of death attributable to a specific cause, for example, homicide; (2) *morbidity*, measured or estimated from the incidence of selected acute diseases and the prevalence of selected chronic conditions, including the occurrence of injuries from assault, industrial accidents, and self-inflicted wounds; (3) *disability*, measured or estimated by days of restricted activity or days of bed confinement; and (4) *emotional distress*, estimated from actual or considered suicide attempts, actual or impending nervous breakdowns, nervousness, inertia, insomnia, trembling or perspiring hands, nightmares, fainting spells or dizziness, headaches, and heart palpitations.

Selected indicators of treatment include the following: (1) *outpatient diagnosis and treatment*–measured by frequency of consultation–by a physician, psychiatrist, dentist, eye, or other, medical specialist; (2) *hospital episodes*, measured by the *per capita* rate of admission and the average length of stay per person admitted to a prison or an outside hospital; (3) *surgical operations*, including both major and minor surgical procedures, but excluding cosmetic plastic surgery; (4) *convalescence*, measured by days of restricted activity or days of bed confinement following a hospital episode or surgery.

A second objective is to observe the differences, if any, at which each of the above indicators of health and treatment occur on the basis of age, race, length of time spent in prison, and other demographic variables. A third objective is to compare some of the rates obtained from the inmate population with rates at which the same indicators may be measured or estimated to occur among adult male probationers and adult male parolees in the same state.

D. Research Setting

The research project was conducted in Tennessee. Tennessee is situated near the latitudinal and longitudinal center of the United States. The location is important since it makes the state a crossroads between northern and southern as well as eastern and western states. Although some Tennessee natives continue to think of their state as southern in character, such a conception is not as accurate now as it may have been in the nineteenth century. Since World War II the American population has migrated in several patterns.[16] People have moved into Tennessee from all areas of the country, but especially from the middle Atlantic states and from states that border on the Great Lakes.[17] In 1970 an estimated 25.9 percent of Tennessee's white population and an estimated 25.5 percent of its non-white population had been born outside the state.[18] Thus, geographic mobility has contributed to making Tennessee a state representative of other states in terms of various social factors.[19]

On 31 December 1970, a total of 3,268 adult criminal offenders of both sexes and all races were confined within six Tennessee prisons.[20] On that date, only eighteen states confined a larger number of adult criminal offenders within state-operated facilities, as is reflected in Table 1-1. Therefore, Tennessee ranked nineteenth among the states in 1970 in terms of the size of its institutionalized adult, criminal-offender population.

The Tennessee State Penitentiary is a large prison. It is referred to as the "Main Prison" by staff of the Tennessee Department of Correction. Indeed, it is Tennessee's principal maximum security facility for adult-male, criminal offenders. Its racial composition is approximately 60 percent white and 40 percent black, although less than one-seventh of the general adult, male population of Tennessee is black. Therefore, the ratio of black prisoners to white prisoners is more balanced here than in many other American prisons.

Table 1-1
Year-End Prison Population in State Institutions, by State: 1970

State	Rank	Inmates	State	Rank	Inmates
California	1	25,033	Kansas	26	1,902
Texas	2	14,331	Oregon	27	1,800
New York	3	12,059	Iowa	28	1,747
			Mississippi	29	1,730
			Minnesota	30	1,585
Florida	4	9,187	Connecticut	31	1,568
Ohio	5	9,185	Arizona	32	1,461
Michigan	6	9,079	District of Columbia	33	1,423
Illinois	7	6,381			
Pennsylvania	8	6,289	Nebraska	34	1,001
North Carolina	9	5,969			
New Jersey	10	5,704			
Maryland	11	5,186	West Virginia	35	938
Georgia	12	5,113	New Mexico	36	742
			Nevada	37	690
			Delaware	38	596
Virginia	13	4,648	Maine	39	516
Louisiana	14	4,196	Utah	40	491
Indiana	15	4,137	Idaho	41	411
Alabama	16	3,790	South Dakota	42	391
Oklahoma	17	3,640	Montana	43	260
Missouri	18	3,413	Hawaii	44	228
Tennessee	19	3,268	New Hampshire	45	244
			Wyoming	46	231
			Vermont	47	162
Wisconsin	20	2,973	North Dakota	48	147
Washington	21	2,864			
Kentucky	22	2,849			
South Carolina	23	2,726	Alaska	–	–
Colorado	24	2,066	Arkansas	–	–
Massachusetts	25	2,053	Rhode Island	–	–

Note: hyphens (–) indicate data missing.

Source: U.S. Department of Justice, Bureau of Prisons, *National Prisoner Statistics: Prisoners in State and Federal Institutions for Adult Felons, 1968, 1969, 1970.*

In 1961 Tennessee adopted a statewide integrated system of probation and parole under the administration of the Division of Probation and Parole within the Tennessee Department of Correction. On 1 January 1972 a total of 1,138 persons of both sexes and all races were on parole in Tennessee,[21] and a total of 1,953 persons were on probation.[22] During the first eleven months of 1972, on a monthly average 142 persons were paroled from prison and 266 persons placed on probation. During the same period, on a monthly average 125 persons were released from parole and 212 persons released from probation.[23] The nature of the present research required that it be conducted in a state with a significantly large number of probationers, parolees, and prisoners. This was necessary in order to support a multivariate analysis of health and safety data according to age within race and other selected demographic variables. As many as two-thirds of the states in the United States could be expected to have populations of adult-male, criminal offenders sufficiently large to facilitate the research objectives. The existence of a sizable criminal offender population allows for a systematic empirical study only if permission to conduct a specific study can be obtained from proper authorities. Permission to conduct the present study was denied in several states before being granted in Tennessee.

E. Populations

The primary objective of the present project was to examine the health and medical treatment characteristics of prisoners confined at the Tennessee State Penitentiary during the course of its research. Therefore, the inmates who were confined there between 1 July 1972 and 30 June 1973 constituted the principal population studied. For the limited objective of making a control comparison between the health and medical characteristics of incarcerated and nonincarcerated criminal offenders, in addition two of Tennessee's nonincarcerated criminal offender populations (probationers and parolees) were observed.

Only adult males who had been convicted of a felony were confined at the Tennessee State Penitentiary during the period in question. No juvenile males under seventeen years of age and no females of any age were confined there at the time; nor was any adult male who had been convicted only of a misdemeanor. For these reasons, only probationers and parolees who were adult-male, felony offenders were studied, since only this class of probationer or parolee could be compared with the class of prisoner then confined at the Tennessee State Penitentiary.

Interstate Compact offenders were omitted from the populations (prisoners, probationers, and parolees) studied for two reasons. First, those offenders who had been convicted of a felony in Tennessee but who were serving their sentences in another state were not available. Secondly, those offenders who had been convicted of a felony in another state but who were serving their current sentences in Tennessee might not have reflected the demographic characteristics of Tennessee's own adult-male, felony populations.

New adult male prisoners who were committed to the Tennessee State Penitentiary but who had not completed the routine intake process known as "classification" (a series of physical and psychological tests, taken over about a six-week period), were omitted from the population of prisoners studied. At the time in question these prisoners were confined separately from the main prisoner population (the classification center was later transferred to another site). Their routine daily activities were different from those of the main prisoner population, and they did not interact with members of the main prisoner population except during some sports events or other on a very limited occasion.

The separate characteristics of Tennessee's main populations of prisoners, probationers, and parolees should be noted.

1. The Prisoner Population

On 1 July 1972, the general population of prisoners confined at the Tennessee State Penitentiary consisted of 1,814 adult male, felony offenders. Of these, 58.8 percent (1,067) were white and 41.2 percent (747) were black. On 30 June 1973, the general population of prisoners confined there consisted of 1,898 adult-male, felony offenders. Of these, 54.9 percent (1,042) were white and 45.1 percent (856) were black.[24] The racial composition of inmates changed from 41.2 percent black to 45.1 percent black within one year, a relative increase of 9.5 percent.

On 30 June 1973, 7.8 percent (148) of the general prisoner population at the Tennessee State Penitentiary possessed maximum security classification; 67.1 percent (1,274) possessed medium security classification; and 25.0 percent (476) possessed minimum security classification. On the same date, 87.0 percent (1,651) of the same population was classified as medically fit for full duty; 8.4 percent (160) classified as medically fit for limited duty; and 4.6 percent (87) classified as medically unfit for duty.[25]

On 30 June 1973, 59.9 percent (1,136) of the general prisoner population there consisted of first offenders; 26.6 percent (504) had one prior conviction; and 13.6 percent (258) had two or more prior convictions. The types of crime for which these prisoners were sentenced were summarized in the 1972-73 Annual Report of the Tennessee Department of Correction.[26] That summary appears in Table 1-2. The data there shows that more prisoners were serving a sentence for robbery than for any other crime; and a nearly equal number were serving a sentence for either homicide or a property crime.

Midway through the present study, a 10.0 percent random sample was obtained from the population of adult male prisoners who had been confined at the Tennessee State Penitentiary continuously between 1 July 1972 and 31 December 1972. The criminal history of each sample prisoner was studied carefully and summarized from the Federal Bureau of Investigation (FBI) record of arrests, charges, convictions and commitments ("the rap sheet"). This data indicated that an estimated 44.3 percent of the inmates confined at the Tennessee State Penitentiary during the entire second half of 1972 had been in

Table 1-2
Offense Percentage Chart: Prisoners at Tennessee State Penitentiary: 30 June 1973

Type of Crime	*N*	Percent
Homicide	422	22.24
Property Crime	408	21.50
Robbery	598	31.50
Drugs	54	2.84
Sex Crimes	191	10.07
Other*	225	11.85

*Includes crimes against persons.
Source: State of Tennessee Department of Correction, *Annual Report: 1972-73.*

some conflict with law enforcement authorities in at least one other state at some time prior to their Tennessee commitment. An estimated 15.1 percent of the same prisoner population had been in conflict with the law in at least two other states, and 14.2 percent in at least three other states.

2. The Probationer and Parolee Populations

On 1 July 1972 a total of 2,444 persons of both sexes and all races were on probation under the supervision of the Tennessee Department of Correction, Division of Probation and Parole.[27] On 30 June 1973, a total of 2,853 persons of both sexes and all races were on probation under the same supervision.[28] During that fiscal year, 2,732 persons were placed on probation by the Tennessee courts, and 2,323 persons were discharged from probation.[29]

On 1 July 1972, a total of 1,203 persons of both sexes and all races were on parole under the supervision of the Tennessee Department of Correction, Division of Probation and Parole.[30] On 30 June 1973, a total of 1,402 persons of both sexes and all races were on parole under the same supervision.[31] During that fiscal year, 1,206 persons were granted parole by the Tennessee Board of Pardons and Paroles,[32] and 1,007 persons ceased to be on parole either because they were released from parole or because they were returned to prison as a result of a parole violation.[33]

According to this data, the average person who is placed on probation or parole in Tennessee spends a little more than one year under the supervision of the Division of Probation and Parole. This is a relatively short period in comparison to the length of time probationers and parolees may remain under supervision in many other states.

Very little additional data was available concerning the characteristics of

Tennessee's population of parolees and probationers. As a result of the samples obtained, however, estimates may be made concerning a number of demographic characteristics for these populations. These estimates are summarized with Appendix A.

F. Sampling Methodology

The present objectives and research design required that a series of multistage samples be obtained for each adult-male, felony offender population (prisoners, probationers, and parolees) in Tennessee. The objectives and the design required also that several multiphase samples be obtained for various subpopulations of prisoners at the Tennessee State Penitentiary.

Six population samples were obtained at two different times. Two samples were obtained for each of the three adult-male, felony-offender populations in Tennessee—two samples of prisoners, two samples of probationers, and two samples of parolees. Each population was sampled on two separate occasions six months apart, and each time the three populations were sampled on the same date. To elaborate: two independent samples were drawn at six month intervals for each of Tennessee's three adult-male, felony-offender populations: prisoners, probationers, and parolees. In this sub-chapter and throughout this study, the two samples obtained for each of the three populations have been combined. The sample adult male prisoners represent a 20.0 percent sampling (two 10.0 percent samples) of inmates confined at the Tennessee State Penitentiary continuously for at least six months during the period studied. The sample adult male probationers represent a 20.0 percent sampling (two 10.0 percent samples) of adult male felons who were then on probation supervision across Tennessee continuously for at least six months. The sample adult male parolees represent a 30.0 percent sampling (one 10.0 percent sample and one 20.0 percent sample) of adult male felons who were then on parole supervision across Tennessee continuously for at least six months.

The three populations were sampled for the first time on 31 December 1972, and for the second time on 30 June 1973. These two dates signify respectively the midpoint and the end of the 1972-73 fiscal year for the Tennessee Department of Correction.

At different times, several subpopulations of prisoners at the Tennessee State Penitentiary were sampled for special reasons. These subpopulations included, inter alia, prisoners who were hospitalized, underwent surgery, visited physicians or clinics outside the prison, or who spent time in a mental hospital for evaluation or commitment.

Offenders who had not been members of the same population continuously for at least six months immediately prior to each sampling date were deleted from the sampling frames of each population or subpopulation sample. This was considered necessary in order to prevent some persons from being represented in the sampling frames (and thereby perhaps even in the samples, also) of two or more different offender populations at the same time. As the criminal justice process is both ongoing and dynamic, the status of some criminal offenders may change abruptly as time moves forward. For example: a prisoner becomes a parolee when he is released from prison and placed under supervision in the community; a parolee who violates a condition of his parole may be returned to prison as a parole violator, and then he becomes a prisoner once again. Now a person who has been both a prisoner and a parolee during the same six month period may reflect the health characteristics of both populations, but he cannot be shown to reflect the health characteristics of either population exclusively. By including only those offenders who were members of the same felony-offender population continuously for at least six months, each of the population sampling frames used was autonomous in relation to the other two sampling frames utilized on the same date. Hence, during the same six month interval no individual person could have been sampled as both prisoner and parolee, and no person could have been sampled as both probationer and prisoner.

One other important reason influenced the decision to remove from each sampling frame offenders who had not been members of the same population continuously for at least six months. The intended objectives were to observe the effects, if any, that each particular penological condition (imprisonment, probation, or parole) may have exerted upon an offender's health, safety, or access to and use of medical treatment facilities. It was felt that at least six months might normally be required for a person to become affected by a particular penological condition. For a probationer who becomes sick during his first few months on probation may have incurred the illness prior to the time when he was placed on probation, during the commission of his crime; or in the period elapsing before discovery of his crime. Similarly, a prisoner who becomes sick during his first few months in prison may have incurred the illness while he was in jail or out in the free world before his arrival at prison. Finally, a parolee who becomes sick during his first few months on parole may have incurred the illness while he was still in prison.

2 Morbidity Trends: Acute Physical Conditions

A. Terms Relating to Acute Conditions

A morbidity condition, or simply a condition, is a person's departure from a state of physical or mental well-being for any reason whatsoever. A condition is "acute" if it has lasted less than three months and has involved either medical attention or restriction of activity.[1] Conditions except impairments are classified by type in the *Eighth Revision International Classification of Diseases, Adapted for Use in the United States* (1968),[2] referred to as the "ICDA." The ICDA distinguishes conditions into those that are illnesses and those that are injuries. A condition is an injury if it was caused by an accident, by poisoning, or from violence;[3] all other conditions are illnesses.[4] Here illnesses are referred to as sicknesses since this word is used more commonly by laymen, and therefore was used in the questionnaires and interviews that formed the basis for this study. Here, but not in the ICDA, some tables combine sicknesses and injuries as "total conditions."

Acute conditions are measured or estimated according to incidence, which is the number or estimated number of conditions having their onset in a particular time period among members of a specific population. A condition is considered to have had its onset when it was first noticed by the person who experienced the condition or by his physician, whoever discovered the condition first.[5] A condition may be, but does not have to be, accompanied by disability or by the need for restricting activity or for treatment.

B. Incidence of Acute Physical Conditions

The incidence of acute physical conditions is measured according to the reported number of separate physical conditions having their onset within a twelve month period among members of a particular population, and is summarized as a rate per 100 persons who were members of that population during the period. This study estimates the incidence of acute physical conditions separately for each adult-male, criminal-offender population (prisoners, probationers, and parolees) which it considers. The estimate of acute physical conditions for these three populations is based on the number of separate, acute physical conditions per 100 members of each population that had their onset during the twelve month period beginning 1 July 1972 and ending 30 June 1973. For each of the three study populations, the incidence of acute physical conditions is estimated separately according to age, race, age within race, marital status, and education. Only the incidence of acute physical conditions is presented in this chapter. The incidence of acute mental conditions is discussed in Chapters Four and Five. For this reason, acute physical conditions will be referred to simply as acute conditions for the balance of this chapter, similarly, sicknesses and injuries mean acute physical sicknesses and injuries.

1. Incidence by Age and Race

As Table 2-1 illustrates, black prisoners of all ages combined reported a higher incidence of sicknesses than did white prisoners of all ages combined. Nevertheless, the reported incidence of injuries was virtually the same for black and white prisoners of all ages combined. Among prisoners of both races combined, those

Table 2-1
Sicknesses and Injuries Reported* in Latest Twelve-Month Period: Adult Male Prisoners, by Age within Race

Race and Age	Sicknesses		Injuries		Total Conditions	
	Sample	Estimated Rate	Sample	Estimated Rate	Sample	Estimated Rate
Both Races						
17 years and over	882	432.4	190	93.1	1072	525.5
17-24 years	248	620.0	58	145.0	306	765.0
25-34 years	358	411.5	74	85.1	432	497.0
35-44 years	94	254.1	36	97.3	130	351.4
45 years and over	182	455.0	22	55.0	204	510.0
White						
17 years and over	466	398.3	110	94.0	576	492.3
17-24 years	94	552.9	32	188.2	126	741.2
25-34 years	178	370.8	38	79.2	216	450.0
35-44 years	52	216.7	26	108.3	78	325.0
45 years and over	142	507.1	14	50.0	156	557.1
Black						
17 years and over	416	478.2	80	92.0	496	570.1
17-24 years	154	669.6	26	113.0	180	782.6
25-34 years	180	461.5	36	92.3	216	553.8
35-44 years	42	323.1	10	76.9	52	400.0
45 years and over	40	333.3	8	66.7	48	400.0

*Rates per 100 persons (estimates based on probability samples).

between 17 and 24 years of age reported by far the highest incidence of sicknesses and injuries. Prisoners between 35 and 44 years of age reported the lowest incidence of sicknesses, but prisoners over 45 years old reported the lowest incidence of injuries.

Black prisoners reported approximately one more sickness per year per person than did white prisoners in all age brackets under 45 years of age. White prisoners who were over 45 years old reported a higher incidence of both sicknesses and injuries than did black prisoners in this age bracket. White prisoners between 35 and 44 years of age reported a higher incidence of injuries than did black prisoners in this age bracket. However, black prisoners between 25 and 34 years of age reported a higher incidence of injuries than did their counterpart white prisoners. This appears to have been true also for black prisoners who were 45 years of age or older compared with white prisoners in this age bracket, although there were only twelve black prisoners who had reached their 45th birthday.

As Table 2-2 illustrates, black parolees of all ages combined reported a slightly higher incidence of sicknesses than did white parolees of all ages combined. On the contrary, white parolees of all ages combined reported a slightly higher incidence of injuries than did black parolees of all ages combined. Among parolees of both races combined, persons between 24 and 34 years of age reported the highest incidence of sicknesses but the lowest incidence of injuries. Parolees between 17 and 24 years of age reported the lowest incidence of sicknesses. The reported injury rate was nearly the same for parolees between 17 and 24 years of age and those between 35 and 44 years of age. Parolees over 45 years old reported the lowest incidence of injuries.

Black and white parolees between 17 and 24 years of age reported sicknesses at about the same rate. So did black and white parolees between 25 and 34 years of age. However, parolees between 25 and 34 years old reported sicknesses at about twice the rate of those under 25 years old. White parolees who were over 45 years old reported the highest incidence of sicknesses among parolees of both races and all age intervals. Black parolees between 25 and 34 years of age reported the highest incidence of sicknesses among black parolees of all age intervals. White parolees between 35 and 44 years of age reported the lowest incidence of sicknesses among parolees of both races and all age intervals. Black parolees between 17 and 24 years of age reported the lowest incidence of sicknesses among black parolees of all age intervals.

Black parolees between 25 and 34 years of age reported about the same incidence of injuries as white parolees in this age bracket and white parolees between 35 and 44 years of age. Black parolees between 35 and 44 years of age reported about the same incidence of injuries as white parolees between 17 and 24 years of age and white parolees who were over 45 years old. Among parolees of both races and all age intervals, black parolees between 35 and 44 years of age reported the highest incidence of injuries, followed closely by white parolees

Table 2-2
Sicknesses and Injuries Reported* in Latest Twelve-Month Period: Adult Male Parolees, by Age within Race

Race and Age	Sicknesses		Injuries		Total Conditions	
	Sample	Estimated Rate	Sample	Estimated Rate	Sample	Estimated Rate
Both Races						
17 years and over	197	55.7	75	21.1	272	76.8
17-24 years	41	36.0	27	24.3	68	59.7
25-34 years	96	76.2	21	16.3	117	90.7
35-44 years	30	41.7	18	25.0	48	66.7
45 years and over	30	71.4	9	21.4	39	92.9
White						
17 years and over	110	53.9	46	23.6	156	76.5
17-24 years	23	35.4	21	35.0	44	67.7
25-34 years	56	75.7	12	16.0	68	33.3
35-44 years	15	32.6	7	16.7	22	47.8
45 years and over	16	84.2	6	33.3	22	115.8
Black						
17 years and over	87	58.0	29	18.2	116	73.0
17-24 years	18	36.7	6	11.8	24	47.1
25-34 years	40	76.9	9	16.7	49	90.7
35-44 years	15	57.7	11	36.7	26	86.7
45 years and over	14	60.9	3	12.5	17	70.8

*Rates per 100 persons (estimates based on probability samples).

between 17 and 24 years of age. Among parolees of both races and all age intervals, black parolees between 17 and 24 years of age reported the lowest incidence of injuries, followed closely by black parolees over 45 years old. Among white parolees of all age intervals, those between 25 and 34 years of age reported the lowest incidence of injuries, followed closely by those between 35 and 44 years of age.

As Table 2-3 illustrates, white probationers of all ages combined reported a minutely higher incidence of sicknesses than black probationers of all ages combined. There was no significant difference between the incidence of reported injuries experienced by black probationers and white probationers of all ages combined. Among probationers of both races combined, those who were 45 years old reported the highest incidence of sicknesses, but the lowest incidence of injuries. Among probationers of both races and combined, those between 25 and 34 years of age reported the lowest incidence of sicknesses. Among probationers of both races combined, those between 17 and 24 years of age

Table 2-3
Sicknesses and Injuries Reported* in Latest Twelve-Month Period: Adult Male Probationers, by Marital Status

Race and Age	Sicknesses		Injuries		Total Conditions	
	Sample	Estimated Rate	Sample	Estimated Rate	Sample	Estimated Rate
Both Races						
17 years and over	129	51.0	65	25.9	194	76.7
17-24 years	79	54.9	41	28.5	120	83.3
25-34 years	19	28.8	19	29.2	38	57.6
35-44 years	10	43.5	4	18.2	14	60.9
45 years and over	21	105.0	1	5.0	22	110.0
White						
17 years and over	104	51.5	52	25.9	156	77.2
17-24 years	64	55.7	34	29.6	98	85.2
25-34 years	16	29.1	13	24.1	29	52.7
35-44 years	7	41.2	4	23.5	11	64.7
45 years and over	17	113.3	1	6.7	18	120.0
Black						
17 years and over	25	49.0	13	26.0	38	74.5
17-24 years	15	51.7	7	24.1	22	75.9
25-34 years	3	27.3	6	54.6	9	81.8
35-44 years	3	50.0	0	0.0	3	50.0
45 years and over	4	80.0	0	0.0	4	80.0

*Rates per 100 persons (estimates based on probability samples).

shared the highest reported incidence of injuries with those between 25 and 34 years of age.

The incidence of reported sicknesses did not vary significantly among probationers by race within age intervals. Among probationers of both races and all age intervals, black probationers between 25 and 34 years of age reported the highest incidence of injuries. Among white probationers in all age intervals, those between 17 and 24 years of age reported the highest incidence of injuries. No sample black probationer over 35 years old reported being injured, but white probationers over 45 years old reported a slight incidence of injuries.

Ratios may be used to depict the differences, if any, and the direction of differences between reported sickness or injury rates for one population in comparison with another population. A ratio of 1.00 indicates that the reported rate of the population represented in the numerator is equal to the reported rate of the population represented in the denominator. A ratio of 1.01 or greater indicates that the reported rate of the population represented in the numerator is greater than that of the population represented in the denominator. A ratio of 0.99 or less indicates that the reported rate of the population represented in the denominator is greater than that of the population represented in the numerator.

The present principal objective is to learn what impact, if any, imprisonment may have upon the sickness or the injury rates of convicted criminal offenders. Thus, reported sickness and injury rates for probationers who have not been imprisoned would seem to be the most suitable base rates with which to compare reported rates for prisoners and parolees. These comparisons are made in Table 2-4, using four sets of ratios, each set being broken down by age within race. Two of the four sets of ratios pertain to reported sickness rates, and two pertain to reported injury rates. One set of sickness ratios and one set of injury ratios represent a comparison of appropriate rates for prisoners (numerator) in relation to comparable rates for probationers (denominator). One set of sickness ratios and one set of injury ratios represent a comparison of appropriate rates for parolees (numerator) in relation to comparable rates for probationers (denominator).

Table 2-4
Reported* Sickness and Injury Rates: Adult Male Prisoners and Parolees Compared with Adult Male Probationers, by Age within Race

Race and Age	Ratio: Rates for Prisoners/Probationers		Ratio: Rates for Parolees/Probationers	
	Sickness	Injury	Sickness	Injury
Both Races				
17 years and over	8.48	3.59	1.09	0.81
17-24 years	11.29	5.09	0.66	0.85
25-34 years	14.29	2.91	2.65	0.56
35-44 years	5.84	5.35	0.96	1.37
45 years and over	4.33	11.00	0.68	4.28
White				
17 years and over	7.73	3.63	1.05	0.91
17-24 years	9.93	6.36	0.64	1.18
25-34 years	12.74	3.29	2.60	0.66
35-44 years	5.26	4.61	0.79	0.71
45 years and over	4.48	7.46	0.74	4.97
Black				
17 years and over	9.76	3.54	1.18	0.70
17-24 years	12.95	4.69	0.71	0.49
25-34 years	16.90	1.69	2.82	0.31
35-44 years	6.46		1.15	–
45 years and over	4.17		0.76	–

*Estimates based on probability samples.

When reported sickness rates for prisoners and probationers are compared, these rates for the prisoners are substantially higher than comparable rates for the probationers at all age brackets of both races. The ratio for offenders of both races and all ages is 8.48, the ratio is higher for black offenders (ratio: 9.76) than for white offenders (ratio: 7.73). Among offenders of both races combined, those between 25 and 34 years of age had the highest ratio (ratio: 14.29) followed by those under 25 years old (ratio: 11.29); those over 45 years old had the lowest ratio (ratio: 4.33) followed by those between 35 and 44 years of age (ratio: 5.84). This pattern remained true for each race when measured separately by age intervals.

When reported injury rates for prisoners and probationers are compared, these rates for the prisoners are substantially higher than comparable rates for the probationers at all age brackets of both races. However, prisoner injury rates are not higher than probationer injury rates by as much as prisoner sickness rates are higher than probationer sickness rates. The ratio for offenders of both races and all ages is 3.59. This ratio is about the same for white (ratio: 3.63) and black (ratio: 3.54) offenders. Among offenders of both races combined, those over 45 years old had the highest ratio (ratio: 11.00), followed by those between 35 and 44 years of age (ratio: 5.35) and those under 25 years old (ratio: 5.09); while those between 25 and 34 years of age had the lowest ratio (ratio: 2.91). This pattern remained somewhat true for each race when measured separately by age intervals. However, white offenders under 25 years old had a higher ratio (ratio: 6.36) than those between 35 and 44 years of age (ratio: 4.61). Black probationers over 35 years old did not report any injuries, so no ratio could be computed for black offenders over 35 years old.

When reported sickness rates for parolees and probationers are compared, these ratios do not form a pattern as consistent as that of the ratios based on a comparison of rates for prisoners and probationers. The ratio for offenders of both races and all ages is 1.09. This ratio is only slightly higher for black offenders (ratio: 1.18) than for white offenders (ratio: 1.05). Among offenders of both races combined, rates for parolees exceed rates for probationers only in the 25 to 34 year-old age bracket (ratio: 2.65); and the ratios are 0.96, 0.68 and 0.66 for the 35 to 44 year-old age group, the age group over 45 years old, and the age group under 25 years old respectively. This pattern remained rather true for each race separately. Unlike white offenders between 35 and 44 years of age, black offenders in this age bracket reflected higher reported sickness rates for parolees than for probationers (white ratio: 0.79; black ratio: 1.15). The 25 to 34 year-old age group of each race reflected higher reported sickness rates for parolees than for probationers (white ratio: 2.60; black ratio: 2.82). In the age groups under 25 years and over 45 years old, black offenders had slightly higher ratios than white offenders (ratios under 25 years old: black: 0.71; white: 0.64; ratios over 45 years old: black: 0.76; white: 0.74).

When reported injury rates for parolees and probationers are compared, the ratios are fairly inconsistent in the same way as the sickness ratios are for the same populations. The ratio for offenders of both races and all ages is 0.81; this ratio is slightly higher for white offenders (ratio: 0.91) than for black offenders (ratio: 0.70). Among offenders of both races combined, those over 45 years old had the highest ratio (ratio: 4.28) followed by those between 35 and 44 years of age (ratio: 1.37); while those between 25 and 34 years of age had the lowest ratio (ratio: 0.56) followed by those under 25 years old (ratio: 0.85). White offenders under 25 years old reflected a higher reported injury rate for parolees than for probationers (ratio: 1.18), but the reverse is true for black offenders in the same age bracket (ratio: 0.49). Sample black probationers over 35 years old did not report any injuries, so no ratio could be computed for black offenders over 35 years old.

2. *Incidence by Marital Status*

Table 2-5 summarizes the reported incidence of sicknesses and injuries for prisoners of both races and all ages by marital status (as listed in records and verified by the respondents). Single prisoners reported the highest incidence of sicknesses, followed by separated prisoners, married prisoners, divorced prisoners, and widowed prisoners.

Married prisoners reported the highest incidence of injuries, followed closely by divorced prisoners, and by single prisoners. Separated prisoners reported a much lower incidence of injuries, and sample widowed prisoners reported no injuries at all.

Table 2-6 summarizes the reported incidence of sicknesses and injuries for parolees of both races and all ages, according to marital status. Married parolees reported the highest incidence of sicknesses, followed by divorced parolees, separated parolees, single parolees, and widowed parolees.

Table 2-5
Sicknesses and Injuries Reported* in Latest Twelve-Month Period: Adult Male Prisoners, by Marital Status

Marital Status	Sicknesses		Injuries		Total Conditions	
	Sample	Estimated Rate	Sample	Estimated Rate	Sample	Estimated Rate
Single	376	522.2	66	91.7	442	613.9
Married	360	395.6	100	109.9	460	505.5
Widowed	24	266.7	0	0.0	24	266.7
Separated	64	492.3	4	30.8	68	523.1
Divorced	58	305.3	18	94.7	76	400.0

*Rates per 100 persons (estimates based on probability samples).

Table 2-6
Sicknesses and Injuries Reported* in Latest Twelve-Month Period: Adult Male Parolees, by Marital Status

Marital Status	Sicknesses		Injuries		Total Conditions	
	Sample	Estimated Rate	Sample	Estimated Rate	Sample	Estimated Rate
Single	42	43.8	27	29.0	69	71.9
Married	93	70.5	15	11.4	108	81.8
Widowed	4	26.7	4	26.7	8	53.3
Separated	31	54.4	15	25.0	46	76.7
Divorced	36	63.2	15	26.3	51	89.5

*Rates per 100 persons (estimates based on probability samples).

Divorced parolees reported the highest incidence of injuries, followed by married parolees, separated parolees, and single parolees. Widowed parolees reported the lowest incidence of injuries.

Table 2-7 summarizes the reported incidence of sicknesses and injuries for probationers of both races and all ages according to marital status. Widowed probationers reported a sickness rate of 100.0 per 100 persons, although only two widowers were included in the sample of probationers. Reported sickness rates for other probationers were about half of that for widowers and did not vary widely by marital status.

Divorced probationers reported the highest incidence of injuries, followed by single probationers; married probationers reported a lower incidence of injuries, as did separated probationers. The two sample probationers who were widowed did not report any injuries at all.

Table 2-7
Sicknesses and Injuries Reported* in Latest Twelve-Month Period: Adult Male Probationers, by Marital Status

Marital Status	Sicknesses		Injuries		Total Conditions	
	Sample	Estimated Rate	Sample	Estimated Rate	Sample	Estimated Rate
Single	44	51.2	29	34.1	73	84.9
Married	59	49.2	22	18.5	81	67.5
Widowed	2	100.0	0	0.0	2	100.0
Separated	8	57.1	2	14.3	10	71.4
Divorced	13	43.3	11	36.7	24	80.0

*Rates per 100 persons (estimates based on probability samples).

Table 2-8 contains ratios of reported sickness and injury rates for prisoners and parolees compared with probationers, each set of ratios being broken down by marital status. In the comparison of reported sickness rates for prisoners and probationers, single offenders had the highest ratio (ratio: 10.20), followed by those who were separated (ratio: 8.62) and those who were married (ratio: 8.04). Widowed offenders had the lowest ratio (ratio: 2.67), followed by divorced offenders (ratio: 7.05).

In the comparison of reported injury rates for prisoners and probationers, married offenders had the highest ratio (ratio: 5.94). Separated offenders had the lowest ratio (ratio: 2.15), followed by those who were divorced (ratio: 2.58) and those who were single (ratio: 2.69). The ratio for offenders who were widowed could not be computed, since the two probationers who were widowed did not report any injuries.

In the comparison of reported sickness rates for parolees and probationers, divorced offenders had the highest ratio (ratio: 1.46) followed closely by married offenders (ratio: 1.43). Widowed offenders had the lowest ratio (ratio: 0.27), followed by those who were single (ratio: 0.86) and those who were separated (ratio: 0.95).

In the comparison of reported injury rates for parolees and probationers, separated offenders had the highest ratio (ratio: 1.75). Married offenders had the lowest ratio (ratio: 0.62), followed by those who were divorced (ratio: 0.72) and those who were single (ratio: 0.85). The ratio for offenders who were widowed could not be computed, since the two probationers who were widowed did not report any injuries.

3. Incidence by Education

Table 2-9 summarizes the reported incidence of sicknesses and injuries for prisoners of both races and all ages by education. Prisoners with twelve years of

Table 2-8
Reported* Sickness and Injury Rates: Adult Male Prisoners and Parolees Compared with Adult-Male Probationers, by Marital Status

Marital Status	Ratio: Rates for Prisoners/Probationers		Ratio: Rates for Parolees/Probationers	
	Sickness	Injury	Sickness	Injury
Single	10.20	2.69	0.86	0.85
Married	8.04	5.94	1.43	0.62
Widowed	2.67		0.27	
Separated	8.62	2.15	0.95	1.75
Divorced	7.05	2.58	1.46	0.72

*Estimates based on probability samples.

Table 2-9
Sicknesses and Injuries Reported* in Latest Twelve-Month Period: Adult Male Prisoners, by Education

Education in Years of School Completed	Sicknesses		Injuries		Total Conditions	
	Sample	Rate	Sample	Rate	Sample	Rate
0-6	164	468.6	4	11.4	168	480.0
7-8	172	409.5	52	123.8	224	533.3
9-11	314	378.3	69	83.1	383	461.4
12 or over	232	527.3	42	95.5	274	622.7

*Rates per 100 persons (estimates based on probability samples).

education (high school graduates) or more reported the highest incidence of sicknesses, followed by those with less than seven years of education (grade school). Prisoners with between nine and eleven years of education (some high school) reported the lowest incidence of sicknesses, followed by those with seven or eight years of education (junior high school).

Prisoners with seven or eight years of education reported the highest incidence of injuries, followed by those with twelve years or more of education, and those with between nine and eleven years of education. Prisoners with less than seven years of education reported the lowest incidence of injuries.

Table 2-10 summarizes the reported incidence of sicknesses and injuries for parolees of both races and all ages by education. Parolees with between nine and eleven years of education reported the highest incidence of sicknesses, followed closely by those with less than seven years of education. Parolees with seven or eight years of education reported the lowest incidence of sicknesses, followed by those with twelve years or more of education.

Table 2-10
Sicknesses and Injuries Reported* in Latest Twelve-Month Period: Adult Male Parolees, by Education

Education in Years of School Completed	Sicknesses		Injuries		Total Conditions	
	Sample	Estimated Rate	Sample	Estimated Rate	Sample	Estimated Rate
0-6	36	85.7	8	19.1	44	104.8
7-8	18	22.2	7	9.0	25	30.9
9-11	78	89.7	36	40.0	114	126.7
12 or over	56	45.5	19	15.5	75	61.0

*Rates per 100 persons (estimates based on probability samples).

Parolees with between nine and eleven years of education reported the highest incidence of injuries. Parolees with seven or eight years of education reported the lowest incidence of injuries, followed by those with twelve years or more of education and those with less than seven years of education.

Table 2-11 summarizes the reported incidence of sicknesses and injuries for probationers of both races and all ages by education. Probationers with less than seven years of education reported the highest incidence of sicknesses, followed by those with twelve years or more of education and those with seven or eight years of education. Probationers with between nine and eleven years of education reported the lowest incidence of sicknesses.

Probationers with twelve years or more of education reported the highest incidence of injuries, followed closely by those with between nine and eleven years of education. Probationers with less than seven years of education reported the lowest incidence of injuries, followed by those with seven or eight years of education.

Table 2-12 contains ratios of reported sickness and injury rates for prisoners and parolees, compared with probationers, each set of ratios being broken down by education. In the comparison of reported sickness rates for prisoners and probationers, offenders with between nine and eleven years of education had the highest ratio (ratio: 10.09) followed by those with twelve years or more of education (ratio: 9.76). The offenders with less than seven years of education had the lowest ratio (ratio: 7.24) followed by those with seven or eight years of education (ratio: 8.19).

In the comparison of reported injury rates for prisoners and probationers, offenders with seven or eight years of education had the highest ratio (ratio: 5.63). Offenders with less than seven years of education had the lowest ratio (ratio: 0.97), followed by those with between nine and eleven years of education (ratio: 2.53) and those with twelve years or more of education (ratio: 2.87).

Table 2-11
Sicknesses and Injuries Reported* in Latest Twelve-Month Period: Adult Male Probationers, by Education

Education in Years of School Completed	Sicknesses		Injuries		Total Conditions	
	Sample	Estimated Rate	Sample	Estimated Rate	Sample	Estimated Rate
0-6	11	64.7	2	11.8	13	76.5
7-8	30	50.0	13	22.0	43	71.7
9-11	30	37.5	26	32.9	56	70.0
12 or over	47	54.0	29	33.3	76	87.4

*Rates per 100 persons (estimates based on probability samples).

Table 2-12
Reported* Sickness and Injury Rates: Adult Male Prisoners and Parolees Compared with Adult Male Probationers, by Education

Education in Years of School Completed	Ratio: Rates for Prisoners/Probationers		Ratio: Rates for Parolees/Probationers	
	Sickness	Injury	Sickness	Injury
0-6	7.24	0.97	1.32	1.62
7-8	8.19	5.63	0.44	0.41
9-11	10.09	2.53	2.39	1.22
12 or over	9.76	2.87	0.84	0.47

*Estimates based on probability samples.

In the comparison of reported sickness rates for parolees and probationers, offenders with between nine and eleven years of education had the highest ratio (ratio: 2.39) followed by those with less than seven years of education (ratio: 1.32). Offenders who had seven or eight years of education had the lowest ratio (ratio: 0.44) followed by those with twelve years or more of education (ratio: 0.84).

In the comparison of reported injury rates for parolees and probationers, offenders with less than seven years of education had the highest ratio (ratio: 1.62) followed by those with between nine and eleven years of education (ratio: 1.22). Offenders with seven or eight years of education had the lowest ratio (ratio: 0.41) followed by those with twelve years or more of education (ratio: 0.47).

4. Incidence by Offense Category

This study initially divided offenses into two descriptive types: violent offenses and nonviolent offenses. Violent offenses were subdivided into four subtypes: (1) homicide, including all offenses causing death; (2) sexual crimes, including all offenses where sexual contact occurred between offender and victim; (3) assaults and (4) robbery. Nonviolent offenses were subdivided into two subtypes: (5) property crimes and (6) public-order crimes, in which no person was injured or threatened, and no property was stolen or destroyed.

The reported incidence of sicknesses and injuries was summarized for offenders of both races and all ages by the offense for which they were serving their current sentences. When an offender was serving a sentence for two or more separate offenses concurrently, the study classified him according to the more or most serious offense. Violent offenses were assumed to be more serious than nonviolent offenses. Homicide was assumed to be more serious than other violent offenses. Sexual assaults were assumed to be more serious than nonsexual assaults. All actual physical assaults (batteries) were assumed to be more serious than robbery, since robbery may include actual physical contact (battery) or it may include only the threat of physical contact. The word "assault" is used here to mean battery, the actual contact by the offender with the victim's body. Among the nonviolent offenses, those against the victim's property were assumed to be more serious than public-order offenses. Violent offenses include all felonies that cause harm or a substantial risk of harm to the victim's body. Nonviolent offenses include all felonies that do not cause harm or a substantial risk of harm to the victim's body. Public-order offenses include all felonies that are nonviolent and do not cause harm or a substantial risk of harm to property (illegal drug use or sale; consensual sexual offenses; gambling; contempt; other simply *mala prohibita* offenses).

Table 2-13 summarizes the reported incidence of sicknesses and injuries for prisoners of both races and all ages by their offense as defined. Prisoners who were serving a sentence for assault reported the highest incidence of both sicknesses and injuries. Prisoners who were serving a sentence for robbery reported the lowest incidence of sicknesses, and prisoners who were serving a sentence for sexual assault reported the lowest incidence of injuries. Among other prisoners, those who were serving a sentence for public-order offenses reported the second highest incidence of sicknesses, followed by prisoners

Table 2-13
Sicknesses and Injuries Reported* in Latest Twelve-Month Period: Adult Male Prisoners, by Type of Offense

Type of Offense	Sicknesses		Injuries		Total Conditions	
	Sample	Estimated Rate	Sample	Estimated Rate	Sample	Estimated Rate
Total Violent Offenses	609	435.0	133	95.0	742	530.0
Homicide	194	404.2	42	87.5	236	491.7
Sexual	124	476.9	18	69.2	142	546.2
Assaults	60	1000.0	12	200.0	72	1200.0
Robbery	231	385.0	61	101.7	292	486.7
Total Nonviolent Offenses	277	432.8	57	89.1	334	521.9
Property	253	421.7	57	95.0	310	516.7
Public-Order	24	600.0	0	0.0	24	600.0

*Rates per 100 persons (estimates based on probability samples).

serving time for sexual assault, property offenses, and homicide. Prisoners who were serving a sentence for robbery reported the second highest incidence of injuries, followed by those serving time for property offenses, homicide, and public-order offenses, none of whom had any injuries. There is very little difference between the reported sickness rates for prisoners serving time for violent offenses generally and nonviolent offenses generally. Similarly, there is only a small difference between the reported injury rates for prisoners serving time for violent offenses generally and nonviolent offenses generally.

Table 2-14 summarizes the reported incidence of sicknesses and injuries for parolees of both races and all ages by their offense as defined. Parolees who were serving a sentence for sexual assault reported the highest incidence of both sicknesses and injuries. Parolees who were serving a sentence for robbery reported the lowest incidence of both sicknesses and injuries. Among other parolees, those who were serving a sentence for assault reported the second highest incidence of sicknesses, followed by those serving a sentence for homicide, property offenses, and public-order offenses. Parolees who were serving a sentence for public-order offenses reported the second highest incidence of injuries, followed by those serving a sentence for property offenses, assault, and homicide. Parolees serving a sentence for violent offenses generally reported a higher incidence of sicknesses than parolees serving a sentence for nonviolent offenses generally. Parolees serving a sentence for violent offenses generally reported a lower incidence of injuries than parolees serving a sentence for nonviolent offenses generally.

Table 2-14
Sicknesses and Injuries Reported* in Latest Twelve-Month Period: Adult Male Parolees, by Type of Offense

Type of Offense	Sicknesses		Injuries		Total Conditions	
	Sample	Estimated Rate	Sample	Estimated Rate	Sample	Estimated Rate
Total Violent Offenses	111	65.3	17	10.0	128	75.3
Homicide	52	58.4	10	11.2	62	69.7
Sexual	7	175.0	2	50.0	9	225.0
Assaults	30	100.0	4	13.3	34	113.0
Robbery	22	46.8	1	2.1	23	48.9
Total Nonviolent Offenses	95	50.0	60	31.6	155	81.6
Property	73	50.7	40	27.8	113	78.5
Public-Order	22	47.8	20	43.5	42	91.3

*Rates per 100 persons (estimates based on probability samples).

Table 2-15 summarizes the reported incidence of sicknesses and injuries for probationers of both races and all ages by their offense as defined. Probationers who were serving a sentence for sexual assault reported the highest incidence of sicknesses, followed by probationers who were serving a sentence for assault. Probationers who were serving a sentence for property offenses reported the third highest incidence of sicknesses, followed by those serving a sentence for homicide and public-order offenses. Probationers who were serving a sentence for robbery did not report any sicknesses at all. Probationers who were serving a sentence for public-order offenses reported the highest incidence of injuries, followed by those serving a sentence for property offenses, homicide, and assault. Probationers who were serving a sentence for sexual assault reported no injuries, nor did those serving a sentence for robbery. As with parolees, probationers serving a sentence for violent offenses generally reported a higher incidence of sicknesses than probationers serving a sentence for nonviolent offenses generally. As with parolees, also, probationers serving a sentence for violent offenses generally reported a lower incidence of injuries than probationers serving a sentence for nonviolent offenses generally.

Table 2-16 contains ratios of reported sickness and injury rates for prisoners and parolees, compared with probationers, each set of ratios being broken down by offense category. In the comparison of reported sickness rates for prisoners and probationers, nonviolent offenders had a higher ratio (ratio: 9.17) than violent offenders (ratio: 6.96). Among violent offenders, those serving a

Table 2-15
Sicknesses and Injuries Reported* in Latest Twelve-Month Period: Adult Male Probationers, by Type of Offense

Type of Offense	Sicknesses		Injuries		Total Conditions	
	Sample	Estimated Rate	Sample	Estimated Rate	Sample	Estimated Rate
Total Violent Offenses	25	62.5	6	15.0	31	77.5
Homicide	10	47.6	5	23.8	15	71.4
Sexual	6	100.0	0	0.0	6	100.0
Assaults	9	90.0	1	10.0	10	100.0
Robbery	0	0.0	0	0.0	0	0.0
Total Nonviolent Offenses	101	47.2	58	27.1	159	74.3
Property	71	50.7	34	24.3	105	75.0
Public-Order	30	40.5	24	32.4	54	73.0

*Rates per 100 persons (estimates based on probability samples).

Table 2-16
Reported* Sickness and Injury Rates: Adult Male Prisoners and Parolees Compared with Adult Male Probationers, by Type of Offense

Type of Offense	Ratio: Rates for Prisoners/ Probationers		Ratio: Rates for Parolees/Probationers	
	Sickness	Injury	Sickness	Injury
Total Violent Offenses	6.96	6.33	1.04	0.67
Homicide	8.49	3.68	1.23	0.47
Sexual	4.77	–	1.75	–
Assaults	11.11	20.00	1.11	1.33
Robbery	–	–	–	–
Total Nonviolent Offenses	9.17	3.29	1.06	1.17
Property	8.32	3.91	1.00	1.14
Public-Order	14.81	–	1.18	1.34

*Estimates based on probability samples.

sentence for non-sexual assault had the highest ratio (ratio: 11.11) followed by those serving a sentence for homicide (ratio: 8.49); while those serving a sentence for sexual assault had the lowest ratio (ratio: 4.77). Since probationers who were serving a sentence for robbery did not report any sicknesses, no ratio could be computed for the offenders who were serving a sentence for robbery. Among nonviolent offenders, those serving a sentence for a public-order offense had a higher ratio (ratio: 14.81) than those serving a sentence for a property offense (ratio: 8.32).

In the comparison of reported injury rates for prisoners and probationers, violent offenders had a higher ratio (ratio: 6.33) than nonviolent offenders (ratio: 3.29). Among violent offenders, those serving a sentence for non-sexual assault had a higher ratio (ratio: 20.0) than those serving a sentence for homicide (ratio: 3.68). Probationers who were serving a sentence for sexual assault and robbery did not report any injuries. Among nonviolent offenders, those serving a sentence for a property crime had a slightly higher ratio (ratio: 3.91) than the ratio for nonviolent offenders generally (ratio: 3.29). No prisoner who was serving a sentence for a public-order crime reported any injury.

In the comparison of reported sickness rates for parolees and probationers, violent offenders and nonviolent offenders had about the same ratio (ratios: 1.04 and 1.06 respectively). Among violent offenders, those serving a sentence for sexual assault had the highest ratio (ratio: 1.75), while those serving a sentence for non-sexual assault had the lowest ratio (ratio: 1.11), followed by those serving a sentence for homicide (ratio: 1.23). Among nonviolent offenders, those serving a sentence for a public-order crime had a slightly higher ratio (ratio: 1.18) than those serving a sentence for a property crime (ratio: 1.00).

In the comparison of reported injury rates for parolees and probationers, nonviolent offenders had a higher ratio (ratio: 1.17) than violent offenders (ratio: 0.67). Among violent offenders, those serving a sentence for non-sexual assault had a higher ratio (ratio: 1.33) than those serving a sentence for homicide (ratio: 0.47). Among nonviolent offenders, those serving a sentence for a public-order crime had a higher ratio (ratio: 1.34) than those serving a sentence for a property crime (ratio: 1.14).

5. Incidence by Length of Imprisonment

The reported incidence of sicknesses and injuries was compared for prisoners of both races and all ages according to the length of time spent in prison, in months. These incidences could not be compared in this way for parolees or for probationers, since the length of time they spent on parole or on probation was rather short, less than eighteen months as a rule.

Table 2-17 summarizes the reported incidence of sicknesses and injuries for prisoners of both races and all ages according to the length of time spent in prison (i.e., concurrent with this study; computed from date of imprisonment to date of sampling). Prisoners who had spent less than 1 year in prison reported the highest incidence of sicknesses, followed closely by prisoners who had spent 10 years or more in prison. Prisoners who had spent 10 years or more in prison

Table 2-17
Sicknesses and Injuries Reported* in Latest Twelve-Month Period: Adult Male Prisoners, by Length of Imprisonment

Length of Time Spent in Prison	Sicknesses		Injuries		Total Conditions	
	Sample	Estimated Rate	Sample	Estimated Rate	Sample	Estimated Rate
10 years or more	90	562.5	36	225.0	126	787.5
5- 9 years	86	430.0	2	10.0	88	440.0
48-59 months	52	288.9	18	100.0	70	388.9
36-47 months	120	400.0	26	86.7	146	486.7
24-35 months	100	454.5	26	118.2	126	572.7
18-23 months	126	315.0	30	75.0	156	390.0
12-17 months	80	400.0	24	120.0	104	520.0
6-11 months	228	600.0	36	94.7	264	694.7

*Rates per 100 persons (estimates based on probability samples).

reported the highest incidence of injuries. Prisoners who had spent between forty-eight and fifty-nine months (more than 4 years but less than 5 years) in prison reported the lowest incidence of sicknesses. Prisoners who had spent between 5 and 10 years in prison reported the lowest incidence of injuries.

Prisoners who had spent between twelve and twenty-three months, between thirty-six and forty-nine months, and between 5 and 10 years in prison had reported sickness rates below the average sickness rate for all prisoners (432.4 per 100, see Appendix, Table A-1). Prisoners who had spent between eighteen and twenty-three months, between thirty-six and forty-seven months, and between 5 and 10 years in prison had reported injury rates below the average injury rate for all prisoners.

Table 2-18 summarizes the reported incidence of sicknesses and injuries for prisoners of both races and all ages according to the proportion of sentence completed (measured by the decile or nearest tenth of minimum sentence completed). Prisoners who had completed six-tenths of their sentence reported the highest incidence of sicknesses. Prisoners who had completed nine-tenths of their sentence reported the highest incidence of injuries. Prisoners who had completed four-tenths of their sentence reported the lowest incidence of sicknesses. Prisoners who had completed three-tenths of their sentence reported the lowest incidence of injuries.

Prisoners who had completed the first, second, fourth, fifth, seventh, and ninth deciles of their sentence had reported sickness rates which were lower than

Table 2-18
Sicknesses and Injuries Reported* in Latest Twelve-Month Period: Adult Male Prisoners, by Proportion of Sentence Completed

Proportion of Sentence Completed	Sicknesses		Injuries		Total Conditions	
Decile	Sample	Estimated Rate	Sample	Estimated Rate	Sample	Estimated Rate
1st	154	427.8	46	127.8	200	555.6
2nd	162	426.3	44	115.8	206	542.1
3rd	94	447.6	2	9.5	96	457.1
4th	70	333.3	22	104.8	92	438.1
5th	32	400.0	10	125.0	42	525.0
6th	126	525.0	14	58.3	140	583.3
7th	68	425.0	4	25.0	72	450.0
8th	98	445.5	26	118.2	124	563.6
9th	78	433.3	26	144.4	104	577.8

*Rates per 100 persons (estimates based on probability samples).

the average reported sickness rate for all prisoners. Prisoners who had completed the third, sixth, and seventh deciles of their sentence had reported injury rates which were lower than the average reported injury rate for all prisoners.

Table 2-19 summarizes the reported incidence of sicknesses and injuries for prisoners of both races and all ages according to the length of time remaining before eligibility for parole (i.e., the time before minimum sentence is completed). Prisoners who had already become eligible for parole but for whom parole had been temporarily denied reported the highest incidence of both sicknesses and injuries. Prisoners who had between thirty-six and forty-seven months (more than 3 but less than 4 years) remaining before parole eligibility reported the lowest incidence of sicknesses. Prisoners who had between forty-eight and fifty-nine months (more than 4 but less than 5 years) remaining before parole eligibility reported the lowest incidence of injuries.

Prisoners who had thirty-six months or more remaining before parole eligibility all had reported sickness rates lower than the average reported sickness rate for all prisoners. Prisoners who had between six and eleven months and between 4 and 10 years remaining before parole eligibility had reported injury rates lower than the average reported injury rate for all prisoners.

6. Incidence by Month

The reported incidence of sicknesses and injuries was compared for prisoners of both races and all ages according to the month during which each sickness or

Table 2-19
Sicknesses and Injuries Reported* in Latest Twelve-Month Period: Adult-Male Prisoners, by Length of Time before Parole Eligibility

Length of Time Left Before Parole Eligibility	Sicknesses		Injuries		Total Conditions	
	Sample	Rate	Sample	Rate	Sample	Rate
Time Arrived	48	800.0	18	300.0	66	1100.0
1- 5 months	64	640.0	10	100.0	74	740.0
6-11 months	134	670.0	6	30.0	140	700.0
12-23 months	190	441.9	46	107.0	236	548.8
24-35 months	114	518.2	26	118.2	140	636.4
36-47 months	32	266.7	14	116.7	46	383.3
48-59 months	38	422.2	2	22.2	40	444.4
5- 9 years	84	300.0	12	42.9	96	342.9
10 years or more	178	329.6	60	111.1	238	440.7

*Rates per 100 persons (estimates based on probability samples).

injury was first reported. The reported incidence of sicknesses and injuries could not be compared in this way for parolees or probationers, because without medical records to refresh their memories these respondents could not cite the specific month over a six-month to 1-year recall period during which they first noticed a particular sickness or injury.

Table 2-20 summarizes the proportion of sickness and injury incidences that prisoners reported between 1 July 1972 and 30 June 1973, according to the month when each incident was first reported. More sicknesses were reported in February than in any other month, and fewer sicknesses were reported in December than in any other month. More injuries were reported in both June and November than in any other months, and fewer injuries were reported in December than in any other month. For both sicknesses and injuries, more incidents were reported in February and fewer incidents were reported in December than in any other months.

C. Percent Distribution of Separate Conditions

In addition to reported sickness and injury rates per 100 members of a population, the incidence of acute physical conditions may be summarized according to the proportion of the members of a population who report specific frequencies of separate sicknesses or injuries. During a twelve month period, for example, some members of a population may report no sickness at all, while others may report one sickness, two separate sicknesses, or three or more separate sicknesses. Similarly, during the same period some members of a population may report no injury at all, while others may report one injury or two or more separate injuries.

This study estimates the percent distribution of separate reported sicknesses and injuries for each adult-male, criminal-offender population (prisoners, probationers, parolees) considered. The estimate of percent distributions covers the period from 1 July 1972 to 30 June 1973. Only 16.1 percent of black prisoners reported avoiding sickness entirely, compared with 24.8 percent of white prisoners. Among prisoners of both races combined, 50.0 percent between 17 and 24 years of age reported three or more separate sicknesses, although the next highest proportion to report this many sicknesses was 30 percent for those 45 years of age or over. An observation of age intervals within each race showed that 42.9 percent of black prisoners 45 years of age or older reported three or more separate sicknesses, while none of the white prisoners in this age bracket reported as many sicknesses.

About the same proportion of black (87.4 percent) and white (87.2 percent) prisoners reported avoiding injury entirely. However, 9.2 percent of black prisoners but only 6.8 percent of white prisoners reported two or more injuries.

Table 2-20
Sickness and Injury Incidence Reported,* July 1972-June 1973: Adult Male Prisoners, by Month First Reported

Month	Incidence of Sickness and Injury (Rank and Percent Distribution by Column)					
	Sicknesses ($N = 443$)		Injuries ($N = 102$)		Total Conditions ($N = 545$)	
	Rank	Percent	Rank	Percent	Rank	Percent
January	8	7.2	(3)	11.8	7	8.1
February	1	12.0	9	5.9	1	10.8
March	(4)	9.7	8	6.9	4	9.2
April	6	8.6	5	10.8	(5)	9.0
May	2	10.4	(3)	11.8	2	10.6
June	10	6.3	(1)	12.7	8	7.5
July	3	10.2	11	3.9	(5)	9.0
August	(4)	9.7	7	7.8	3	9.4
September	9	6.8	6	8.8	11	7.2
October	7	7.9	10	4.9	(9)	7.3
November	11	6.1	(1)	12.7	(9)	7.3
December	12	5.2	12	2.0	12	4.6
		100.1		100.0		100.0

*Estimates based on probability samples.

Among prisoners of both races combined, 15.0 percent of persons between 17 and 24 years of age reported two or more injuries, although not more than 8.0 percent of prisoners in other age brackets reported as many injuries. An observation of age intervals within each race indicated that 13.0 percent of black prisoners between 17 and 24 years old reported two or more injuries, compared with 11.8 percent for white prisoners in this age bracket. In addition, 10.3 percent of black prisoners between 25 and 34 years old reported two or more injuries, compared with 6.3 percent for white prisoners in this age bracket.

Of black parolees 70.0 percent compared with 63.2 percent of white parolees reported avoiding sickness entirely. On the other hand, 7.3 percent of black parolees compared with 2.0 percent of white parolees reported three or more sicknesses. Among parolees of both races, only 57.1 percent of those between 25 and 34 years of age and only 50.0 percent of those over 45 years of age reported avoiding sickness entirely, compared with over 70.0 percent of those in the other age brackets. An observation of age intervals within each race showed that 15.4 percent of black parolees between 25 and 34 years of age reported three or more sicknesses, although no parolees of either race over 35 years old reported as many sicknesses. Only 36.8 percent of white parolees who were 45 years of age or older reported avoiding sickness entirely, but over 50.0 percent of the parolees in all other age brackets and 60.9 percent of black parolees in this age bracket did so.

Of black parolees 83.6 percent compared with 77.9 percent of white parolees reported avoiding injury entirely. About the same proportion of black and white parolees reported two or more injuries (1.9 and 1.5 percent respectively). No parolees of either race over 45 years of age reported more than one injury. Only 63.3 percent of black parolees between 35 and 44 years of age reported avoiding injury entirely, as did only 66.6 percent of white parolees over 45 years old and only 70.0 percent of white parolees between 17 and 24 years of age. Over 80.0 percent of the parolees of both races in all other age brackets reported avoiding injury altogether.

Of black probationers 68.6 percent compared with 65.3 percent of white probationers reported avoiding sickness entirely. About the same proportion of black (3.9 percent) and white (3.5 percent) probationers reported three or more sicknesses. Among probationers of both races, only 40.0 percent of those who were over 45 years old reported avoiding sickness entirely, but more than 60.0 percent of those in all other age brackets did so. An observation of age intervals within each race showed that only 33.3 percent of white probationers over 45 years old reported avoiding sickness entirely, although over 60.0 percent of other probationers did so. In addition, 20.0 percent of black probationers over 45 years of age reported three or more sicknesses, while not more than 6.7 percent of probationers in other age brackets reported as many sicknesses.

Of black probationers 82.0 percent compared with 78.6 percent of white probationers reported avoiding injury entirely, but 6.0 percent of black probationers compared with 3.5 percent of white probationers reported two or more injuries. Only 54.4 percent of black probationers between 25 and 34 years of age reported avoiding injury entirely, although all black probationers over 35 years old reported this. Nevertheless, 9.1 percent of black probationers between 25 and 34 years of age and 6.9 percent of those between 17 and 24 years of age reported two or more injuries.

Prisoners of both races and all ages reported no sickness 3.1 times less frequently than parolees or probationers of both races and all ages. Black prisoners reported no sickness 4.3 times less frequently than black parolees or black probationers. White prisoners reported no sickness 2.5 times less frequently than white parolees and 2.6 times less frequently than white probationers. Probationers and parolees of both races and all ages reported no sickness during the same interval at nearly the same frequency. Prisoners, parolees, and probationers reported no injury at nearly the same frequency.

Prisoners of both races and all ages reported three or more separate sicknesses per person 7.5 times more frequently than parolees and 8.7 times more frequently than probationers. White prisoners reported three or more separate sicknesses 15.4 times more frequently than white parolees and 8.8 times more frequently than white probationers. Black prisoners reported three or more sicknesses 4.4 times more frequently than black parolees and 8.3 times more frequently than black probationers. The rate at which persons reported three or more separate sicknesses was 16.7 percent higher for parolees than for probationers of both races and all ages; 42.9 percent lower for white parolees than for white probationers; 87.2 percent higher for black parolees than for black probationers.

Prisoners of both races and all ages reported two or more separate injuries per person 4.9 times more frequently than parolees, and 2.1 times more frequently than probationers. White prisoners reported two or more separate injuries 4.5 times more frequently than white parolees and 1.9 times more frequently than white probationers. Black prisoners reported two or more separate injuries 4.8 times more frequently than black parolees and 1.5 times more frequently than black probationers. The rate at which persons reported two or more separate injuries was 57.5 percent lower for parolees than for probationers of both races and all ages; 57.1 percent lower for white parolees than for white probationers; and 3.2 times lower for black parolees than for black probationers.

D. Comparison Statistics

The report of the U.S. Public Health Service, *Current Estimates From The Health Interview Survey, United States, 1972*, suggests that acute conditions (both sicknesses and injuries) occur at the rate of 186.4 per 100 persons for males between 17 and 44 years of age, and at the rate of 124.8 per 100 persons for males 45 years of age and over.[6] These estimates suggest also that acute injuries occur at the rate of 44.1 per 100 persons for males between 17 and 45 years of age, and at the rate of 22.8 per 100 persons for males 45 years of age and over.[7] Subtracting the number of acute injuries from the number of acute conditions in general and then retabulating, these estimates would suggest that acute sicknesses occur at the rate of 142.3 per 100 persons for males between 17 and 44 years of age, and at the rate of 101.9 per 100 persons for males 45 years of age or over.[8]

On the basis of this data, prisoners under 45 years old reported sickness at a rate that was 3.2 times higher than the estimated 1972 sickness rate for the general (noninstitutionalized), adult (over 17), male, United States population under 45 years old.[9] Prisoners over 45 years old reported sickness at a rate that was 4.5 times higher than the estimated sickness rate of the general adult-male United States population over 45 years old in 1972. However, the general adult male United States population under 45 years old had an estimated sickness rate in 1972 that was 2.7 times higher than the sickness rate reported by parolees sampled; and 3.1 times higher than the sickness rate reported by sampled probationers under 45 years old. The general adult-male United States population over 45 years old had an estimated sickness rate in 1972 that was 6.4 times higher than the sickness rate reported by parolees sampled; and 4.3 times higher than the sickness rate reported by sampled probationers over 45 years old.

Similarly, prisoners under 45 years old reported injury at a rate that was 2.5 times higher than the estimated injury rate for the general adult-male United States population in 1972 under 45 years old. The prisoners over 45 years old reported injury at a rate 2.5 times higher than the estimated injury rate for the general adult-male United States population over 45 years old in 1972. However, the general adult-male United States population under 45 years old had an estimated injury rate in 1972 that was 2.1 times higher than the injury rate reported by parolees; and 60.9 percent higher than the injury rate reported by probationers under 45 years old. The general, adult-male United States population over 45 years old had an estimated injury rate in 1972 that was about the same as the injury rate reported by parolees in this age bracket; but 4.6 times higher than the injury rate reported by probationers over 45 years old.

3 Morbidity Trends: Specific Acute and Chronic Conditions

A. Classification of Conditions

From the definition in Chapter Two, a morbidity condition is a person's departure from a state of physical or mental well-being, for any reason whatsoever. An acute condition is one that has lasted less than three months and has involved either medical attention or restricted activity. On the other hand, a chronic condition is one that the respondent describes as having been first noticed more than three months prior to the week of the interview, unless it is one of a list of conditions always classified as chronic regardless of onset.[1]

Conditions except impairments are classified by type in the U.S. Public Health Service Publication, ICDA.[2] Chapter Two summarized the incidence of acute conditions for the three criminal-offender populations (prisoners, parolees, and probationers) sampled. However, the summary of the reported incidence of acute conditions disregarded the cause of the condition, except for distinguishing illnesses (sicknesses) from injuries. This chapter will summarize the reported incidence of selected acute conditions and the reported prevalence of selected chronic conditions, and analyze them according to specific ICDA categories.

The ICDA classifies all conditions (chronic and acute) into 17 main categories. The last of these is subdivided according to internal or external causation. The following is a list of ICDA categories, followed by the three-digit, inclusive numerical codes that ICDA assigns to each category:

I.	Infective and Parasitic Diseases	000 - 136
II.	Neoplasms	140 - 239
III.	Endocrine, Nutritional, and Metabolic Diseases	240 - 279
IV.	Diseases of the Blood and Blood-Forming Organs	280 - 289
V.	Mental Disorders	290 - 315
VI.	Diseases of the Nervous System and Sense Organs	320 - 389
VII.	Diseases of the Circulatory System	390 - 458
VIII.	Diseases of the Respiratory System	460 - 519
IX.	Diseases of the Digestive System	520 - 577
X.	Diseases of the Genito-urinary System	580 - 629
XI.	Complications of Pregnancy, Childbirth, and the Puerperium	630 - 678

XII.	Diseases of the Skin and Subcutaneous Tissue	680 - 709
XIII.	Diseases of the Musculoskeletal System and Connective Tissue	710 - 738
XIV.	Congenital Anomalies	740 - 759
XV.	Certain Causes of Perinatal Morbidity and Mortality	760 - 779
XVI.	Symptoms and Ill-Defined Conditions	780 - 796
XVII.	Accidents, Poisonings, and Violence (Nature of Injury)	800 - 999
EXII.	Accidents, Poisonings, and Violence (External Cause)	E800 - E999

These categories do not necessarily distinguish between acute and chronic conditions, unless a condition is always classified as chronic.[3] Moreover, the classifications employ a decimal system so that each three-digit category may be subdivided into ten separate parts.

Some of the ICDA categories of conditions are not of concern here. For example, all the subjects studied here being males, Category XI, Complications of pregnancy, childbirth, and the puerperium (630-678), is irrelevant. Similarly, because of the relatively small sizes of the populations sampled, many ICDA condition categories are not reflected at all among offenders (prisoners, parolees, and probationers), and many others are reflected so infrequently that they do not permit summarization.

This chapter, like Chapter Two, summarizes or analyzes only physical conditions; acute and chronic mental conditions will be dealt with in Chapters Four and Five. The acute and chronic physical conditions summarized and analyzed in this chapter will be the major conditions that exert the most impact on morbidity and mortality. While acute conditions are measured according to incidence, chronic conditions are measured according to prevalence. The prevalence of chronic conditions is the number of chronic conditions reported or estimated to be present among members of a population at a specific point in time.

B. Specific Acute Conditions

As any analysis of morbidity conditions becomes more specific, fewer members of any particular class or group of persons may be expected to have experienced them. It is not possible to tabulate specific acute condition groups (except injuries) by age within race for offender populations according to ten-year age intervals. Instead, specific acute condition groups are summarized by age within race according to only two age brackets: persons who were 44 years of age or younger, and persons who were 45 years of age or older.

This chapter summarizes the incidence of conditions for parolees combined with probationers, and then compares this combined summary with the incidence of conditions summarized for prisoners. Parolees do not differ markedly from probationers in their experience of most acute conditions, as Chapter Two shows.

Table 3-1 summarizes the incidence of acute conditions reported to have been incurred during the latest twelve-month period among prisoners at Tennessee State Penitentiary, by specific condition groups according to age within race. In this table as in Table 3-2, acute conditions are broken down into four specific groups, one nonspecific group, and two specific subgroups. The specific groups are: infective and parasitic diseases; respiratory conditions; digestive system conditions; and injuries. In turn, the respiratory conditions group is subdivided into two sub-groups: upper respiratory conditions and influenza. Finally, the fifth but nonspecific group is added to summarize the incidence of acute conditions that could not be classified into one of the four specific groups.

Among prisoners of all ages and both races, acute respiratory conditions were reported more frequently than other specific conditions. Injury conditions were reported almost as frequently as others. Digestive system conditions were reported less frequently than others, and infective and parasitic diseases were reported least frequently of all.

Among prisoners of both races under 45 years old, injury conditions were reported most frequently, followed by respiratory conditions. Infective and parasitic diseases were reported least frequently, followed by digestive system conditions.

Among prisoners of both races 45 years of age or older, respiratory conditions were reported most frequently, and infective and parasitic conditions were reported least frequently. This group of prisoners reported injury conditions at the same rate as digestive system conditions.

White prisoners of all ages reported injury conditions more frequently than other specific conditions. On the other hand, black prisoners of all ages reported acute respiratory conditions more frequently than other specific conditions. White prisoners of all ages reported acute respiratory conditions at the rate of 85.5 per 100 persons, and black prisoners of all ages reported injury conditions at the rate of 92.0 per 100 persons.

White prisoners of all ages reported acute digestive system conditions the least frequently of specific acute conditions, but black prisoners of all ages reported infective and parasitic diseases least frequently. Black prisoners of all ages reported infective and parasitic diseases at a rate twice as high as the rate for white prisoners of all ages.

White prisoners under 45 years old reported injury conditions more frequently than other specific conditions. Black prisoners under 45 years old reported acute respiratory conditions more frequently than other specific conditions.

White prisoners under 45 years old reported acute digestive system conditions the least frequently of specific acute conditions, while black prisoners in this age

Table 3-1
Acute Conditions Reported* in Latest Twelve-Month Period: Adult Male Prisoners, by Condition Group, according to Age within Race

Race and Condition Group	Ages 17 Years and Over		Ages 17-44 Years		Ages 45 Years and Over	
	Sample	Estimated Rate	Sample	Estimated Rate	Sample	Estimated Rate
Both Races						
All Acute Conditions	1072	525.5	868	529.3	204	510.0
Infective and parasitic	92	45.1	84	51.2	8	20.0
Respiratory	192	94.1	156	95.1	36	90.0
Upper-respiratory	120	58.8	98	59.8	22	55.0
Influenza	72	35.3	58	35.4	14	35.0
Digestive system	116	56.9	94	57.3	22	55.0
Injuries	190	93.1	168	102.4	22	55.0
All other acute	482	236.3	366	223.2	116	290.0
White						
All Acute Conditions	576	492.3	420	471.9	156	557.1
Infective and parasitic	52	44.4	48	53.9	4	14.3
Respiratory	100	85.5	68	76.4	32	114.3
Upper-respiratory	68	58.1	46	51.7	22	78.6
Influenza	32	27.4	22	24.7	10	35.7
Digestive system	44	37.6	24	27.0	20	71.4
Injuries	110	94.0	96	107.9	14	50.0
All other acute	270	230.8	184	206.7	86	307.1
Black						
All Acute Conditions	496	570.1	448	597.3	48	400.0
Infective and parasitic	40	46.0	36	48.0	4	33.3

Respiratory	92	105.7	88	117.3	4	33.3
Upper-respiratory	52	59.8	52	69.3	–	–
Influenza	40	46.0	36	48.0	4	33.3
Digestive system	72	82.8	70	93.3	2	16.7
Injuries	80	92.0	72	96.0	8	66.7
All other acute	212	243.7	182	242.7	30	250.0

*Rates per 100 persons (estimates based on probability samples).

bracket reported infective and parasitic diseases least frequently. White prisoners over 45 years old reported acute respiratory conditions more frequently than other specific conditions, while black prisoners in this age bracket reported injury conditions more frequently.

White prisoners over 45 years old reported infective and parasitic diseases least frequently of specific acute conditions, while black prisoners of this age group reported digestive system conditions least frequently.

Black and white prisoners of all ages reported upper respiratory conditions at the similar rates. However, black prisoners of all ages reported influenza at the rate of 46.0 per 100 persons, while white prisoners of all ages reported this at the rate of 27.4 per 100 persons. Black prisoners under 45 years old reported influenza at the rate of 48.0 per 100 persons, while white prisoners of this age group reported this at the rate of 24.7 per 100 persons.

Black and white prisoners over 45 years old reported influenza at about the same rate. White prisoners over 45 years old had a higher reported incidence of respiratory conditions than did those under 45 years old, and this was true also of acute digestive system condtitions. Black prisoners over 45 years old had a lower reported incidence of all specific acute conditions than did those under 45 years of age. This was true also of white prisoners over 45 compared with those under 45 years old for infective and parasitic diseases as well as for injuries. Reported incidence of nonspecific acute conditions was shared rather equally among both races of prisoners in most age brackets. The meaning of the nonspecific category of acute conditions will be clarified later in this chapter.[4]

Table 3-2 summarizes the incidence of acute conditions reported to have been incurred during the latest twelve-month period among parolees and probationers in Tennessee, but specific condition groups according to age within race. This table, like Table 3-1, breaks down acute conditions into four specific groups, one nonspecific group, and two specific subgroups. This chapter combines probationers and refers to them as nonincarcerated offenders. Among nonincarcerated offenders of both races and all ages, acute respiratory conditions were reported more frequently than other specific acute conditions; while infective and parasitic diseases were reported least frequently, followed by acute digestive system conditions.

Among nonincarcerated offenders of both races who were over 45 years old, respiratory conditions were reported more frequently than other specific acute conditions, and among them also digestive system conditions and injury conditions were next; while infective and parasitic diseases were reported least frequently.

Black and white nonincarcerated offenders of all ages reported respiratory conditions more frequently than other specific acute conditions. Black and white nonincarcerated offenders of all ages reported infective and parasitic diseases least frequently. Acute digestive system conditions were reported rather evenly by black and white nonincarcerated offenders. This was true of injury conditions, also. Reported incidence of specific acute conditions varied only slightly by age within race.

Black and white nonincarcerated offenders of all ages reported upper respiratory conditions at about the same rate. Black nonincarcerated offenders had a slightly higher reported incidence of influenza than did white nonincarcerated offenders. The reported incidence of these conditions varied only slightly by age within race.

White nonincarcerated offenders who were over 45 years old reported a higher incidence of respiratory conditions than did those under 45 years old. This was true also of acute digestive system conditions. Black nonincarcerated offenders over 45 years old reported a slightly higher incidence of respiratory conditions than did those under 45 years old, but they reported a lower incidence of both digestive system conditions and injury conditions. Both black and white nonincarcerated offenders under 45 and over 45 years old reported about the same incidence of infective and parasitic diseases. White nonincarcerated offenders under 45 and over 45 years old reported about the same incidence of injuries. Black nonincarcerated offenders under 45 and over 45 years old reported about the same incidence of acute digestive system conditions.

Reported incidence of nonspecific acute conditions was rather equal among black and white nonincarcerated offenders under 45 years old. Black nonincarcerated offenders under 45 years old reported nonspecific acute conditions at a lower rate, while white nonincarcerated offenders over 45 years old reported a higher rate of nonspecific acute conditions.

Table 3-3 contains ratios of reported acute-condition rates by condition groups for prisoners compared by age within race with nonincarcerated offenders. Comparing reported acute condition rates by condition groups for prisoners and nonincarcerated offenders of both races under 45 years old, the highest ratios for specific-condition groups were observed for acute digestive system conditions (ratio: 7.85) and for infective and parasitic diseases (ratio: 7.31). The lowest ratios for specific-condition groups were observed for upper respiratory conditions (ratio: 2.62) and influenza (ratio: 3.93), followed by injuries (ratio: 4.28). Reported acute-condition rates for all specific, acute-condition groups are noticeably higher for prisoners under 45 years old compared separately by race with nonincarcerated offenders in this age bracket. Among prisoners compared with nonincarcerated offenders under 45 years old, few ratio variations were observed by race. There is a striking exception to this statement: the ratio for acute, digestive-system conditions is only 3.91 for white prisoners compared with white nonincarcerated offenders under 45 years old, however, the ratio for acute-digestive system conditions is an alarming 11.24 for black prisoners compared with black nonincarcerated offenders under 45 years old.

In the comparison of acute-condition rates by condition groups for prisoners and nonincarcerated offenders of both races over 45 years old, the highest ratios

Table 3-2
Acute Conditions Reported in Latest Twelve-Month Period: Adult Male Parolees and Probationers, by Condition Group, according to Age within Race

Race and Condition Group	Ages 17 Years and Over		Ages 17-44 Years		Ages 45 Years and Over	
	Sample	Estimated Rate	Sample	Estimated Rate	Sample	Estimated Rate
Both Races						
All Acute Conditions	466	76.8	405	74.3	61	98.4
Infective and parasitic	42	6.9	38	7.0	4	6.5
Respiratory	199	32.8	173	31.7	26	41.9
Upper-respiratory	138	22.7	124	22.8	14	22.6
Influenza	61	10.0	49	9.0	12	19.4
Digestive system	52	8.6	40	7.3	12	19.4
Injuries	140	23.1	130	23.9	10	16.1
All other acute	33	5.4	24	4.4	9	14.8
White						
All Acute Conditions	312	78.8	272	74.9	40	121.2
Infective and parasitic	27	6.8	25	6.9	2	6.1
Respiratory	126	31.8	112	30.9	14	42.4
Upper-respiratory	89	22.5	79	21.8	10	30.3
Influenza	37	9.3	33	9.1	4	12.1
Digestive system	35	8.8	25	6.9	10	30.3
Injuries	98	24.7	91	25.1	7	21.2
All other acute	26	6.6	19	5.2	7	21.2
Black						
All Acute Conditions	154	73.7	133	73.9	21	72.4

Infective and parasitic	15	7.2	13	7.2	2	6.9
Respiratory	73	34.9	61	33.9	12	41.4
Upper-respiratory	49	23.4	45	25.0	4	13.8
Influenza	24	11.5	16	8.9	8	27.6
Digestive-system	17	8.1	15	8.3	2	6.9
Injuries	42	20.1	39	21.7	3	10.3
All other acute	7	3.3	5	2.8	2	6.9

Note: rates per 100 persons (estimates based on probability samples).

Table 3-3
Reported* Acute-Condition Rates by Condition Groups: Adult Male Prisoners Compared with Adult Male, Nonincarcerated Offenders

Race and Condition Group	Ratio: Rates for Prisoners/Nonincarcerated Offenders		
	Ages 17 Years and Over	Ages 17-44 Years	Ages 45 Years and Over
Both Races			
All Acute Conditions	6.84	7.12	5.18
Infective and parasitic	6.54	7.31	3.08
Respiratory	2.87	3.00	2.15
Upper-respiratory	2.59	2.62	2.43
Influenza	3.53	3.93	1.80
Digestive system	6.62	7.85	2.84
Injuries	4.03	4.28	3.42
All other acute	43.76	50.73	19.59
White			
All Acute Conditions	6.25	6.30	4.60
Infective and parasitic	6.53	7.81	2.34
Respiratory	2.69	2.47	2.70
Upper-respiratory	2.58	2.37	2.59
Influenza	2.95	2.71	2.95
Digestive system	4.27	3.91	2.36
Injuries	3.81	4.30	2.36
All other acute	34.97	39.75	14.49
Black			
All Acute Conditions	7.74	8.08	5.52
Infective and parasitic	6.39	6.67	4.83
Respiratory	3.03	3.46	0.80
Upper-respiratory	2.56	2.77	–
Influenza	4.00	5.39	1.21
Digestive system	10.22	11.24	2.42
Injuries	4.58	4.42	6.48
All other acute	73.85	86.68	36.23

*Estimates based on probability samples.

for specific condition groups were observed for injuries (ratio: 3.42) and for infective and parasitic diseases (ratio: 3.08). The lowest ratio for a specific-condition group was observed for influenza (ratio: 1.80), followed by upper respiratory conditions (ratio: 2.43), and acute, digestive-system conditions (ratio: 2.84). A few differences seem to be attributable to race. Black offenders (prisoners compared with nonincarcerated offenders) over 45 years old had a ratio of 6.48 for injuries, while white offenders over 45 years old had a ratio of 2.36 for injuries. White offenders over 45 years old had a ratio of 2.95 for influenza, while black offenders over 45 years old had a ratio of 1.21 for influenza.

Some acute morbidity conditions cannot be classified into one of the four specific condition categories. Instead, these conditions are relegated to the nonspecific category, "all other acute conditions." This does not mean automatically that such conditions have no identity of their own. Instead, these conditions pertain to a variety of categories, too numerous to be tabulated separately. Many of the conditions summarized in the category of "all other acute conditions" are from ICDA codes 780-796, labeled "Symptoms and Ill-Defined Conditions."[5]

In the comparison of prisoners with nonincarcerated offenders by age within race for the nonspecific category labeled "all other acute conditions," the highest ratio was observed for black offenders under 45 years old (ratio: 86.68), and the lowest ratio was observed for white offenders over 45 years old (ratio: 14.49). Similar ratios were observed for black offenders over 45 years old (ratio: 36.23) and white offenders under 45 years old (ratio: 39.75).

Injury conditions were reported in sufficient quantity among prisoners and nonincarcerated offenders to be studied according to areas of the body that were injured. Table 3-4 summarizes the percentage distribution of injury conditions by part(s) of the body reported to have been injured during the latest twelve-month period by age within race for prisoners. According to Table 3-4, more prisoners of both races and all ages experienced upper limb (shoulder, arm, hand, and finger) injuries than injuries to other parts of the body. This remained true for prisoners at all age intervals within both races. Prisoners of both races and all ages next reported head injuries more frequently than injuries to other parts of the body. This remained true for prisoners of both races combined at all age intervals except the 35 to 44 year old age group, which reported injuries to the lower limbs (hip, leg, foot, and toe) more frequently than injuries to other parts of the body, except to the upper limbs. Prisoners of both races and all ages reported injuries first to the back then to abdomen or chest at a lower rate than injuries to all other areas of the body. This remained true for prisoners of both races combined under 35 years old. Prisoners of both races combined between 35 and 44 yearss of age reported injuries to the back at about the same rate as injuries to the abdomen or chest; but those over 45 years old reported back injuries at a higher rate than abdomen or chest injuries.

According to Table 3-5, more nonincarcerated offenders of both races and all ages reported back injuries than injuries to other parts of the body. This remained true for nonincarcerated offenders under 45 years old, but those of both races over 45 years old reported an equal number of injuries to the back and to the lower limbs. Nonincarcerated offenders of both races and all ages reported injuries to the lower limbs more frequently than to other parts of the body except the back; this remained true also for those under 45 years old. Nonincarcerated offenders of both races and all ages reported the fewest injuries

Table 3-4
Injury Conditions, according to Parts of the Body, Reported* in Latest Twelve-Month Period: Adult Male Prisoners, by Age within Race

Age and Race	Parts of Body Injured (Percent Distribution By Row)						
	Head	Back	Upper Limb	Lower Limb	Abdomen or Chest	Total	Sample
Both Races[a]							
17 years and over	20.5	6.3	50.5	14.7	7.9	99.9	190
17-24 years	25.9	3.4	50.0	13.8	6.9	100.0	58
25-34 years	20.3	4.1	48.6	17.6	9.4	100.0	74
35-44 years	13.9	8.3	50.0	19.4	8.3	99.9	36
45 years and over	18.2	18.2	59.1	0.0	4.5	100.0	22
White[b]							
17 years and over	20.9	5.5	53.6	11.8	8.2	100.0	110
17-24 years	34.4	3.1	43.8	12.5	6.3	100.1	32
25-34 years	18.4	2.6	57.9	10.5	10.5	99.9	38
35-44 years	15.4	7.7	50.0	19.2	7.7	100.0	26
45 years and over	7.1	14.3	71.4	0.0	7.1	99.9	14
Black[c]							
17 years and over	20.0	7.5	46.2	18.8	7.5	100.0	80
17-24 years	15.4	3.8	57.7	15.4	7.7	100.0	26
25-34 years	22.2	5.6	38.9	25.0	8.3	100.0	36
35-44 years	10.0	10.0	50.0	20.0	10.0	100.0	10
45 years and over	37.5	25.0	37.5	0.0	0.0	100.0	8

[a] $X^2 = 13.35$ $DF = 12$ $P = >.30$

[b] $X^2 = 12.61$ $DF = 12$ $P = >.30$

[c] $X^2 = 10.54$ $DF = 12$ $P = >.50$

*Estimates based on probability samples.

to the abdomen or chest compared with other parts of the body; this remained true for all age brackets of both races. These offenders of both races and all ages reported injuries to the head at a lower rate than injuries to other parts of the body except the abdomen and chest. This remained true for all age brackets of both races, except that black nonincarcerated offenders under 45 years old reported an equal number of injuries to the head and upper limbs.

The percent distributions of injury conditions by the part(s) of the body reported to have been injured during the latest twelve-month period may be compared by age and race for prisoners and nonincarcerated offenders by comparing Tables 3-4 and 3-5. Prisoners of both races and all ages reported head injuries, upper limb injuries, and abdomen and chest injuries at rates higher than nonincarcerated offenders of both races and all ages. Nonincarcerated offenders

Table 3-5
Injury Conditions, according to Parts of the Body, Reported* in Latest Twelve-Month Period: Adult Male Parolees and Probationers, by Age within Race

Age and Race	Parts of Body Injured (Percent Distribution by Row)						
	Head	Back	Upper Limb	Lower Limb	Abdomen or Chest	Total	Sample
Both Races[a]							
17 years and over	7.8	39.3	22.1	28.6	2.1	99.9	140
17-44 years	8.5	39.2	22.3	27.7	2.3	100.0	130
45 years and over	0.0	40.0	20.0	40.0	0.0	100.0	10
White[b]							
17 years and over	5.1	40.8	25.5	26.5	2.0	99.9	98
17-44 years	5.5	40.7	25.3	26.4	2.2	100.1	91
45 years and over	0.0	42.8	28.6	28.6	0.0	100.0	7
Black[c]							
17 years and over	14.3	35.7	14.3	33.3	2.4	100.0	42
17-44 years	15.4	35.9	15.4	30.8	2.6	100.1	39
45 years and over	0.0	33.3	0.0	66.6	0.0	99.9	3

[a]$\chi^2 = 1.59$ $DF = 4$ $P = >.80$
[b]$\chi^2 = 0.59$ $DF = 4$ $P = >.99$
[c]$\chi^2 = 2.08$ $DF = 4$ $P = >.70$
*Estimates based on probability samples.

of both races and all ages reported back injuries and lower limb injuries at rates higher than prisoners of both races and all ages.

C. Selected Chronic Conditions

It is more difficult to tabulate specific chronic conditions than to tabulate specific acute conditions according to demographic factors. This is true because only a small proportion of any population or subsection thereof may be expected to suffer from a particular class of chronic ailment. A few of the chronic conditions that were found to be most prevalent among the criminal-offender populations sampled are selected for summary and analysis. By far the most reported chronic conditions relate to the digestive system, and incidence of other chronic conditions was too infrequent to warrant inclusion.

As Table 3-6 shows, prisoners of both races and all ages reported more

Table 3-6
Selected, Chronic Digestive Conditions Reported:* Adult Male Prisoners, by Age within Race

Race and Chronic Condition	Ages 17 Years and Over		Ages 17-44 Years		Ages 45 Years and Over	
	Sample	Rate	Sample	Rate	Sample	Rate
Both Races						
Ulcer of stomach or duodenum	21	102.9	15	91.5	6	150.0
Hernia of abdominal cavity	11	53.9	7	42.7	4	250.0
Upper gastrointestinal disorder	18	88.2	14	85.4	4	250.0
Gallbladder condition	0	–	0	–	0	–
Enteritis/ulcerative colitis	11	53.9	7	42.7	4	250.0
Gastritis and duodenitis	19	93.1	15	91.5	4	250.0
Frequent constipation	16	78.4	12	73.2	4	250.0
Intestinal condition (n.o.s.)	25	122.5	21	128.0	4	250.0
Liver condition	5	24.5	2	12.2	3	75.0
Stomach condition (n.o.s.)	16	78.4	9	54.9	7	175.0
White						
Ulcer of stomach or duodenum	12	102.6	8	89.9	4	142.9
Hernia of abdominal cavity	5	42.7	3	33.7	2	71.4
Upper gastrointestinal disorder	11	94.0	8	90.0	3	107.1
Gallbladder condition	0	–	0	–	0	–
Enteritis/ulcerative colitis	5	42.7	3	33.7	2	71.4
Gastritis and Duodenitis	12	102.6	8	90.0	4	142.9
Frequent constipation	7	59.8	4	44.9	3	107.1
Intestinal condition (n.o.s.)	13	111.1	10	112.4	3	107.1
Liver condition	4	34.2	2	22.5	2	71.4
Stomach condition (n.o.s.)	8	68.4	3	33.7	5	178.6
Black						
Ulcer of stomach or duodenum	9	103.4	7	93.3	2	166.7
Hernia of abdominal cavity	6	69.0	4	53.3	2	166.7
Upper gastrointestinal disorder	7	80.5	6	80.0	1	83.3
Gallbladder condition	0	–	0	–	0	–
Enteritis/ulcerative colitis	6	69.0	4	53.3	2	166.7
Gastritis and Duodenitis	7	80.5	7	93.3	0	–
Frequent constipation	9	103.4	8	106.7	1	83.3
Intestinal condition (n.o.s.)	12	137.9	11	146.7	1	83.3
Liver condition	1	11.5	0	–	1	83.3
Stomach condition (n.o.s.)	8	92.0	6	80.0	2	166.7

*Rates per 1,000 persons (estimates based on probability samples).

intestinal conditions "n.o.s." (not otherwise specified, i.e., not so localized as to allow identification of their specific causes) than other selected chronic conditions, followed by ulcers of the stomach or duodenum. Prisoners of both races and all ages reported a number of other selected chronic conditions in significant quantity, but surprisingly they reported no gallbladder conditions. Black prisoners of all ages reported more hernia conditions than white prisoners of all ages reported, as well as frequent constipation, enteritis or ulcerative colitis, stomach (n.o.s.) and intestinal (n.o.s.) conditions more often. White prisoners of all ages reported liver conditions more frequently than black prisoners of all ages. White prisoners over 45 years old reported most selected chronic conditions at a higher rate than white prisoners under 45 years old. This was true for some but not for other conditions among black prisoners over 45 compared with those under 45 years old. It was not true for gastritis and duodenitis, frequent constipation, or intestinal conditions (n.o.s.).

As Table 3-7 shows, nonincarcerated offenders of both races under 45 years old reported stomach conditions (n.o.s.) more frequently than other selected chronic conditions, followed by ulcers of the stomach or duodenum. Nonincarcerated offenders of both races over 45 years old reported upper gastrointestinal disorders more frequently than other selected chronic conditions, followed by stomach conditions (n.o.s.). Nonincarcerated white offenders under 45 years old reported gallbladder conditions and enteritis or ulcerative colitis very infrequently, those who are black did not report either of these conditions or herniae at all. Nonincarcerated offenders of both races over 45 years old did not report any liver conditions. Black nonincarcerated offenders over 45 years old did not report any gallbladder conditions, enteritis or ulcerative colitis, or any intestinal conditions (n.o.s.).

The reported rate of all selected chronic conditions was higher for white nonincarcerated offenders over 45 years old than for black nonincarcerated offenders in this age bracket (except for liver conditions, which none of either race reported). The reported rate of most selected chronic conditions was higher for white nonincarcerated offenders under 45 years old than for black nonincarcerated offenders in this age bracket. The opposite was true for stomach or duodenal ulcers, liver conditions, and intestinal conditions (n.o.s.).

Table 3-8 contains ratios of selected chronic digestive condition rates reported for prisoners compared by age within race with nonincarcerated offenders. Comparing chronic digestive condition rates reported for prisoners and nonincarcerated offenders of both races under 45 years old, the highest ratios were observed for enteritis or ulcerative colitis (ratio: 23.72) and for intestinal conditions (n.o.s.) (ratio: 23.27). Ratios could not be obtained for gallbladder conditions, since no prisoners of either race reported them. The lowest ratios were observed for stomach conditions (n.o.s.) (ratio: 1.07) and

Table 3-7
Selected, Chronic Digestive Conditions Reported:* Adult Male Parolees and Probationers, by Age within Race

Race and Chronic Condition	Ages 17 Years and Over		Ages 17-44 Years		Ages 45 Years and Over	
	Sample	Estimated Rate	Sample	Estimated Rate	Sample	Estimated Rate
Both Races						
Ulcer of stomach or duodenum	28	46.1	22	40.4	6	96.8
Hernia of abdominal cavity	9	14.8	6	11.0	3	48.4
Upper gastrointestinal disorder	21	34.5	10	18.3	11	177.4
Gallbladder condition	3	4.9	1	1.8	2	32.3
Enteritis/ulcerative colitis	2	3.3	1	1.8	1	16.1
Gastritis and duodenitis	13	21.4	10	18.3	3	48.4
Frequent constipation	20	32.9	16	29.4	4	64.5
Intestinal condition (n.o.s.)	4	6.6	3	5.5	1	16.1
Liver condition	4	6.6	4	7.3	0	–
Stomach condition (n.o.s.)	37	61.0	28	51.4	9	145.2
White						
Ulcer of stomach or duodenum	16	40.4	12	33.1	4	121.2
Hernia of abdominal cavity	8	20.2	6	16.5	2	60.6
Upper gastrintestinal disorder	15	38.0	9	24.9	6	181.8
Gallbladder condition	3	7.6	1	2.8	2	60.6
Enteritis/ulcerative colitis	2	5.1	1	2.8	1	30.3
Gastritis and duodenitis	10	25.3	8	22.0	2	60.6
Frequent constipation	14	35.4	11	30.3	3	90.9
Intestinal condition (n.o.s.)	3	7.6	2	5.5	1	30.3
Liver condition	3	7.6	3	8.3	0	–
Stomach condition (n.o.s.)	26	65.7	20	55.1	6	181.8
Black						
Ulcer of stomach or duodenum	12	57.4	10	55.6	2	69.0
Hernia of abdominal cavity	1	4.8	0	–	1	34.5
Upper gastrointestinal disorder	6	28.2	1	5.4	5	172.4
Gallbladder condition	0	–	0	–	0	–
Enteritis/ulcerative colitis	0	–	0	–	0	–
Gastritis and duodenitis	3	14.4	2	11.1	1	34.5
Frequent constipation	6	28.7	5	27.8	1	34.5
Intestinal condition (n.o.s.)	1	4.8	1	11.1	0	–
Liver condition	1	4.8	1	11.1	0	–
Stomach condition (n.o.s.)	11	52.6	8	44.4	3	103.4

*Rates per 1,000 persons (estimates based on probability samples).

Table 3-8
Reported,* Selected, Chronic Digestive-Condition Rates: Adult Male Prisoners Compared with Adult Male, Nonincarcerated Offenders, by Age within Race

Race and Chronic Condition	Ratio: Rates for Prisoners/Nonincarcerated Offenders		
	Ages 17 Years and Over	Ages 17-44 Years	Ages 45 Years and Over
Both races			
Ulcer of stomach or duodenum	2.23	2.26	1.55
Hernia of abdominal cavity	3.64	3.88	5.17
Upper gastrointestinal disorder	2.56	4.67	1.41
Gall bladder condition			
Enteritis/ulcerative colitis	16.33	23.72	15.53
Gastritis and duodenitis	4.35	5.00	5.17
Frequent constipation	2.38	2.49	3.88
Intestinal condition (n.o.s.)	18.56	23.27	15.53
Liver condition	3.71	1.67	
Stomach condition (n.o.s.)	1.29	1.07	1.21
White			
Ulcer of stomach or duodenum	2.54	2.72	1.18
Hernia of abdominal cavity	2.11	2.04	1.18
Upper gastrointestinal disorder	2.47	3.61	0.60
Gallbladder condition			
Enteritis/ulcerative colitis	8.37	12.04	2.36
Gastritis and duodenitis	4.06	4.09	2.36
Frequent constipation	1.69	1.48	1.18
Intestinal condition (n.o.s.)	14.62	20.44	3.53
Liver condition	4.50	2.71	
Stomach condition (n.o.s.)	1.04	0.61	0.98
Black			
Ulcer of stomach or duodenum	1.80	1.68	2.42
Hernia of abdominal cavity	14.38		4.83
Upper gastrointestinal disorder	2.85	14.81	0.48
Gallbladder condition			
Enteritis/ulcerative colitis			
Gastritis and duodenitis	5.59	8.41	
Frequent constipation	3.60	3.84	2.41
Intestinal condition (n.o.s.)	28.73	13.72	
Liver condition	2.40		
Stomach condition (n.o.s.)	1.75	1.80	1.61

*Estimates based on probability samples.

liver conditions (ratio: 1.67). Black offenders had a high ratio (ratio: 14.81) for upper gastrointestinal disorders, white offenders, a lower ratio (ratio: 3.61).

A similar pattern prevailed in the comparison of chronic digestive condition rates reported for prisoners and nonincarcerated offenders of both races over 45 years old. However, as cells became smaller and responses became fewer for offenders over 45 compared with those under 45 years of age, it became more difficult to analyze items of information for specific chronic conditions according to race or age within race.

Discomfort attributable to toothaches or sore gums is an excellent indicator[6] of a chronic disorder of the upper gastrointestinal system. Prisoners of both races and all ages reported these conditions in a much lower proportion (24.0 percent) than did probationers of both races and all ages (70.0 percent). This difference remained true in all age brackets of both races combined, except for the 35 to 44 year-old group where this difference was much less pronounced. White prisoners and probationers between 35 and 44 years of age reported discomfort attributable to toothaches or sore gums in about the same proportion (29.2 and 29.4 percent respectively). Black prisoners under 35 years old reported these conditions in a higher proportion than did non-black probationers in this age bracket.

Parolees of both races and all ages reported discomfort attributable to toothaches or sore gums in a much lower proportion (23.0 percent) than did probationers of both races and all ages (70.0 percent). This difference remained true in all age brackets for both races combined, except for the 35 to 44 year-old group, where this difference was much less pronounced (as it also was between probationers and prisoners). White parolees and probationers between 35 and 44 years of age reported discomfort attributable to toothaches or sore gums in about the same proportion (and in about the same proportion as prisoners in this age bracket). Black parolees between 25 and 34 years of age reported these conditions in a higher proportion than black probationers in this age bracket.

The inability of a person to read ordinary newspaper print without wearing eyeglasses represents a chronic condition of the eyes.[7] Among prisoners of both races and all ages, 22.1 percent reported a need for wearing glasses to read, compared with 20.9 percent of probationers of both races and all ages, and compared with 20.3 percent of parolees of both races and all ages. More white probationers of all ages (37.7 percent) than black probationers of all ages (20.0 percent) reported this need for eyeglasses, as did more black prisoners of all ages (33.3 percent) than white prisoners of all ages (13.7 percent).

Fewer proportions of parolees than probationers in most age brackets of both races reported a need for wearing eyeglasses to read. White parolees over 45 years old reported this need in a higher proportion than white probationers in this age bracket. Black parolees under 25 years old reported this need in a higher proportion than black probationers in this age bracket. The reason may be that more white than black parolees over 45 years old, and more black than white parolees under 25 and between 35 and 44 years of age, reported the need for wearing eyeglasses to read.

D. Comparison Statistics

Table 3-9 summarizes the estimated incidence of acute conditions per 100 persons per year, by condition groups according to age for the United States population of adult males in 1972.[8] Prisoners of both races between 17 and 44 years of age reported infective and parasitic diseases at a rate that was 3.2 times higher than this estimate rate for the general adult-male United States population in this age bracket in 1972; acute digestive-system conditions at a rate that was 7.7 times higher; and injuries at a rate that was 2.3 times higher. Prisoners of both races between 17 and 44 years of age reported a slightly lower rate of acute respiratory conditions than did the general adult-male United States population in this age bracket in 1972.

Prisoners of both races over 45 years old reported infective and parasitic diseases at a rate that was 2.2 times higher than this estimated rate for the general adult-male United States population in this age bracket in 1972; acute respiratory conditions at a rate 33.5 percent higher; acute digestive conditions at a rate 6.8 times higher; and injuries at a rate 2.4 times higher.

Nonincarcerated offenders of both races between 17 and 44 years of age reported acute digestive conditions at a rate similar to that estimated for the

Table 3-9
Acute Conditions per 100 Persons per Year, by Condition Groups According to Age: United States Population of Adult Males, 1972

Condition Group	Ages 17-44 Years	Ages 45 Years and Over
All Acute Conditions	186.4	124.8
Infective and parasitic	15.9	8.9
Respiratory	100.2	67.4
Upper-respiratory	48.8	30.8
Influenza	47.7	30.8
All other respiratory	3.6	5.9
Digestive system	7.4	8.1
Injuries	44.1	22.8
All other acute conditions	18.9	17.5

Source: U.S. Public Health Service, *Current Estimates from the Health Interview Survey, United States, 1972.* Publication no. (HRA) 74-1512. Washington: 1973, U.S. Government Printing Office. (Adapted for use here.)

general adult-male United States population in this age bracket in 1972. However, the general adult-male United States population in this age bracket in 1972 had a rate of infective and parasitic diseases 2.3 times higher than this rate for sample nonincarcerated offenders; a rate of acute respiratory conditions 3.1 times higher; and a rate of injuries 84.5 percent higher.

Nonincarcerated offenders of both races over 45 years old reported acute digestive conditions at a rate 2.4 times higher than this rate for the general adult-male United States population in this age bracket in 1972. However, the general adult-male United States population in this age bracket in 1972 had an estimated rate of infective and parasitic diseases 36.9 percent higher than this rate for nonincarcerated offenders; a rate of acute respiratory conditions 60.9 percent higher; and a rate of injuries 41.6 percent higher.

Table 3-10 summarizes the estimated prevalence of selected, chronic digestive conditions per 1,000 persons by age for the United States population of adult males in the second half of 1968.[9] Prisoners of both races between 17 and 44 years of age reported all selected, chronic digestive conditions (except gallbladder conditions) at substantially higher rates than did the general adult-male United States population in this age bracket in 1968. Prisoners between 17 and 44 years old reported stomach or duodenal ulcers at a rate 3.5 times higher than this rate for the general adult male population in 1968; a rate of abdominal herniae 3.0 times higher; a rate of gastrointestinal disorders 5.9 times higher; a rate of chronic enteritis or ulcerative colitis 13.9 times higher; a rate of frequent

Table 3-10
Selected, Chronic Digestive Conditions per 1,000 Persons, by Age: United States Population of Adult Males, July to December 1968

Chronic Digestive Condition	Ages 17-44 Years	Ages 45-64 Years
Ulcer of stomach or duodenum	26.5	45.0
Hernia of abdominal cavity	14.1	34.0
Upper gastrintestinal disorder	14.5	25.5
Gallbladder condition	3.2	11.8
Enteritis/ulcerative colitis	5.0	12.2
Gastritis and duodenitis	6.6	14.5
Frequent constipation	6.9	19.6
Intestinal condition (n.o.s.)	1.9	3.5
Liver condition	–	2.2
Stomach condition (n.o.s.)	2.3	5.3

Source: U.S. Public Health Service, *Prevalence of Selected Chronic Digestive Conditions, United States, July-December, 1968.* Publication no. 1 (HRA) 74-1510. Washington: 1973, U.S. Government Printing Office.

constipation 10.6 times higher; a rate of intestinal conditions (n.o.s.) 67.4 times higher; and a rate of stomach conditions (n.o.s.) 23.5 times higher than the estimated rate for the general adult-male United States population in 1968.

Prisoners of both races over 45 years old reported rates of selected, chronic digestive conditions that were even more substantially higher than the rates for the general adult-male United States population in this age bracket in 1968. On the average, prisoners over 45 years old reported chronic digestive conditions at a rate more than 20 times higher than the estimated rate of each comparable condition for the general adult-male United States population in this age bracket in 1968. (Compare Table 3-6 with Table 3-10.)

Nonincarcerated offenders of both races between 17 and 44 years of age reported selected, chronic digestive conditions at rates sometimes higher and sometimes lower than similar condition rates estimated for the general adult-male United States population in this age bracket in 1968. Nonincarcerated offenders reported stomach or duodenal ulcers at a rate 52.5 percent higher than the estimated rate for the adult-male United States general population rate in 1968; a rate of upper gastrointestinal disorders 20.8 percent higher; a rate of gastritis and duodenitis 2.8 times higher; a rate of frequent constipation 4.3 times higher; a rate of intestinal conditions (n.o.s.) 2.9 times higher; and a rate of stomach conditions (n.o.s.) 22.3 percent higher. On the other hand, in 1968 the general adult-male United States population in this age bracket is estimated to have had abdominal herniae at a rate 28.2 percent higher than the rate reported by nonincarcerated offenders; a rate of chronic gallbladder conditions 77.8 percent higher; and a rate of chronic enteritis or ulcerative colitis 2.8 times higher.

Nonincarcerated offenders over 45 years old reported chronic digestive conditions at rates higher than comparable estimated rates for the general adult-male United States population in this age bracket in 1968, but less substantially higher than the rate for prisoners over 45 years old. Nonincarcerated offenders in this age bracket reported chronic stomach or duodenal ulcers at a rate 2.2 times higher than this estimated rate for the general adult-male United States population in this age bracket in 1968; a rate of abdominal herniae 42.4 percent higher; a rate of upper gastrointestinal disorders 7.0 times higher; a rate of chronic gallbladder conditions 2.7 times higher; a rate of chronic enteritis or ulcerative colitis 32.0 percent higher; a rate of frequent constipation, gastritis and duodenitis was 3.3 times higher; a rate of intestinal conditions (n.o.s.) 4.6 times higher; and a rate of stomach conditions (n.o.s.) 27.4 times higher.

4 Chronic Mental Disorders

A. Classification of Mental Disorders

No workable, satisfactory classification of mental disorders had been devised prior to 1968, when the *Eighth Revision International Classification of Diseases, Adapted for Use in the United States* (ICDA) was published.[1] The earlier ICDA revisions failed to classify mental disorders into categories sufficiently autonomous and explicit.[2] They failed particularly to classify many mental disorders according to the relationship of these disorders to organic and physical factors associated with physical disorders.[3] Coincidentally, the American Psychiatric Association also in 1968 published its second edition of the *Diagnostic and Statistical Manual of Mental Disorders* (DSM-II), revising the earlier edition (DSM-I) to conform to the eighth revision of the ICDA.

The new diagnostic nomenclature that appeared in DSM-II divided mental disorders into ten categories, to each of which is applied a three-digit numerical code, divisible into ten subdivisions, to correspond to the ICDA disease categories. The following is the list of DSM-II categories and their three-digit, inclusive numerical codes, which correspond to the ICDA disease codes:[4]

	Category	Codes
I.	Mental Retardation	310 - 315
II.	Organic Brain Syndromes	
	A. Psychotic	290 - 294
	B. Non-Psychotic	309
III.	Psychoses not Attributed to Physical Conditions Listed Previously	295 - 298
IV.	Neuroses	300
V.	Personality Disorders and Certain Other Non-Psychotic Mental Disorders	301 - 304
VI.	Psychophysiologic Disorders	305
VII.	Special Symptoms	306
VIII.	Transient Situational Distrubances	307
IX.	Behavior Disorders of Childhood and Adolescence	308
X.	Conditions without Manifest Psychiatric Disorder and Non-Specific Conditions	316 - 318

DSM-II replaced the DSM-I term "mental defect" with the term "mental retardation." The specific meanings which DSM-II employs for several terms need to be indicated here. Within the DSM-II meaning a person is considered to be mentally retarded if he has been shown to have an intelligence quotient (IQ) of 83 or below.[5] The DSM-II divides mental retardation into five degrees, as follows: borderline (IQ 68-83); mild (IQ 52-67); moderate (IQ 36-51); severe (IQ 20-35); and profound (IQ under 20).[6]

It divides organic brain syndromes into two categories: those with which psychoses are associated, and the non-psychotic.[7] Organic brain syndromes (OBS) are manifested by five symptoms: (a) impairment of orientation; (b) impairment of memory; (c) impairment of the intellectual functions of comprehension, calculation, knowledge, and learning; (d) impairment of judgment; and (e) lability and shallowness of affect.[8] The psychoses associated with organic brain syndromes are caused primarily by alcohol intoxication, syphilis of the central nervous system, senility, intracranial neoplasms (tumors), or brain trauma (following injury or surgery).[9] The non-psychotic organic brain syndromes are associated with schizophrenia, paranoia, and manic-depressive illnesses.[10]

Neuroses are characterized by anxiety and will be discussed in Chapter Five in greater detail. As contrasted to psychoses, neuroses manifest neither gross distortion or misinterpretation of external reality, nor gross personality disorganization.[11] Personality disorders are characterized by deeply ingrained maladaptive patterns of behavior that are lifelong and often recognizable by the time of adolescence or earlier.[12] Psychophysiologic disorders are characterized by physical symptoms that are caused by emotional states.[13] Transient situational disturbances occur in persons who have no apparent underlying mental disorders, and they represent an acute reaction to overwhelming environmental stress.[14] Conditions without manifest psychiatric disorder may be the result of marital, occupational, or social maladjustment.[15]

B. Statistical Tabulations

Statistics on the diagnostic characteristics of patients admitted to psychiatric facilities have usually been prepared according to the underlying or primary psychiatric disorder.[16] However, the recording of multiple diagnoses for a single patient makes it possible to obtain more extensive information on the simultaneous occurrence of more than one mental disorder. This is particularly important in providing more information on the occurrence of such disorders as alcohol and drug dependence among persons with specific types of psychoses, neuroses, and personality disorders.[17]

The maintenance of accurate records on the mental disorders of institutionalized patients is a difficult task for the personnel of mental hospitals, whose traditional function this has been. This task is more difficult for a prison administration to accomplish, since it requires the cooperation of personnel in agencies outside the prison, unless the prison employs a psychiatrist. At the time of this study Tennessee State Penitentiary did not employ one; but during its early stages the psychological services section under the supervisor of counseling began to accumulate the psychiatric records of prisoners. There were still not sufficient psychiatric records available throughout 1972, but there were by the spring of 1973 at the close of field research.

Some attention should be focused here on the procedures used by Tennessee State Penitentiary personnel to obtain the psychiatric records of prisoners. Four classes of inmates should be distinguished: (1) prisoners with a history of a mental disorder prior to imprisonment, and manifesting signs of it during imprisonment; (2) prisoners with no history of mental disorder prior to imprisonment, but manifesting signs of one during imprisonment and referred to a mental hospital for admission or evaluation; (3) prisoners with a history of a mental disorder prior to imprisonment, but manifesting no signs of it during imprisonment; and (4) prisoners with no history of a mental disorder prior to imprisonment, and manifesting no signs of one during imprisonment, the so-called normal prisoners. (Of course latent mental disorders could be present.)

Prior to early 1973, prison personnel were concerned with obtaining only psychiatric records of prisoners in the first two categories mentioned. In other words, prison personnel did not attempt to do a psychiatric profile on each prisoner upon intake, but waited until a prisoner became involved in an altercation or otherwise displayed some indication of a mental disorder. Early in 1973, the prison counseling section began a fairly systematic process of requests to all psychiatric institutions in Tennessee for any psychiatric records that might exist for prisoners in the third class mentioned. In this way, the prison would have access to the psychiatric case histories of some prisoners before they displayed evidence of a mental disorder in their behavior during imprisonment. By June 1973 all available data was in. (Probably no psychiatric records would exist for the fourth class of prisoner listed above.)

In this way, the prison began to accumulate and index the psychiatric records of prisoners in the first three (rather than only the first two) of the above listed classes. This effort enlarged their files and facilitated a cursory quantification of the mental disorders of prisoners. Still, psychiatric records of the prisoners at Tennessee State Penitentiary were not completely obtained by prison personnel. The prison did not routinely solicit the records of mental hospitals outside of the state, or of psychiatrists in private practice. In addition, even state hospitals in Tennessee were slipshod in their compliance with the request that they furnish the prison with records; in a few instances requests were denied, since they were not based on a compulsory court process.[a]

[a]Psychiatric records (including diagnoses, prognoses, impressions, and other data) are held by most agencies under the cloak of secrecy. While the reasons for maintaining such data on a confidential basis are obvious, it seems ludicrous for one state agency to deny another access to records as important as these. Most of these records were supplied by the agency that had evaluated the patient originally, and many of the records supplied were marked "eyes only" for "authorized personnel." Some were limited to the eyes of psychiatrists or

Table 4-1 summarizes: the number of times each specified diagnosis of a mental disorder appeared on record as the only disorder or in combination with other disorders, according to the time when the diagnosis was first made (before or since imprisonment); and for the population of prisoners confined at Tennessee State Penitentiary during the entire first half of 1973. This summary undoubtedly is more complete for prisoners in the indicated first two classes than for those in the third. Nevertheless, the summary provides a firm delineation of those most prevalent mental disorders diagnosed for inmates of this prison. In Table 4-1, all diagnoses are listed according to ICDA code number and according to the title and category set forth in DSM-II. By reason of the small size of each cell, these diagnoses are not broken down by any demographic variables, an unwise procedure in any event, since it might jeopardize the privacy of the information.[b] Data is based on an estimated 1,040 inmates confined at Tennessee State Penitentiary during the entire period beginning 1 January 1973 and ending 30 June 1973.

Of these estimated 1,040 inmates, 172 had at least one diagnosis of a mental disorder that was known to prison personnel, and 39 had two or more known diagnoses. As has been mentioned, this data should be considered a minimum, but not necessarily a maximum, since the records of psychiatric history may not have been complete because of lack of agency cooperation. The substantial percentage of diagnoses noted is a significant minimum boundary. If the records had been complete, 16.5 percent of the prisoners confined for the entire first half of 1973 at Tennessee State Penitentiary would have had a record of a diagnosed mental disorder, and 3.8 percent would have had a record of two or more diagnosed mental disorders. In addition, 32 of the 172 diagnosed persons received their first known, but not necessarily most recent diagnosis before imprisonment for their current sentence, while 140 of these 172 diagnosed persons received their first known diagnosis of a mental disorder since being imprisoned for their current sentence. If the records were complete, then 18.6 percent of those prisoners who had a diagnosed mental disorder would have received their first diagnosis prior to imprisonment for their current sentence,

licensed social workers. The administration granted this researcher access to all such records, notwithstanding the constraints purported by the contributing agencies. A few agencies refused to send psychiatric evaluations to the prison administration, nor could they be obtained for the present study.

[b]There is some justification for the common psychiatric practice of denying a patient access to his own psychiatric evaluation. Reasons vary from the desire not to alarm a patient to a precaution against a libel action by a patient who contests the truth of a diagnosis. In any event, this study should not be the format for the disclosure of confidential information. If demographic variables were associated with some of the data in Table 4-1, the risk would be high that a prisoner-patient might infer accurately or not, that a particular diagnosis pertained to himself.

and 81.4 percent would have received their first diagnosis since the beginning of their current prison term.

Of the 172 prisoners who had a diagnosed mental disorder, 24 had a diagnosis of mental retardation; 15 had a diagnosis of an organic brain syndrome of which 12 had been determined to be psychoses and 3 had been determined to be non-psychotic; 30 had a diagnosis of a psychosis not attributed to an organic brain syndrome; 8 had a diagnosis of a neurosis; 57 had a diagnosis of a personality disorder, 11 of a sexual deviation, 13 of alcohol dependence, and 10 of drug dependence. In addition, two prisoners had a diagnosis of a transient situational disturbance, and one of a behavior disorder of childhood or adolescence.

If the records were complete, and even if not, as a minimum, 2.3 percent of the population of prisoners who spent all of the first half of 1973 at Tennessee State Penitentiary had been diagnosed as mentally retarded; 4.0 percent had been diagnosed as suffering from a psychosis; 2.2 percent had been diagnosed as being dependent upon alcohol or drugs; and 1.1 percent had been diagnosed as suffering from a mental disorder associated with a sexual deviation. In addition, 5.5 percent had been diagnosed as suffering from a personality disorder.[18]

No systematic comparison on the number of diagnosed mental disorders can be made between prisoners and parolees or probationers, since the Division of Probation and Parole did not possess any psychiatric records on its clients, and these records could not be obtained for sample parolees or sample probationers in any other way.[c] That prisoners seem to have received fewer psychiatric diagnoses before imprisonment than during imprisonment would seem to suggest a hypothesis: in the absence of contrary evidence, probationers have received fewer psychiatric diagnoses than prisoners in Tennessee. No statement can be made regarding parolees, since the parolees studied had been released from prison prior to 1973, when the prison began to accumulate psychiatric records on a systematic basis.

Among the 254 probationers responding to questions on whether they had received any outpatient consultation with a psychiatrist, 27 answered affirmatively. Among 360 parolees who responded to the same questions, 11 answered affirmatively. The assumption is that a person who consults with a psychiatrist has a psychiatric record, although the diagnosis may be that no

[c]The Division of Probation and Parole undoubtedly should try to obtain psychiatric records of its clients. Again, the difficulties are manifold. First, persons are placed on probation and parole for relatively short periods of time, and it may take at least six months for an agency to acquire records for a substantial proportion of its population. Secondly, a probation or a parole officer is not in as authoritative position as a prison administration. While psychiatric evaluations may be ordered by a court as part of a presentence report, this practice is not followed uniformly in Tennessee, and without it the probation officer or the parole officer lacks the leverage sufficient to demand that this data be supplied.

Table 4-1
Diagnoses of Mental Disorders, Specified by Time First Diagnosed: Prisoners Confined during Entire First Half of 1973

		Diagnosis	No Other Mental Disorder	With Other Mental Disorder	Times Diagnosis Listed	Diagnosed Before Prison	Diagnosed Since Prison
		Total, All Mental Disorders	133	39	172	32	140
	I.	Mental Retardation					
31x.5*		Mental retardation, all grades, with chromosomal abnormality					
31x.7		Mental retardation, all grades, following major psychiatric disorder					
31x.8		Mental retardation, all grades, with psychosocial deprivation	4	3	7	2	5
31x.0-31x.4) 31x.6,31x.9)		Mental retardation, all grades, with other conditions	16	1	17	1	16
	II.	Organic Brain Syndromes					
	A.	Psychoses					
290		Senile and presenile dementia					
291		Alcoholic psychosis	2	1	3	1	2
292.0-.1		Psychosis associated with syphilitic infection					
292.2-.9		Psychosis with other intracranial infection					
293.0		Psychosis with cerebral Arteriosclerosis	1		1		1
293.1-.9		Psychosis with other cerebral condition	4	1	5	1	4
294.3		Psychosis with a drug or poison intoxication		1	1		1

294.0-.2) 294.4-.9)		Psychosis with other physical condition (excluding alcohol)	2		2	1	1
	B.	Nonpsychotic					
309		Nonpsychotic organic brain syndromes	2	1	3	1	2
	III.	Psychoses Not Attributed To Physical Conditions					
295		Shizophrenia	22	3	25	6	19
296		Major affective disorders	1		1		1
297		Paranoid states	2		2		2
298		Other psychoses	2		2	1	1
	IV.	Neuroses					
300		Neuroses	7	1	8	1	7
	V.	Personality Disorders And Other Nonpsychotic Mental Disorders					
301		Personality disorders	38	19	57	5	52
302		Sexual deviations	7	4	11	3	8
303		Alcoholism	10	3	13	5	8
304		Drug dependence	9	1	10	1	9
	VI.	Other Disorders					
305		Psychophysiologic disorders					
306		Special symptoms					
307		Transient situational disturbances	2		2	2	
308		Behavior disorders of childhood and adolescence	1		1	1	

*This indicates the total for all grades of mental retardation within a given ICDA etiological category. Thus, the total of 310.5, 311.5, 312.5, 313.5, 314.5, 315.5 is represented as simply 31x.5.

mental disorder exists. Again, these responses by parolees and probationers would seem to evidence a minimum rather than a maximum proportion of those with a psychiatric case history. On the basis of this data, at least 3.1 percent of parolees and 10.6 percent of probationers had received a psychiatric evaluation.[d]

C. Self-Destruction

The existence of a mental disorder may be evidenced by behavior that identifies a person as a danger to himself or to others.[19] Indeed, in some states a person must be diagnosed as both mentally ill and in need of treatment, and a danger to himself or to others, in order to be committed civilly to a mental hospital.[20] In 1972, twenty-one prisoners at Tennessee State Penitentiary were sent to Tennessee's Central State Hospital at Nashville for a psychiatric evaluation, out of them thirteen were committed to the mental hospital. Only three of the twenty-one prisoners who received a psychiatric evaluation were suspected of being a danger to themselves rather than to others. Only two of the thirteen prisoners who were committed to the mental hospital were suspected of being a danger to themselves rather than to others. The remaining prisoners were evaluated and/or committed as a result of altercations that included assaults upon other prisoners.

Self-destruction may include a desire on the part of the actor to cause his own death, but suicide does not have to be the objective of the self-mutilator. This study distinguishes two kinds of self-destruction. The form of self-destruction most commonly known outside prison may be labeled the "Mortality Type" or simply "Type One." The form of self-destruction more commonly known inside prison may be labeled the "Morbidity Type" or simply "Type Two." In Type One, the actor's principal objective in the ultimate analysis seems to be to cause his own death, and if he fails, his act still is a genuine attempted suicide. In Type Two, the actor's principal objective is not to cause his own death at all, but instead to cause a non-fatal injury to his own body.

Naturally, the Type One actor may harbor secondary objectives besides the causation of death. This actor may desperately want to be discovered and saved,

---

[d]Again, these estimates are very minimal. Is there any reason to presume that a population of parolees would have received psychiatric evaluations at a lower rate than a population of prisoners in the same state? Only if the rate at which prisoners received evaluations increased over time (since the average parolee could be expected to have begun imprisonment prior to the time when the average inmate still in prison began imprisonment). On the other hand, probationers could be expected to have received psychiatric evaluations at a higher rate than either prisoners or parolees under certain conditions: first, if the practice of courts were to order a psychiatric evaluation only for those offenders convicted of less serious offenses, as a means of justifying release back into the community; secondly, if persons on probation had been convicted of crimes involving bizarre behavior—such as drug offenses—more frequently than those in prison or on parole.

so that his incomplete act may be viewed as a warning, drawing the attention of family or friends to his depression.[21] Still, the true Type One actor seems to risk almost certain death by such actions as hanging, shooting in the head, or inhaling carbon monoxide to the point of unconsciousness. If the Type One actor is saved, that is attributable to chance or to unforeseeable factors, for example, skillfull surgery.

The Type Two actor may harbor secondary objectives also, and one may be death. However, the Type Two actor seems to calculate precisely the risk that his act may result in his own death, in order to minimize that risk. On occasion, the Type Two actor may lose the gamble and his life. Much more often, however, the Type Two actor survives his injury only to repeat the self-injurious act many times. Although the Type Two actor may create the appearance of impending death by severing a major artery (commonly the heelstring), he notifies at least one other person, or may scream loudly as soon as he has completed his charade, and the ensuing clamor invites rescue rather than danger. Quite clearly, therefore, the Type Two actor differs from the Type One actor, not only by his state of mind, but also by his method of activity.

Emile Durkheim observed that a person who commits or attempts to commit suicide may display either an egoistic, an altruistic, or an anomic pattern.[22] Unlike the Type One actor, the Type Two actor seems to display only an egoistic pattern, although a pseudoanomic pattern may be discernible. Whether or not a trace of depression (such as a need for drugs) may be a cause of the Type Two act, the clear objective of the Type Two actor appears to be to attract attention, especially attention on the part of medical personnel.[e]

1. Type One Activity

Type One activity, or attempted suicide in the sense of its traditional meaning, must involve more than a mere threat to take one's own life. With or without a threat, there must be an overt physical manifestation leading to some self-inflicted physical injury. Prisoners, parolees and probationers were asked to respond to questions that probed whether they had ever attempted to commit suicide or felt like committing suicide since being imprisoned or since being placed on parole or probation. No difficulty was encountered over the ordinary meaning of suicide and attempt to commit suicide.

No prisoner responding reported having attempted to commit suicide since being sent to prison for his current sentence. Similarly, no black parolee or black probationer responding reported having attempted to commit suicide since being

[e]Certainly, the objective is not altruistic, since no possible good results from Type Two activity. Perhaps the objective might be anomic, but the actor would have to be extremely masochistic, since only greater anomie (rather than relief in the form of death) results from Type Two activity.

placed on parole or probation for his current sentence. All the attempts to commit suicide documented here were reported by white parolees and white probationers under 35 years old. Among white offenders under 25 years old reporting an attempted suicide, one was a parolee and four were probationers. Among white offenders between 25 and 34 years of age reporting an attempted suicide, one was a parolee and two were probationers. Both the parolees were married; one had less than seven and the other had between nine and eleven years of education. Three of the six probationers were single, one was married, one separated, one divorced. Two of the probationers had seven or eight years of education; two had between nine and eleven years; and one had less than seven and one more than twelve years of education.

Although none of the prisoners reported an attempted suicide during imprisonment, some did report having feelings of a desire to commit suicide during imprisonment. A higher percentage (32.5 percent) of white prisoners reported these feelings than did black prisoners of all ages (3.4 percent). White prisoners under 25 years old reported these feelings more frequently than prisoners of other ages (58.8 percent), followed by white prisoners between 25 and 34 years of age (43.8 percent), and by white prisoners between 35 and 44 years of age (20.8 percent). Among black prisoners those under 25 years old (8.7 percent) and over 45 years old (8.3 percent) reported these feelings most frequently.

Among nonincarcerated offenders, black probationers under 25 years old reported feelings of a desire to commit suicide most frequently (10.3 percent), followed by white probationers under 25 years old (9.7 percent) and between 25 and 34 years of age (7.5 percent). Among parolees, whites over 45 years old (3.7 percent) and under 25 years old (3.2 percent) reported these feelings most frequently.

Table 4-2 contains ratios of reported suicide desire rates for prisoners and for parolees compared by age within race to probationers. In the comparison of prisoners with probationers showed a ratio of 2.68 for offenders of both races and all ages. Thus, prisoners of both races and all ages reported feelings of a desire to commit suicide at a higher rate than did probationers of both races and all ages. The highest ratio was for white offenders under 25 years old (ratio: 6.06), followed closely by the ratio for white offenders between 25 and 34 years of age (ratio: 5.84). The lowest ratios appearing were for black offenders under 25 years old (ratio: 0.84) and for white offenders over 45 years old (ratio: 1.34). However, ratios could not be computed for black offenders over 25 years old or for white offenders between 35 and 44 years of age, since probationers of these groups reported no such feelings. White offenders of all ages combined had a much higher ratio (ratio: 4.01) than black offenders of all ages combined (ratio: 0.58).

In the comparison of parolees with probationers, a ratio of 0.22 was observed for offenders of both races and all ages. Thus, parolees of both races and all ages

Table 4-2
Suicide Desires Reported:* Adult Male Prisoners and Parolees Compared with Adult Male Probationers, by Age within Race

Age and Race	Ratio: Rates for Prisoners/Probationers	Ratio: Rates for Parolees/Probationers
Both Races		
17 years and over	2.68	0.22
17-24 years	3.03	0.18
25-34 years	4.02	0.25
35-44 years	–	–
45 years and over	1.42	0.42
White		
17 years and over	4.01	0.30
17-24 years	6.06	0.33
25-34 years	5.84	0.17
35-44 years	–	–
45 years and over	1.34	0.70
Black		
17 years and over	0.58	0.12
17-24 years	0.84	–
25-34 years	–	–
35-44 years	–	–
45 years and over	–	–

*Estimates based on probability samples.

reported feelings of a desire to commit suicide at a lower rate than did probationers of both races and all ages. The ratio for white offenders of all ages combined (ratio: 0.30) was somewhat higher than the ratio for black offenders of all ages combined (ratio: 0.12). Ratios could not be computed for black offenders. The highest ratio observed was for white offenders over 45 years old (ratio: 0.70).

Prisoners who were married reported these feelings more frequently (26.4 percent) than other prisoners, followed by those who were single (20.8 percent). Prisoners who were separated reported these feelings at a lower rate (7.7 percent), as did those who were divorced (10.5 percent). Sample prisoners who were widowed reported no such feelings at all. Probationers who were separated reported these feelings more frequently (21.4 percent) than other probationers, followed by those who were divorced (10.3 percent), and those who were single (9.3 percent). Probationers who were married reported these feelings at a lower rate (3.4 percent), and those who were widowed reported no such feelings at all. Widowed parolees reported these feelings more frequently (16.7 percent) than other parolees, followed by the single (8.6 percent) and the married (6.7 percent). Separated parolees reported these feelings at a lower rate (2.0 percent), as did the divorced (2.1 percent).

Table 4-3 contains ratios of reported suicide-desire rates for prisoners and parolees compared by marital status to probationers. In the comparison of prisoners with probationers, married offenders had the highest ratio (ratio: 7.76), while separated offenders had the lowest observed ratio (ratio: 0.36). Single offenders had a ratio of 2.24, while divorced offenders had a ratio of 1.02. In the comparison of parolees with probationers, married offenders had the highest ratio (ratio: 1.97), followed by single offenders (ratio: 0.92). Separated offenders had the lowest ratio (ratio: 0.09), followed by divorced offenders (ratio: 0.20).

Prisoners with between nine and eleven years of education reported these feelings more frequently (38.6 percent) than other prisoners, followed by those with twelve years or more of education (13.6 percent). Prisoners with less than seven years of education reported these feelings less frequently (5.7 percent), and those with seven or eight years reported these feelings still less frequently (4.8 percent). Probationers with less than seven years of education reported these feelings more frequently (17.6 percent) than other probationers, followed by those with between nine and eleven years (7.7 percent), and those with seven or eight and those with twelve years or more of education (6.8 percent). Parolees with seven or eight years of education reported these feelings more frequently (11.6 percent) than other parolees, followed by those with less than seven years (7.7 percent), twelve years or more (6.5 percent), and between nine and eleven years of education (2.6 percent).

Table 4-4 contains ratios of reported suicide-desire rates for prisoners and parolees compared by education with probationers. In the comparison of prisoners with probationers, offenders with between nine and eleven years of education had the highest ratio (ratio: 5.01), followed by those with twelve years or more of education (ratio: 2.00). Offenders with less than seven years of education had the lowest ratio (ratio: 0.32), followed by those with seven or eight years (ratio: 0.71). In the comparison of parolees with probationers,

Table 4-3
Suicide Desires Reported:* Adult-Male Prisoners and Parolees Compared with Adult-Male Probationers, by Marital Status

Marital Status	Ratio: Rates for Prisoners/Probationers	Ratio: Rates for Parolees/Probationers
Single	2.24	0.92
Married	7.76	1.97
Widowed		
Separated	0.36	0.09
Divorced	1.02	0.20

*Estimates based on probability samples.

Table 4-4
Suicide Desires Reported:* Adult Male Prisoners and Parolees Compared with Adult Male Probationers, by Education

Education in Years of School Completed	Ratio: Rates for Prisoners/Probationers	Ratio: Rates for Parolees/Probationers
0-6	0.32	0.44
7-8	0.71	1.71
9-11	5.01	0.34
12 or over	2.00	0.96

*Estimates based on probability samples.

offenders with seven or eight years of education had the highest ratio (ratio: 1.71), followed by those with twelve years or more (ratio: 0.96). Offenders with between nine and eleven years of education had the lowest ratio (ratio: 0.34), followed by those with less than seven years (ratio: 0.44).

2. *Type Two Activity*

Type Two activity, or self-mutilation without the desire to take one's own life, must still involve some degree of self-inflicted injury. Under some conditions, the distinction between a Type One and a Type Two self-inflicted injury might seem vague. One test for making this distinction with high accuracy rests in the number of a given actor's prior self-inflicted injuries. Another test relates to the part of the body an actor has injured. One who repeatedly injures himself on multiple occasions must be assumed to intend to live rather than to die, since without his will to live the law of averages would seem to ensure death. This assumption is buttressed by evidence that an actor injures parts of the body to which injury is unlikely to result in immediate death, or which are easily restorable through simple corrective surgery.[23]

Among those prisoners who spent six months or longer at Tennessee State Penitentiary during 1972, twenty-two persons were reported to have inflicted upon themselves at least one injury matching the Type Two criteria. Sixteen of these self-mutilators were white prisoners; five were black prisoners; and one was a Native American prisoner. The majority of these self-mutilators were between 25 and 34 years of age at the time of their mutilations. These included ten whites, four blacks, and the Native American. Four white self-mutilators and one black self-mutilator were under 25 years old. One white self-mutilator was between 35 and 44 years of age, and one was over 45 years old.

The majority of these self-mutilators lacerated either their wrists, hands, or arms. Thirteen self-mutilators followed this pattern. Four punctured the stomach; three severed the heelstring; and two punctured the eye. Five of the self-mutilators injured themselves intentionally more than once during 1972. Among these twenty-two prisoners there were forty-three reported incidents of self-inflicted injury. One individual prisoner injured himself intentionally on 16 separate occasions during 1972. Another had injured himself intentionally on 13 separate occasions during 1971 and on the same number of occasions during 1970. One self-mutilator injured himself intentionally on at least 66 separate occasions documented during the course of the sixty-three months of his continuous imprisonment at Tennessee State Penitentiary.[f] Most of these incidents consisted of the reopening of a pre-existing wound that had become ulcerated. Another prisoner injured himself intentionally on more than 20 separate occasions in about as many months of confinement at the same prison.

Self-mutilations occurred on multiple occasions during the same day, both on the part of the same actor and on the part of two or more different actors. For instance, two chronic self-mutilators either reopened a pre-existing wound or started a fresh wound twice on the same day on at least five separate days during 1972. Similarly, two different self-mutilators intentionally injured themselves on the same day on at least four separate occasions in 1972. The same instruments[g] are known to have been used by two different self-mutilators to inflict injury on at least three separate occasions during 1972. Hence, Type Two self-mutilations may be viewed as being collective ventures quite frequently.

Seven self-mutilators were admitted to an outside general hospital during 1972 for emergency surgery to correct a self-inflicted injury. One of these prisoners and another prisoner were admitted to the maximum security ward of a state mental hospital, and a third prisoner was sent to the same hospital for a psychiatric evaluation, all as a result of self-inflicted injuries. Each of these prisoners, however, was returned to Tennessee State Penitentiary before the end of 1972.

Only eight of the twenty-two prisoners who were reported to have inflicted injury on themselves intentionally during 1972 had a psychiatric record on file at the prison in 1973. These eight prisoners included five chronic repeaters. Of

[f]This prisoner's wound, of which he seemed to be very proud, consisted of an opening in the abdomen perhaps three inches in diameter and with the upper circumference extending to perhaps an inch below the navel. This researcher was introduced to the prisoner, who offered to expose the wound for observation. He proceeded to unfasten a wide belt, which in turn released several pieces of four inch gauze used to plug the opening. He reclined on his back, removed the final gauze, and several fluid ounces of liquid feces were ejaculated into the air, because of puncture holes in his colon. Then the feces drained back into the cavity, which the prisoner repacked with gauze.

[g]These instruments, which were wires, on at least two occasions seem to have been smuggled between self-mutilators by means of a third party who enjoyed greater freedom than these actors. Other instruments which self-mutilators have used include nails, scrap metal pieces, bedsprings, and even pieces of torn fingernails (used to reopen a sensitive pre-existing wound).

the five chronic repeaters, three had been diagnosed as having an antisocial personality (ICDA and DSM-II Code 301.7), and one of these had also been diagnosed as being addicted to alcohol (303.2). Out of the other two chronic repeaters, one had been diagnosed as having a passive-aggressive personality (301.81) together with a manic-depressive psychosis (296.3). The other had been diagnosed as having a mental defect (the term used in DSM-I that became mental retardation in DSM-II). The remaining three self-mutilators who had received a psychiatric evaluation were diagnosed respectively as having: a passive-aggressive personality (51.1 in DSM-I); a psychoneurotic depression (300.4); and a psychosis associated with an organic brain syndrome resulting from brain trauma (293.5).

5 Neurotic Conditions: Selected Symptoms of Psychological Distress

A. The Meaning of Neurosis

Anxiety is the chief characteristic of a neurosis; one suffering a neurosis may feel and express anxiety directly, or may control it subconsciously by conversion, displacement, or other psychological defense mechanisms.[1] In addition to anxiety, neuroses may manifest themselves in feelings of depression, shame, or guilt, from which a person may desire relief. In contrast to psychoses, neuroses do not manifest gross personality disorganization or gross distortion or misinterpretation of reality.[2] Symptoms of a severe neurosis include hysteria, phobia, depression, neurasthenia (weakness), depersonalization, and hypochondria, alone or in combination with these or other symptoms.[3]

Not every form of neurosis can be isolated and distinguished separately from other forms, and this is especially difficult for a layman. On the other hand, ordinary people use such words as "nervousness" and "nervous breakdown" to describe their perceptions of anxiety and emotional crisis. The average person is quite capable of describing certain feelings of psychological distress associated with mild to moderate forms of neurosis. Specific physical, psychological, or psychosomatic symptoms have been used repeatedly in other studies as valid and reliable indicators of general psychological distress.[4] Twelve symptom items that have been used in studies of psychological distress are selected for replication here; they are:

1. nervous breakdown
2. feelings of an impending nervous breakdown
3. nervousness
4. inertia
5. insomnia
6. trembling hands
7. nightmares
8. perspiring hands
9. fainting
10. headaches
11. dizziness
12. heart palpitations

The first two items are not mutually exclusive, in the sense that a person making a positive response to the first must also make a positive response to the second, although the reverse may not be necessarily true. A nervous breakdown is characterized as an emotional crisis that involves multiple symptoms of psychological distress without a physical basis, and that culminates in complete emotional collapse. Although this term is both nonmedical and nonspecific, it is widely used and its meaning commonly understood. A person who reports he has felt an impending nervous breakdown but that he has resolved the emotional crisis short of complete emotional collapse is classified as exhibiting symptom number 2 instead of symptom number 1. Nervousness is the condition of being easily excited or agitated, and is associated with anxiety and tension. Inertia is the condition of psychological immobilization, and is associated with resistance to action and may or may not be sufficient to reach neurasthenia. Insomnia is the condition of experiencing difficulty getting to sleep or staying asleep. Hand trembling is the condition of being unable to prevent one's hands from shaking or twitching involuntarily. Nightmares are fright reactions that occur during sleep. Perspiring hands are characterized by unusual accumulations of sweat on the hands in the absence of direct exertion or fright. Fainting is the temporary loss of consciousness—sometimes referred to as blacking out—that occurs without warning. A headache is a constricting sensation about the skull. Dizziness is the feeling that consciousness may be about to be lost, and is accompanied often by blurred vision or shortness of breath. A heart palpitation is a sensation that the heart is beating unusually hard, but not on account of any physical basis or of any identifiable fear.

Each of these 12 symptom items is an independent indicator of some form of psychological distress. Symptom items 1 (nervous breakdown) and 2 (impending nervous breakdown) are combined into a single symptom item. The combination of items 1 and 2, plus the remaining 10 items, is used to form an 11-point omnibus stress index. Respondents were asked to report whether they experienced 1 or more of these 11 symptom items separately. Then the percentage of respondents who answered affirmatively to each of the 11 items individually was averaged for all eleven items combined. The mean percentage of affirmative responses becomes the omnibus stress score.[a]

Each adult male criminal offender (prisoner, probationer, parolee) was asked to answer questions relating to the frequency and intensity at which he suffered from each symptom of psychological distress. Respondents were asked to make a choice among either three or four possible answers to such questions as the following:

"Do you ever have any trouble getting to sleep or staying asleep?"

Often _______ Sometimes ____ Almost Never ____ Never _____

[a]Responses to each symptom-item question are tabulated separately, and then combined into an average response for all symptom-item questions combined.

"Have you ever had spells of dizziness?"

Every Few Days __________ Less Often __________ Never _____

"Do these bother you?"

Quite a Bit _________ Just a Little _________ Not at All ______

Crude responses were summarized on either a three- or a four-point scale, and then these scales were polarized into affirmative or negative responses. Such responses as "Often" and "Sometimes" were coded together as a single affirmative response, and such responses as "Almost Never" and "Never" were coded together as a single negative response. In the same way, responses to such other questions as "Every Few Days" and "Quite a Bit" were interpreted as affirmative, and such responses as "Less Often" or "Just a Little" were interpreted as negative, so were "Not at All" and "Never."

Two questions were asked separately for symptom items no. 10 (headaches), no. 11 (dizziness), and no. 12 (heart palpitations). In addition to being asked to assess the frequency of their being bothered by these conditions ("Every Few Days," "Less Often," "Never"), respondents were asked also to assess the intensity of their being bothered by these conditions ("Quite a Bit," "Just a Little," "Not at All"). An affirmative response to either question was interpreted as an affirmative response to the condition.

B. The Omnibus Stress Scores

Affirmative responses to each psychological stress symptom were averaged to produce the mean percentage of affirmative responses for all 11 symptom items combined. This mean percentage is the omnibus stress score. Omnibus stress scores are summarized separately for prisoners compared with probationers and for parolees compared with probationers. Within each of these two comparisons, omnibus stress scores are summarized separately according to age, race, age within race, marital status, and education.

From the comparison between the omnibus stress scores of prisoners and the scores of probationers, an inference may be drawn concerning the differential frequency and intensity of anxiety among incarcerated adult males in comparison to nonincarcerated, adult-male criminal offenders. From the comparison between the omnibus stress scores of parolees and the scores of probationers, an inference may be drawn concerning the differential frequency and intensity of anxiety among two populations of nonincarcerated, adult-male criminal offenders—one of which has experienced imprisonment and the other of which has not. No comparison has been made between parolees and prisoners according to omnibus stress scores, since the scores of parolees could be expected to be dependent upon the scores of prisoners.

1. Omnibus Scores of Probationers and Prisoners

As Table 5-1 shows, the omnibus stress score reported by probationers of both races and all ages is 19.6 percent. Among probationers of both races combined, those who were over 45 years old had the highest omnibus score, followed by those who were under 25 years old; while those who were between 35 and 44 years of age had the lowest omnibus score, followed by those between 25 and 34 years of age. This pattern remained virtually true for both races separately.

Table 5-1
Prevalence of General Psychological Distress from Responses* to Omnibus Stress Questionnaire: Adult Male Prisoners Compared with Adult Male Probationers and Parolees, by Age within Race

Race and Age	Average (Mean) Percentage Reporting Psychological Distress					
	Probationers		Prisoners		Parolees	
	Sample	%	Sample	%	Sample	%
Both Races						
17 years and over	(248)	19.6	(204)	51.2	(357)	19.1
17-24 years	(142)	19.5	(40)	48.3	(114)	17.1
25-34 years	(64)	18.6	(87)	51.1	(129)	21.1
35-44 years	(23)	15.4	(37)	40.0	(69)	14.2
45 years and over	(19)	29.2	(40)	64.8	(45)	26.5
White						
17 years and over	(197)	19.5	(117)	56.9	(207)	20.0
17-24 years	(113)	19.1	(17)	60.0	(63)	19.5
25-34 years	(53)	18.0	(48)	59.8	(75)	20.4
35-44 years	(17)	17.6	(24)	36.3	(42)	14.9
45 years and over	(14)	30.5	(28)	67.9	(27)	27.9
Black						
17 years and over	(51)	20.1	(87)	43.6	(150)	18.0
17-24 years	(29)	21.0	(23)	39.5	(51)	14.1
25-34 years	(11)	21.5	(39)	40.5	(54)	22.1
35-44 years	(6)	9.1	(13)	46.9	(27)	13.1
45 years and over	(5)	25.5	(12)	57.5	(18)	24.2

*Estimates based on probability samples.

Table 5-1 also shows that the omnibus stress score reported by prisoners of both races and all ages is 51.2 percent. Among prisoners of both races combined, those who were over 45 years old had the highest omnibus score, followed by those who were between 25 and 34 years of age; while those who were between 35 and 44 years of age had the lowest omnibus score, followed by those who were under 25 years old. Among white prisoners those over 45 years old had the highest omnibus score, as did black prisoners in the same age bracket among black prisoners. However, among white prisoners those between 35 and 44 years of age had the lowest omnibus score, whereas among black prisoners those under 25 years old had the lowest omnibus score. White prisoners under 25 years old had an omnibus score of 60.0 percent, and black prisoners between 35 and 44 years of age had an omnibus score of 46.9 percent.

Table 5-2 shows that among probationers those who were widowed had the highest omnibus stress score, although this data is based on only two respondents. Among probationers the divorced had the next highest omnibus score, followed by the separated; the married had the lowest omnibus score, followed by the unmarried. Among prisoners the divorced had the highest omnibus stress score, followed by the widowed and the separated; those who were married had the lowest omnibus score, followed by those who were single.

As Table 5-3 shows, among probationers those with less than seven years of education had the highest omnibus stress score, followed by those with between nine and eleven years of education, and those with seven or eight years of education; those with twelve years or more of education had the lowest omnibus stress score. Among prisoners those with less than seven years of education had the highest omnibus stress score, followed by those with twelve years or more of education; those with seven or eight years of education had the lowest omnibus score, followed by those with between nine and eleven years of education.

Table 5-2
Prevalence of General Psychological Distress from Responses* to Omnibus Stress Questionnaire: Adult Male Prisoners Compared with Adult Male Probationers and Parolees, by Marital Status

Marital Status	Average (Mean) Percentage Reporting Psychological Distress					
	Probationers		Prisoners		Parolees	
	Sample	%	Sample	%	Sample	%
Single	(85)	21.6	(72)	50.1	(93)	17.7
Married	(119)	15.3	(91)	36.5	(132)	17.5
Widowed	(2)	36.4	(9)	78.9	(15)	33.3
Separated	(14)	22.1	(13)	77.7	(60)	13.8
Divorced	(30)	25.0	(19)	82.6	(57)	26.7

*Estimates based on probability samples.

Table 5-3
Prevalence of General Psychological Distress from Responses* to Omnibus Stress Questionnaire: Adult Male Prisoners Compared with Adult Male Probationers and Parolees, by Education

Education in Years of School Completed	Average, Mean, Percentage Reporting Psychological Distress					
	Probationers		Prisoners		Parolees	
	Sample	%	Sample	%	Sample	%
0-6	(17)	24.1	(35)	94.6	(42)	27.4
7-8	(60)	20.2	(42)	27.4	(81)	23.0
9-11	(78)	21.2	(83)	38.7	(90)	17.9
12 or over	(87)	15.5	(44)	54.8	(120)	15.1

*Estimates based on probability samples.

Table 5-4 shows the ratio of omnibus stress scores for prisoners compared with probationers according to age within race. The ratio for prisoners compared with probationers of both races and all ages is 2.61. Thus, prisoners of both races and all ages had an omnibus stress score that was more than two and one half times higher than the omnibus score of probationers. The highest ratio for prisoners of both races compared with probationers (ratio: 2.75) appeared among those between 25 and 34 years of age, followed by those between 35 and 44 years of age (ratio: 2.60); those over 45 years old had the lowest ratio (ratio: 2.22), followed by those under 25 years old (ratio: 2.48). The ratio for white prisoners compared with white probationers of all ages (ratio: 2.92) is higher than the ratio of black prisoners compared with black probationers of all ages (ratio: 2.17). Among white prisoners compared with white probationers, those between 25 and 34 years of age had the highest ratio (ratio: 3.32) of omnibus stress scores, followed by those under 25 years old (ratio: 3.14); those between 35 and 44 years of age had the lowest ratio (ratio: 2.06), followed by those over 45 years old (ratio: 2.23). Among black prisoners compared with black probationers, those between 35 and 44 years of age had the highest ratio (ratio: 5.15) of omnibus stress scores, followed by those over 45 years old (ratio: 2.25); those under 35 years old had a ratio of 1.88.

Table 5-5 shows the ratio of omnibus stress scores for prisoners compared with probationers according to marital status. Among prisoners compared with probationers, those who were separated had the highest ratio (ratio: 3.52) of omnibus stress scores, followed by those who were divorced (ratio: 3.30); those who were widowed had the lowest ratio (ratio: 2.17), followed by those who were single (ratio: 2.32) and those who were married (ratio: 2.39).

Table 5-6 shows the ratio of omnibus stress scores for prisoners compared with probationers according to education. Among prisoners compared with

Table 5-4
General Psychological Distress Rates Reported:* Adult Male Prisoners and Parolees Compared with Adult Male Probationers, by Age within Race

Age and Race	Ratio: Rates for Prisoners/Probationers	Ratio: Rates for Parolees/Probationers
Both Races		
17 years and over	2.61	0.97
17-24 years	2.48	0.88
25-34 years	2.75	1.13
35-44 years	2.60	0.92
45 years and over	2.22	0.91
White		
17 years and over	2.92	1.03
17-24 years	3.14	1.02
25-34 years	3.32	1.13
35-44 years	2.06	0.85
45 years and over	2.23	0.91
Black		
17 years and over	2.17	0.90
17-24 years	1.88	0.67
25-34 years	1.88	1.03
35-44 years	5.15	1.44
45 years and over	2.25	0.95

*Estimates based on probability samples.

Table 5-5
General Psychological Distress Rates Reported:* Adult Male Prisoners and Parolees Compared with Adult Male Probationers, by Marital Status

Marital Status	Ratio: Rates for Prisoners/Probationers	Ratio: Rates for Parolees/Probationers
Single	2.32	0.82
Married	2.39	1.14
Widowed	2.17	0.91
Separated	3.52	0.62
Divorced	3.30	1.07

*Estimates based on probability samples.

probationers, those with less than seven years of education had the highest ratio (ratio: 3.93) of omnibus stress scores, followed by those with twelve years or more of education (ratio: 3.54); those with seven or eight years of education had the lowest ratio (ratio: 1.36), followed by those with between nine and eleven years of education (ratio: 1.83).

Table 5-6
General Psychological Distress Rates Reported:* Adult Male Prisoners and Parolees Compared with Adult Male Probationers, by Education

Education in Years of School Completed	Ratio: Rates for Prisoners/Probationers	Ratio: Rates for Parolees/Probationers
0-6	3.93	1.14
7-8	1.36	1.14
9-11	1.83	0.84
12 or over	3.54	0.97

*Estimates based on probability samples.

2. Omnibus Scores of Probationers and Parolees

As Table 5-1 shows, the omnibus stress score reported by parolees of both races and all ages is 19.1 percent. Among parolees of both races combined, those over 45 years old had the highest omnibus score, followed by those between 25 and 34 years of age; those between 35 and 44 years of age had the lowest omnibus score, followed by those under 25 years old. This pattern remained virtually true for both races separately.

Table 5-2 shows that among parolees the widowed had the highest omnibus stress score, followed by the divorced; the separated had the lowest omnibus score, followed by the married and the single. Table 5-3 shows that among parolees those with less than seven years of education had the highest omnibus stress score, followed by those with seven or eight years of education; those with twelve years or more of education had the lowest omnibus score, followed by those with between nine and eleven years of education.

Table 5-4 shows the ratio of omnibus stress scores for parolees compared with probationers according to age within race. The ratio for parolees compared with probationers of both races and all ages is 0.97. Thus, parolees of both races and all ages had an omnibus stress score that was slightly lower than the omnibus score of probationers. The highest ratio for parolees of both races compared with probationers (ratio: 1.13) appeared among those between 25 and 34 years of age, who were followed by those between 35 and 44 years of age (ratio: 0.92) and those over 45 years old (ratio: 0.91); those under 25 years old had the lowest ratio (ratio: 0.88).

The ratio for white parolees compared with white probationers of all ages (ratio: 1.03) is slightly higher than the ratio for black parolees compared with black probationers of all ages (ratio: 0.90). Among white parolees compared with white probationers, those between 25 and 34 years of age had the highest ratio (ratio: 1.13) of omnibus stress scores, followed by those under 25 years old (ratio: 1.02); those between 35 and 44 years of age had the lowest ratio (ratio: 0.85) of omnibus stress scores, followed by those over 45 years old (ratio: 0.91). Among black parolees compared with black probationers, those between 35 and 44 years of age had the highest ratio (ratio: 1.44) of omnibus stress scores, followed by those between 25 and 34 years of age (ratio: 1.03); those under 25 years old had the lowest ratio (ratio: 0.67) of omnibus stress scores, followed by those over 45 years old (ratio: 0.95).

Table 5-5 shows the ratio of omnibus stress scores for parolees compared with probationers according to marital status. Among parolees compared with probationers, the married had the highest ratio (ratio: 1.14) of omnibus stress scores, followed by the divorced (ratio: 1.07); the separated had the lowest ratio (ratio: 0.62) of omnibus scores, followed by the single (ratio: 0.82) and the widowed (ratio: 0.91).

Table 5-6 shows the ratio of omnibus stress scores for sample parolees compared with probationers according to education. Among parolees compared with probationers, those with less than eight years of education had the highest ratio (ratio: 1.14) of omnibus stress scores, while those with between nine and eleven years of education had the lowest ratio (ratio: 0.84) of omnibus scores, followed by those with twelve years or more of education (ratio: 0.97).

C. Comparison Statistics

No study of psychological distress is known to be available for Tennessee. The latest national study of psychological distress known to have been published was conducted between 1960 and 1962 on a national sample of 7,710 persons, and was published in August, 1970.[5] A useful addendum here is a comparison of some of its data with the data of this chapter. Prisoners of both races and all ages reported psychological distress by a proportion 3.6 times higher (average, mean, percent 51.2) than that reported for the general adult-male United States population of both races and all ages in 1960-62 (average, mean, percent 14.1). Parolees of both races and all ages reported distress by a proportion 35.5 percent higher (average, mean, percent 19.1). Probationers of both races and all ages reported distress by a proportion 39.0 percent higher (average, mean, percent 19.6).

6 Disability and Hospitalization

A. Components of Disability

Disability, the effect of a morbidity condition, is a measurement of the impact of illness (sickness) and injury. This study defines disability, following the (National) Health Interview Survey (HIS), as any temporary or long-term reduction or restriction of a person's activity as a result of illness (sickness) or injury.[1] Disability is not limited to clinically determined abnormality resulting in incapacity,[2] nor to prolonged limitations of an individual's functional ability,[3] although these and other definitions have been used in some previous studies. Here the concept of disability encompasses a variety of situations. An episode of disability may last only a few days or it may endure for years. Some persons are disabled from birth, while others become disabled only late in life. Restrictions imposed by disability may affect work, activities other than work, or both. A person may be restricted to the house, confined in bed, or hospitalized during his period of disability.

This chapter will study disability as it relates to acute conditions (short-term disability) and chronic conditions (long-term disability). Short-term disability is measured according to (1) days of restricted activity, (2) days of bed disability, and (3) days of short-stay hospitalization because of acute conditions. Long-term disability is measured by the proportion of a population who (1) are limited in either the kind or the amount of (a) work or (b) activities other than work which they can perform; (2) have been confined to bed for more than three out of twelve months; or (3) have been hospitalized because of chronic conditions.

A day of restricted activity is one on which a person cuts down on his usual activities for the whole of that day by reason of sickness or injury. The term "usual activities" for any day means the things that person would ordinarily do on that day.[4] Even though some persons usual activities consist of almost no activity, cutting down on even a small amount for as much as a day is counted as restricted activity. For noninstitutionalized populations, restricted activity usually means confinement to the house. A day spent in bed or in the hospital is a day of restricted activity, but following standard practice, to avoid overlapping measurements, days of bed disability and hospital days are not included here in the tabulation of restricted activity.[5]

A day of bed disability is one on which a person stays in bed for all or most of the day because of sickness or injury. The phrase "all or most of the day" is defined as more than half the daylight hours of a day.[6] All hospital days for inpatients are considered to be days of bed disability even if the patient was not actually in bed at the hospital.[7]

A hospital episode is any continuous period of stay of one night or more in a hospital as an inpatient. A hospital day is a day on which a person is confined to a hospital, but the day is counted as a hospital day only if the patient stays overnight.[8] Thus, a patient who enters a hospital on Monday afternoon and leaves Wednesday noon is considered to have had two hospital days. A hospital may include the hospital department of an institution,[9] and here does include the prison hospital.

A person is limited in the kind or the amount of work he can do if he needs special working aids or special rest periods at work, cannot work full time or for long periods of time, or cannot do strenuous work.[10] A person is limited in the kind or the amount of activities other than work that he can perform if he is not limited in regular work activities, but is limited in such other activities as sports, games, or hobbies.[11]

Disability may be measured also in terms of work-loss days. A day lost from work is a day on which a person did not work at his job or business for at least half of his normal workday because of illness (sickness) or injury.[12] The number of days lost from work is determined only for persons currently employed at the time of a sickness or injury.

Each component of disability may be measured separately for specific acute and chronic conditions, but here it is more feasible to measure short-term disability for all acute conditions combined, and long-term disability for all chronic conditions combined.

B. Short-Term Disability

Short-term disability is measured by (1) days of restricted activity, (2) days of bed disability, and (3) days of short-stay hospitalization. Restricted activity here does not include bed disability or hospitalization. Bed disability among prisoners does not include hospitalization at an outside hospital, but it does include confinement in the prison hospital's medical ward.[a]

1. Days of Restricted Activity

Days of restricted activity may be measured in several ways and by different methods. Among noninstitutionalized populations, days of restricted activity are

[a]This adjustment from the U.S. Public Health Service definition of bed disability was necessary: prisoners confined within the general medical ward (not the surgical or psychiatric wards) of the prison hospital, as opposed to an outside hospital, are presumed to be disabled to the same degree as a free-world person would be when he is confined to bed, but disabled to a lesser extent than a person who is hospitalized in an outside hospital.

associated with house confinement. For parolees and probationers an appropriate question was how many days they were confined to their house due to sickness or injury. Among members of an institutionalized population such as prisoners, restricted activity cannot be measured according to house confinement, since in a way they are always confined. Instead, days of restricted activity are measured for prisoners by the number of short-term, work-loss days.[b] An assumption was made that prisoners who did not work regularly at a job were disabled on a long-term rather than on a short-term basis, since all inmates of Tennessee State Penitentiary, unlike those of many prisons, are required to work if they are physically able to do so. Work-loss days were not measured for parolees or probationers, because only a small proportion of these sample populations reported that they worked regularly at a job, not by choice but by reason of resistance to employing convicted offenders.

Table 6-1 summarizes reported days of restricted activity, per 100 persons per year, associated with acute conditions (short-term, work-loss days) for prisoners by age within race. Prisoners of both races and all ages reported 485.3 days of restricted activity per 100 persons during the period between 1 July 1972 and 30 June 1973. Black prisoners of all ages reported restricted activity at more than twice the rate for white prisoners.

Among prisoners of both races combined, those between 25 and 34 years of age reported restricted activity at the highest rate, followed by those over 45 years old. Among prisoners of both races combined, those between 35 and 44 years of age reported restricted activity at the lowest rate, followed by those under 25 years old.

Among white prisoners, those under 25 years old reported restricted activity at the highest rate, followed by those between 25 and 34 years of age; those between 35 and 44 years of age reported the lowest rate, followed by those over 45 years old. Among black prisoners, those between 25 and 34 years of age reported restricted activity at the highest rate, followed by those over 45 years old; those under 25 years old reported the lowest rate, followed by those between 35 and 44 years of age.

Table 6-2 summarizes reported days of restricted activity (house confinement), per 100 persons per year, associated with acute conditions for parolees by age within race. Parolees of both races and all ages reported 675.8 days of restricted activity per 100 persons during the period beginning 1 July 1972 and ending 30 June 1973. White parolees of all ages reported 540.6 days of restricted activity per 100 persons, while black parolees reported 858.8 days per 100 persons. Among parolees of both races combined, those under 45 years old reported restricted activity at a higher rate than those over 45 years old. This remained true for both black and white parolees.

Table 6-3 summarizes reported days of restricted activity (house confine-

[b]At Tennessee State Penitentiary confinement does not mean lingering in the cell; a bedridden prisoner is hospitalized; a mild acute condition may bring a reprieve from work. The work reprieve was taken to be the best indicator of short-term disability.

Table 6-1
Days of Restricted Activity Reported:* Adult Male Prisoners, by Age within Race

Age and Race	Number of Days and Rate of Restricted Activity		
	Days of Restricted Activity Per Year	Number of Persons Sampled	Estimated Days of Restricted Activity Per 100 Persons Per Year
Both Races			
17 years and over	990	204	485.3
17-24 years	137	40	342.5
25-34 years	601	87	690.8
35-44 years	76	37	205.4
45 years and over	176	40	440.0
White			
17 years and over	395	117	337.6
17-24 years	120	17	705.9
25-34 years	178	48	370.8
35-44 years	39	24	162.5
45 years and over	58	28	207.1
Black			
17 years and over	595	87	683.9
17-24 years	17	23	73.9
25-34 years	423	39	1084.6
35-44 years	37	13	284.6
45 years and over	118	12	983.3

*Estimates based on probability samples.

ment), per 100 persons per year, associated with acute conditions for probationers by age within race. Probationers of both races and all ages reported 412.6 days of restricted activity per 100 persons during the period beginning 1 July 1972 and ending 30 June 1973. White probationers of all ages reported 427.2 days of restricted activity per 100 persons, while black probationers of all ages reported 355.8 days per 100 persons. Among probationers of both races combined, those under 45 years old reported restricted activity at a lower rate than those over 45 years old. This remained true for both black and white probationers separately.

Table 6-4 contains ratios of reported restricted activity day rates associated with acute conditions for prisoners and for parolees compared with probationers by age within race. The comparison of prisoners with probationers, showed a ratio of 1.18 for offenders of both races and all ages. Thus, prisoners of both races and all ages reported restricted activity at a slightly higher rate than did probationers of both races and all ages. A higher ratio (ratio: 1.38) appeared for

Table 6-2
Days of House Confinement Reported:* Adult Male Parolees, by Age within Race

Age and Race	Number of Days and Rate of House Confinement		
	Days of House Confinement Per Year	Number of Persons Sampled	Estimated Days of House Confinement Per 100 Persons Per Year
Both Races			
17 years and over	2433	360	675.8
17-44 years	2259	315	717.1
45 years and over	174	45	386.7
White			
17 years and over	1119	207	540.6
17-44 years	1050	180	583.3
45 years and over	69	27	255.6
Black			
17 years and over	1314	153	858.8
17-44 years	1209	135	895.6
45 years and over	105	18	583.3

*Estimates based on probability samples.

offenders of both races under 45 years old than for those over 45 years old (ratio: 0.43). This remained true for offenders of each race separately. Similarly, a higher ratio (ratio: 1.92) showed for black offenders of all ages than for white offenders of all ages (ratio: 0.79). It is important to note that black offenders under 45 years old had the highest ratio by far (ratio: 2.39), while white offenders over 45 years old had the lowest ratio (ratio: 0.22).

In the comparison of parolees with probationers, a ratio of 1.64 was observed for offenders of both races and all ages. Thus, parolees of both races and all ages reported restricted activity at a higher rate than did probationers of both races and all ages. A higher ratio (ratio: 1.99) emerged for offenders of both races under 45 years old than for those over 45 years old (ratio: 0.38). This remained true for offenders of each race separately. Similarly, a higher ratio (ratio: 2.41) was observed for black offenders of all ages than for white offenders of all ages (ratio: 1.27). Again, it is important to note that black offenders under 45 years old had the highest ratio by far (ratio: 3.37), while white offenders over 45 years old had the lowest ratio (ratio: 0.27). In general, the comparison of parolees with probationers revealed a pattern similar to that shown by comparing prisoners with probationers.

It is of value to consider the proportions of each population not reporting

Table 6-3
Days of House Confinement Reported:* Adult Male Probationers, by Age within Race

Age and Race	Number of Days and Rate of House Confinement		
	Days of House Confinement Per Year	Number of Persons Sampled	Estimated Days of House Confinement Per 100 Persons Per Year
Both Races			
17 years and over	1048	254	412.6
17-44 years	844	234	360.7
45 years and over	204	20	1020.0
White			
17 years and over	863	202	427.2
17-44 years	719	187	384.5
45 years and over	144	15	960.0
Black			
17 years and over	185	52	355.8
17-44 years	125	47	266.0
45 years and over	60	5	1200.0

*Estimates based on probability samples.

any days of restricted activity during the twelve month period studied. Among offenders of both races and all ages, 73.5 percent of probationers, 72.0 percent of parolees, and 47.5 percent of prisoners reported no days of restricted activity. Among offenders of both races combined, there was very little variation by age intervals for parolees or for probationers. However, prisoners of both races combined showed considerable variation by age, since only 13.8 percent of those between 25 and 34 years of age reported no days of restricted activity, while at least 70.0 percent of those in all other age brackets reported no days of restricted activity.[c] Among parolees and probationers, there was very little variation by race in the proportion of those reporting no restricted activity. However, 62.4 percent of white prisoners reported no days of restricted activity, but only 27.6 percent of black prisoners reported no days of restricted activity.[d] Thus, some variations by both age and race emerged.

It is crucially important to note that days of restricted activity as measured in

[c]Are such prisoners more susceptible to acute conditions necessitating restricted activity; or less inclined to want regular work?

[d]Are black prisoners more prone than white to acute conditions necessitating restricted activity; or more prone to seek reprieve from working at jobs that, with some justification, they consider inferior to those assigned to whites?

Table 6-4
Days of Restricted Activity Reported:* Adult Male-Prisoners and Parolees Compared with Adult Male Probationers, by Age within Race

Age and Race	Ratio: Rates for Prisoners/Probationers	Ratio: Rates for Parolees/Probationers
Both Races		
17 years and over	1.18	1.64
17-44 years	1.38	1.99
45 years and over	0.43	0.38
White		
17 years and over	0.79	1.27
17-44 years	0.98	1.52
45 years and over	0.22	0.27
Black		
17 years and over	1.92	2.41
17-44 years	2.39	3.37
45 years and over	0.82	0.49

*Estimates based on probability samples.

this section are associated with acute conditions attributable to all causes. Thus, the work-loss days used as indicators of restricted activity for sample prisoners may have been (and most of them were) caused by sicknesses and injuries not related to work in any way. On the other hand, some concern should be directed toward measuring the number of work-loss days attributable to injuries sustained on the job. Industrial work-loss days, as these are known, are measured by the number of lost days (caused by job-related injuries) per 1 million man-hours of work at a particular industrial operation.

Table 6-5 summarizes according to job type the industrial work-loss days per 1 million man-hours that were reported between 1 July 1972 and 30 June 1973 (fiscal year 1972-73) by prisoners employed at the Tennessee State Industries. The highest incidence of industrial work-loss days (from the untabulated records of shop foremen) occurred among prisoners who worked in the warehouse and shipping division, followed by those who worked in the soap plant. The lowest reported incidence of industrial work-loss days occurred among prisoners who worked in the print shop, followed by those who worked in manufacturing services,[e] and those who worked in the shoe shop.

The average rate of reported industrial work-loss for all job areas of the

[e]Are some jobs intrinsically more dangerous than others; or do some jobs, by reason of lower pay, monotony, or drudgery, cause a differentially higher motivation for work-loss?

Table 6-5
Work-Loss Days, Fiscal Year 1972-73; Inmate Employees, by Type of Work

Type of Work	Total Industrial Work-Loss Days	Total Number of Industrial Man-Hours	Number of Days Lost From Work Per 1,000,000 Man-Hours
Total, Tennessee State Industries	334	883,518	378.0
Manufacturing services	21	104,823	200.3
Accounts	0	3,156	–
Warehouse and shipping	48	33,691	1,424.7
Sign	13	20,850	623.5
Soap	20	15,784	1,267.1
Shoe	8	36,946	216.5
Wood	122	324,544	375.9
Metal	71	258,972	274.1
Print	5	27,696	180.5
Paint	23	48,579	473.4
Knitting and clothing	3	8,477	353.8

Tennessee State Industries was 378.0 days per 1 million man-hours. This rate is 21.6 percent less than the rate sustained by federal prisoners (482 days per 1 million man-hours) who worked during 1972 for the Federal Prison Industries Corporation.[13] The Tennessee State Industries rate is 50.2 percent less than the rate for persons across the nation who worked in outside, "free-world" manufacturing industries (759 days per 1 million man-hours) during 1972.[14]

2. *Days of Bed Disability*

Days of bed disability may be measured in several ways and by different methods. Among noninstitutionalized populations, days of bed disability are associated with confinement to bed at home or in a hospital.[15] To avoid overlapping measurements, bed disability for parolees and probationers is associated here with confinement to bed at home but not in the hospital. Prisoners at Tennessee State Penitentiary are not permitted to remain in their cells if they become so sick or injured as to be bedridden. For this reason, admission to the general medical ward of the prison hospital is a good indicator of bed disability for prisoners. Admission to the general medical ward of the prison hospital is distinguished from admission to the prison hospital's convalescent, psychiatric, or surgical wards, these are indicators of hospitalization rather than of bed disability.[f]

Table 6-6 summarizes reported days of bed disability, per 100 persons per year, associated with acute conditions for prisoners by age within race. Prisoners of both races and all ages reported 600.0 days of bed disability per 100 persons between 1 July 1972 and 30 June 1973. Black and white prisoners reported bed disability at about the same rate during this time period. Among prisoners of both races combined, those under 45 years old reported 584.1 days of bed disability per 100 persons, compared with 665.0 days per 100 persons for those over 45 years old. White prisoners over 45 years old reported bed disability at a higher rate than did those under 45 years of age, but black prisoners under 45 years reported a slightly higher rate than did their counterparts over 45 years of age.

Table 6-7 summarizes reported days of bed disability, per 100 persons per year, associated with acute conditions for parolees by age within race. Parolees of both races and all ages reported 363.3 days of bed disability per 100 persons between 1 July 1972 and 30 June 1973. White parolees reported bed disability

Table 6-6
Days of Bed Disability Reported:* Adult Male Prisoners, by Age within Race

Age and Race	Number of Days and Rate of Bed Disability		
	Days of Bed Disability Per Year	Number of Persons Sampled	Days of Bed Disability per 100 Persons per Year
Both Races			
17 years and over	1224	204	600.0
17-44 years	958	164	584.1
45 years and over	266	40	665.0
White			
17 years and over	710	117	606.8
17-44 years	511	89	574.2
45 years and over	199	28	710.7
Black			
17 years and over	514	87	590.8
17-44 years	447	75	596.0
45 years and over	67	12	558.3

*Estimates based on probability samples.

[f]They are so taken throughout; the convalescent ward is taken throughout as an indicator of hospitalization in the case of the few, short-term convalescents there; as an indicator of long-term (chronic) bed disability for convalescents remaining for more than three months.

Table 6-7
Days of Bed Disability Reported:* Adult Male Parolees, by Age within Race

Age and Race	Number of Days and Rate of Bed Disability		
	Days of Bed Disability Per Year	Number of Persons Sampled	Days of Bed Disability per 100 Persons per Year
Both Races			
17 years and over	1308	360	363.3
17-44 years	1179	315	374.3
45 years and over	129	45	286.7
White			
17 years and over	960	207	463.8
17-44 years	891	180	495.0
45 years and over	69	27	255.6
Black			
17 years and over	348	153	227.5
17-44 years	288	135	213.3
45 years and over	60	18	333.3

*Estimates based on probability samples.

at twice the rate for black parolees during this time period. Among parolees of both races combined, those under 45 years old reported 374.3 days of bed disability per 100 persons, compared with 286.7 days per 100 persons for those over 45 years old. Parolees over 45 years old reported bed disability at nearly twice the rate for those under 45 years of age. Black parolees over 45 reported bed disability at a slightly higher rate than did those under 45 years old.

Table 6-8 summarizes reported days of bed disability, per 100 persons per year, associated with acute conditions for probationers by age within race. Probationers of both races and all ages reported 283.5 days of bed disability per 100 persons between 1 July 1972 and 30 June 1973. White probationers reported 328.2 days of bed disability, while black probationers reported 109.6 days per 100 persons. Among probationers of both races combined, those under 45 years old reported 270.1 days of bed disability per 100 persons, compared with 440.0 days per 100 persons for those over 45 years old. White probationers under 45 years old reported 319.8 days of bed disability per 100 persons, compared with 433.3 days per 100 persons for those over 45 years old. Black probationers under 45 years old reported only 72.3 days of bed disability per 100 persons, compared with 460.0 days per 100 persons for those over 45 years old.

Table 6-9 contains ratios of reported bed disability day rates associated with

Table 6-8
Days of Bed Disability Reported:* Adult Male Probationers, by Age within Race

Age and Race	Number of Days and Rate of Bed Disability		
	Days of Bed Disability Per Year	Number of Persons Sampled	Days of Bed Disability per 100 Persons per Year
Both Races			
17 years and over	720	254	283.5
17-44 years	632	234	270.1
45 years and over	88	20	440.0
White			
17 years and over	663	202	328.2
17-44 years	598	187	319.8
45 years and over	65	15	433.3
Black			
17 years and over	57	52	109.6
17-44 years	34	47	72.3
45 years and over	23	5	460.0

*Estimates based on probability samples.

acute conditions for prisoners and for sample parolees compared with probationers, by age within race. In the comparison of prisoners with probationers, a ratio of 2.12 was observed for offenders of both races and all ages. Thus, prisoners of both races and all ages reported bed disability at a higher rate than did probationers of both races and all ages. A substantially higher ratio (ratio: 5.39) appeared for black offenders of all ages than for white offenders of all ages (ratio: 1.85). In addition, a substantially higher ratio (ratio: 8.24) showed for black offenders under 45 years old than for those over 45 years old (ratio: 1.21). White offenders under 45 and over 45 years old had similar ratios.

In the comparison of parolees with sample probationers, a ratio of 1.28 was observed for offenders of both races and all ages. Thus, parolees of both races and all ages reported bed disability at a slightly higher rate than did probationers of both races and all ages. A higher ratio (ratio: 1.39) was observed for offenders of both races under 45 years old than for those over 45 years old (ratio: 0.65). This remained true for offenders of each race separately. A higher ratio (ratio: 2.08) was observed for black offenders of all ages than for white offenders of all ages (ratio: 1.41). Black offenders under 45 years old had the highest ratio (ratio: 2.95), while white offenders over 45 years old had the lowest ratio (ratio: 0.59).

It is of value to consider the proportions of each population not reporting

Table 6-9
Days of Bed-Disability Rates Reported:* Adult Male Prisoners and Parolees Compared with Adult Male Probationers, by Age within Race

Age and Race	Ratio: Rates for Prisoners/Probationers	Ratio: Rates for Parolees/ Probationers
Both Races		
17 years and over	2.12	1.28
17-44 years	2.16	1.39
45 years and over	1.51	0.65
White		
17 years and over	1.85	1.41
17-44 years	1.80	1.55
45 years and over	1.64	0.59
Black		
17 years and over	5.39	2.08
17-44 years	8.24	2.95
45 years and over	1.21	0.74

*Estimates based on probability samples.

any days of bed disability during the twelve month period studied. Among offenders of both races and all ages, 71.3 percent of probationers, 69.5 percent of parolees, but only 29.4 percent of prisoners reported no days of bed disability. There was very little variation by race for any of the offender populations. There was very little variation by age intervals, except for parolees and probationers over 45 years old. Only about half of the probationers (50.0 percent) and the parolees (57.1 percent) over 45 years old reported no days of bed disability, but over 65.0 percent of those under 45 years old in all age brackets reported no days of bed disability.

3. Days of Short-Stay Hospitalization

Days of short-stay hospitalization are measured generally in two ways for any population studied. First, hospital discharges are tabulated per 100 persons who are members of the population.[g] Secondly, the number of hospital days is computed per person with one hospital episode or more. In the present case both of these rates are based on a twelve month period. It is very important to note that discharges rather than admissions are calculated, so that in the event a person enters the hospital and dies before being discharged, he would be

[g]Hospital discharge rates reflect frequency, but not average length of episodes.

excluded from the hospital discharge rate. Moreover, the number of hospital days calculated for a population is based on the number of persons from the population spending one day or longer in a hospital, rather than on the number of members of the population.[h]

While the meaning of hospitalization usually includes confinement in such an institution, as a prison hospital, this study necessarily deviates from the usual usage. Obviously, prisoners would be likely to spend more time in the prison hospital than parolees or probationers would be likely to spend in an outside hospital, since the prison hospital is easier to enter and free of cost. On the other hand, it is less easy for a prisoner to obtain admission to an outside hospital, since his condition must conform to the admission standards of the hospital, and the state must pay the cost of outside hospitalization. For these reasons, in the case of prisoners the term "hospitalization" is limited here to mean admission to and discharge from hospitals outside the prison–with several minor exceptions. The exceptions include admission to the prison hospital for surgery that would necessitate hospitalization for a noninstitutionalized person, for example, an appendectomy, tonsilectomy, hernia operation, or the ligation and stripping of veins (all performed in the prison hospital at Tennessee State Penitentiary). There exists also one exception to this exception–admission for plastic surgery. Although a significant number of plastic surgery operations are performed at the prison hospital, prisoners receiving this treatment are not here considered as hospitalized, even though noninstitutionalized persons normally receive this treatment as inpatients in a hospital. The reasons for the exception are that no parolees or probationers studied received plastic surgery treatment; and that the purely cosmetic plastic surgery undergone by the prisoners studied here[16] is not considered to be a disability. Thus, it would be false to count plastic surgery in a comparison of the hospitalization of prisoners with that of probationers or parolees.

a. Hospital Discharges. Table 6-10 summarizes the rate per 100 persons of reported hospital discharges, by age within race for the year 1972; for the estimated total population of prisoners at Tennessee State Penitentiary who had spent six months or longer in prison at the time they were hospitalized. In order to achieve four age intervals within each race, hospital discharges had to be measured for the entire population of these prisoners, rather than for a sample thereof. Nevertheless, this should not affect the comparisons to be made between prisoners and nonincarcerated offenders.[i] According to Table 6-10, prisoners of both races and all ages had a reported hospital discharge rate of

[h]Hospital-day rates per person hospitalized with one episode or more reflect average length of time for each hospitalized person during the total period measured.

[i]For maximum accuracy, validity and reliability, hospital measurements for prisoners covered the entire population; for probationers and parolees, however, samples had to suffice, since they were not in one place.

Table 6-10
Hospital Discharges Reported* 1972: Adult-Male Prisoners, by Age within Race

Age and Race	Number and Rate of Hospital Discharges		
	Number of Hospital Discharges	Estimated Number of Prisoners	Number of Hospital Discharges per 100 Persons per Year
Both Races			
17 years and over	126	1000	12.6
17-24 years	14	150	9.3
25-34 years	61	500	12.2
35-44 years	27	200	13.5
45 years and over	24	150	16.0
White			
17 years and over	76	610	12.5
17-24 years	6	80	7.5
25-34 years	38	250	15.2
35-44 years	13	170	7.6
45 years and over	19	110	17.3
Black			
17 years and over	50	390	12.8
17-24 years	8	70	11.4
25-34 years	23	250	9.2
35-44 years	14	30	46.7
45 years and over	5	40	12.5

*Estimates based on validated prison records.

12.6 per 100 persons for the period between 1 January and 31 December 1972.[j] Among prisoners of both races combined, those under 25 years old had the lowest reported hospital discharge rate, while those over 45 years old had the highest rate. White prisoners of all ages had a reported hospital discharge rate of 12.5 per 100 persons, while black prisoners of all ages had a rate of 12.8 per 100 persons. Among white prisoners those under 25 and between 35 and 44 years of age shared the lowest reported hospital discharge rates, while those over 45 years old had the highest rate, followed by those between 25 and 34 years of age. Among black prisoners those between 25 and 34 years of age had the lowest reported hospital discharge rate, followed by those under 25 and those over 45 years old. Among black prisoners those between 35 and 44 years of age had the highest reported hospital discharge rate.

Table 6-11 summarizes the rate of reported hospital discharges for parolees by age within race for the period between 1 July 1972 and 30 June 1973.

[j]These rates were tabulated for 12 consecutive months for all three populations; but using calendar year 1972-73 for prisoners; fiscal year 1972-73, for the nonincarcerated.

Table 6-11
Hospital Discharges Reported:* Adult Male Parolees, by Age within Race

Age and Race	Number and Rate of Hospital Discharges		
	Number of Hospital Discharges	Number of Persons Sampled	Number of Hospital Discharges per 100 Persons per Year
Both Races			
17 years and over	30	360	8.3
17-44 years	24	315	7.6
45 years and over	6	45	13.3
White			
17 years and over	19	207	9.2
17-44 years	16	180	8.9
45 years and over	3	27	11.1
Black			
17 years and over	11	153	7.2
17-44 years	8	135	5.9
45 years and over	3	18	16.7

*Estimates based on probability samples.

Parolees of both races and all ages had a reported hospital discharge rate of 8.3 per 100 persons. White parolees of all ages had a reported discharge rate of 9.2 per 100 persons, while black parolees of all ages had a rate of 7.3 per 100 persons.

Table 6-12 summarizes the rate of reported hospital discharges for probationers by age within race for the period between 1 July 1972 and 30 June 1973. Probationers of both races and all ages had a reported discharge rate of 10.6 per 100 persons. White probationers of all ages had a reported discharge rate of 12.9 per 100 persons, while black probationers of all ages had a rate of 1.9 per 100 persons. None of the 47 black probationers under 45 years old sampled reported any hospital discharges.

Table 6-13 contains ratios of reported hospital discharge rates for prisoners and parolees compared by age within race with probationers. From comparing prisoners with probationers a ratio of 1.19 was observed for offenders of both races and all ages. Thus, prisoners of both races and all ages reported hospital discharges at a slightly higher rate than did probationers of both races and all ages. A higher ratio (ratio: 6.74) was observed for black offenders of all ages than for white offenders of all ages (ratio: 0.97). This higher ratio for black offenders is attributable to the absence of any reported hospital discharges among black probationers under 45 years old who were questioned. In contrast,

Table 6-12
Hospital Discharges Reported:* Adult Male Probationers, by Age within Race

Age and Race	Number and Rate of Hospital Discharges		
	Number of Hospital Discharges	Number of Persons Sampled	Number of Hospital Discharges per 100 Persons per Year
Both Races			
17 years and over	27	254	10.6
17-44 years	23	234	9.8
45 years and over	4	20	20.0
White			
17 years and over	26	202	12.9
17-44 years	23	187	12.3
45 years and over	3	15	20.0
Black			
17 years and over	1	52	1.9
17-44 years	0	47	–
45 years and over	1	5	20.0

*Estimates based on probability samples.

black prisoners under 45 years old reported hospital discharges at the rate of 12.9 discharges per 100 persons. White offenders under 45 years old and over 45 years old had similar ratios (ratios: 0.93 and 0.87 respectively), which in turn were only slightly higher than the ratio observed for black offenders over 45 years old (ratio: 0.63). In the comparison of parolees with probationers, a ratio of 0.78 was observed for offenders of both races and all ages. Thus, parolees of both races and all ages had a slightly lower rate of reported hospital discharges than probationers of both races and all ages. A higher ratio (ratio: 3.79) was observed for black offenders of all ages than for white offenders of all ages (ratio: 0.71), again because none of the questioned black probationers under 45 years old reported being discharged from a hospital. In contrast, black parolees under 45 years old reported hospital discharges at the rate of 5.9 discharges per 100 persons. White offenders under 45 and over 45 years old had similar ratios (ratios: 0.72 and 0.56 respectively), which in turn were slightly lower than the ratio observed for black offenders over 45 years old (ratio: 0.84).

b. Hospital Days. Table 6-14 summarizes the rate of reported hospital days, by age within race, for the estimated total population of prisoners at Tennessee State Penitentiary who had spent six months or longer in prison at the time they were hospitalized, and who had one hospital episode or more during 1972. As

Table 6-13
Hospital-Discharge Rates Reported:* Adult Male Prisoners and Parolees Compared with Adult Male Probationers, by Age within Race

Age and Race	Ratio: Rates for Prisoners/Probationers	Ratio: Rates for Parolees/Probationers
Both Races		
17 years and over	1.19	0.78
17-44 years	1.22	0.78
45 years and over	0.80	0.67
White		
17 years and over	0.97	0.71
17-44 years	0.93	0.72
45 years and over	0.87	0.56
Black		
17 years and over	6.74	3.79
17-44 years	–	–
45 years	–	–
45 years and over	0.63	0.84

*Estimates based on validated prison records and on probability sample.

with hospital discharges, hospital days are measured for the entire population of these prisoners rather than for only a sample thereof, in order to achieve four age intervals within each race. According to Table 6-14, prisoners of both races and all ages had 12.6 reported hospital days per person during the period between 1 January and 31 December 1972. Among prisoners of both races combined, those under 25 years old had the fewest reported hospital days, and those over 45 years old had the most reported hospital days. White prisoners of all ages had 15.1 reported hospital days per person, while black prisoners of all ages had 8.5 reported days per person. Among white prisoners those under 25 years old had the fewest reported hospital days, while those between 25 and 34 years of age had the most days, followed by those between 35 and 44 years of age and those over 45 years old. Black prisoners between 25 and 34 years of age had the fewest reported hospital days, followed by those under 25 years old and those between 35 and 44 years of age. Among black prisoners those over 45 years old had the most reported hospital days.

Table 6-15 summarizes the rate of reported hospital days, by age within race, for sampled parolees who had one hospital episode or more between 1 July 1972 and 30 June 1973. Parolees of both races and all ages had 9.3 reported hospital days per person. White parolees of all ages had 7.9 reported hospital days per person, while black parolees of all ages had 11.6 reported hospital days per person.

Table 6-14
Hospital Days Reported:* Adult Male Prisoners, by Age within Race

Age and Race	Number and Rate of Hospital Days		
	Number of Hospital Days	Number of Hospitalized Persons	Number of Hospital Days per Person
Both Races			
17 years and over	1396	111	12.6
17-24 years	66	9	7.3
25-34 years	742	56	13.3
35-44 years	288	25	11.5
45 years and over	300	21	14.3
White			
17 years and over	1030	68	15.1
17-24 years	31	5	6.2
25-34 years	616	35	17.6
35-44 years	152	11	13.8
45 years and over	231	17	13.6
Black			
17 years and over	366	43	8.5
17-24 years	35	4	8.8
25-34 years	126	21	6.0
35-44 years	136	14	9.7
45 years and over	69	4	17.3

*Estimates based on validated prison records.

Table 6-16 summarizes the rate of reported hospital days, by age within race, for sample probationers who had one hospital episode or more between 1 July 1972 and 30 June 1973. Probationers of both races and all ages had 13.7 reported hospital days per person. White probationers of all ages had 14.0 reported hospital days per person, while black probationers of all ages had only 5.0 days per person.

Table 6-17 contains ratios of reported hospital day rates per person, by age within race, with one hospital episode or more, for prisoners and for parolees compared with probationers. By comparing prisoners with probationers, a ratio of 0.92 was observed for offenders of both races and all ages. Thus, prisoners of both races and all ages had only slightly fewer days of reported hospitalization than probationers of both races and all ages. White offenders over 45 years old had a ratio (ratio: 3.40) almost identical with the ratio for black offenders over 45 years old (ratio: 3.46). White offenders under 45 years old had a lower ratio (ratio: 1.03). No ratio could be computed for black offenders under 45 years old, since no sample black probationers under 45 years old reported any hospital

Table 6-15
Hospital Days Reported:* Adult Male Parolees, by Age within Race

Age and Race	Number and Rate of Hospital Days		
	Number of Hospital Days	Sample of Hospitalized Persons	Estimated Number of Hospital Days per Person
Both Races			
17 years and over	278	30	9.3
17-44 years	249	24	10.4
45 years and over	29	6	4.8
White			
17 years and over	150	19	7.9
17-44 years	127	16	7.9
45 years and over	23	3	7.7
Black			
17 years and over	128	11	11.6
17-44 years	122	8	15.3
45 years and over	6	3	2.0

*Estimates based on probability samples.

days at all. In the comparison of parolees with probationers, a ratio of 0.68 was observed for offenders of both races and all ages. Thus, parolees of both races and all ages had fewer days of reported hospitalization than probationers of both races and all ages. A higher ratio (ratio: 2.32) was observed for black offenders of all ages than for white offenders of all ages (ratio: 0.56). Again, part of this high ratio for black offenders is attributable to the absence of any reported days of hospitalization among black probationers under 45 years old, while black parolees under 45 years old had a rate of 15.3 days per person reported hospitalized with one episode or more. White offenders under 45 and black offenders over 45 years old had similar ratios (ratios: 0.52 and 0.40 respectively), but white offenders over 45 years old had a higher ratio (ratio: 1.93).

c. Onset of Hospitalization. It may be of interest to determine how soon members of a criminal-offender population are hospitalized after becoming members of the population.[17] This study could not determine that for parolees or probationers, because too few members of these nonincarcerated-offender populations were hospitalized during the period studied. However, hospitalization was measured for the entire population of prisoners who had spent six months or longer in prison prior to being hospitalized, rather than for a sample of this population. Therefore, a larger number of hospital episodes became available for measurement relating to these prisoners.

Table 6-16
Hospital Days Reported:* Adult Male Probationers, by Age within Race

Age and Race	Number and Rate of Hospital Days		
	Number of Hospital Days	Sample of Hospitalized Persons	Estimated Number of Hospital Days per Person
Both Races			
17 years and over	369	27	13.7
17-44 years	352	23	15.3
45 years and over	17	4	4.3
White			
17 years and over	364	26	14.0
17-44 years	352	23	15.3
45 years and over	12	3	4.0
Black			
17 years and over	5	1	5.0
17-44 years	0	0	0.0
45 years and over	5	1	5.0

*Estimates based on probability samples.

The total number of short-stay hospital episodes was obtained for all prisoners at Tennessee State Penitentiary for the period between 1 July 1972 and 31 December 1972, as were the total number of hospital discharges, hospital days, persons hospitalized, and dollars spent to hospitalize prisoners (according to statements to the Department of Correction from hospitals in the Nashville area). From each of these totals, sub-totals pertaining to prisoners who had spent six months or longer in prison prior to being hospitalized were subtracted. This produced two sets of sub-totals: one set for prisoners who had spent six months or longer in prison, and one set for prisoners who had spent less than six months in prison prior to being hospitalized. Then follows a comparison of the two sets of sub-totals.

During the second half of 1972, 88 prisoners of both races and all ages who had spent six months or longer in prison were hospitalized at Nashville General or Baptist Hospital (data on Vanderbilt and Veterans Hospital was insuffcent) for a total of 515 nights at a total cost of $52,000.65. This represents an average (mean), number of 5.9 hospital days per person with one hospital episode or more (compared with 26.3 days for prisoners hospitalized in their first six months), at a cost of $590.92 per person (compared with $2,304.65 per person for prisoners hospitalized in their first six months). During the same period, 28 prisoners of both races and all ages who had spent less than six months in prison

Table 6-17
Hospital-Day Rates Reported:* Adult Male Prisoners and Parolees Compared with Adult Male Probationers, by Age within Race

Age and Race	Ratio: Rates for Prisoners/Probationers	Ratio: Rates for Parolees/Probationers
Both Races		
17 years and over	0.92	0.68
17-44 years	0.80	0.68
45 years and over	3.33	1.12
White		
17 years and over	1.08	0.56
17-44 years	1.03	0.52
45 years and over	3.40	1.93
Black		
17 years and over	1.70	2.32
17-44 years		
45 years and over	3.46	0.40

*Estimates based on validated prison records and probability samples.

were hospitalized at the same hospitals for a total of 737 nights at a total cost of $64,530.06. This represents an average (mean) number of 26.3 hospital days per person with one hospital episode or more, at a cost of $2,304.65 per person.

The above data shows that prisoners of both races and all ages who had one hospital episode or more during the second half of 1972, but who had been in prison less than six months had 4.5 times more hospital days than prisoners of both races and all ages who had one hospital episode or more during the second half of 1972, but who had been in prison for six months or longer.

C. Long-Term Disability

Long-term disability is measured by the members of a population who (1) are limited in either the kind or the amount of (a) work or (b) activities other than work they can perform; (2) have been confined to bed for more than three months out of twelve; or (3) have been hospitalized due to chronic conditions.

1. Limited in Kind or Amount of Work

A person is limited in the kind or the amount of work he can perform if he is unable on account of his health to do the type of work or the amount of work that ordinary people do routinely. A person may be limited in the kind but not the amount of work he can do, or in the amount but not the kind of work he can do; here, however, both of these work limitations are grouped together.

Table 6-18 summarizes the proportion of prisoners by age who reported a disability limiting the kind or the amount of work they could do. Among prisoners of both races and all ages, 15.7 percent reported this kind of disability. Among prisoners of both races combined, those over 45 years old reported this kind of disability most frequently, and those between 25 and 34 years of age reported this kind of disability least frequently, next were those between 35 and 44 years of age and those under 25 years old.

Table 6-19 summarizes the proportion of parolees by age who reported a

Table 6-18
Percent Distribution of Reported* Work-Limiting Disability: Adult Male Prisoners, according to Age

Age in Years	Disability Limiting Work (Percent Distribution By Row)			
	No	Yes	Total	*N*
17 and over	84.3	15.7	100.0	204
17-24	87.5	12.5	100.0	40
25-34	93.1	6.9	100.0	87
35-44	91.9	8.1	100.0	37
45 and over	55.0	45.0	100.0	40

$X^2 = 32.98$ $DF = 3$ $P = < .001$
*Estimates based on probability samples.

Table 6-19
Percent Distribution of Reported* Work-Limiting Disability: Adult Male Parolees, according to Age

Age in Years	Disability Which Limits Work (Percent Distribution By Row)			
	No	Yes	Total	*N*
17 and over	87.3	12.7	100.0	354
17-24	89.5	10.5	100.0	114
25-34	90.5	9.5	100.0	126
35-44	95.8	4.2	100.0	72
45 and over	50.0	50.0	100.0	42

$X^2 = 55.65$ $DF = 3$ $P = <.001$
*Estimates based on probability samples.

disability limiting the kind or the amount of work they could do. Among parolees of both races and all ages, 12.7 percent reported this kind of disability. Among parolees of both races combined, those over 45 years old reported this kind of disability most frequently, while those between 35 and 44 years of age reported this kind of disability least frequently; next were those between 25 and 34 years of age and those under 25 years old.

Table 6-20 summarizes the proportion of probationers by age who reported a disability limiting the kind or the amount of work they could do. Among probationers of both races and all ages, 12.6 percent reported this kind of disability. Among probationers of both races combined, those over 45 years old reported this kind of disability most frequently, and those between 35 and 44 years of age reported this kind of disability least frequently; next were those between 25 and 34 years of age and those under 25 years old.

Table 6-21 summarizes the proportion of prisoners by race who reported a

Table 6-20
Percent Distribution of Reported* Work-Limiting Disability: Adult Male Probationers, according to Age

Age in Years	Disability Limiting Work (Percent Distribution By Row)			
	No	Yes	Total	*N*
17 and over	87.4	12.6	100.0	254
17-24	88.9	11.1	100.0	144
25-34	92.5	7.5	100.0	67
35-44	95.7	4.3	100.0	23
45 and over	50.0	50.0	100.0	20

$X^2 = 28.72$ $DF = 3$ $P = <.001$
*Estimates based on probability samples.

Table 6-21
Percent Distribution of Reported* Work-Limiting Disability: Adult Male Prisoners, according to Race

Race	Disability Limiting Work (Percent Distribution By Row)			
	No	Yes	Total	*N*
White	83.8	16.2	100.0	117
Black	85.1	14.9	100.0	87

$X^2 = 0.003$ $DF = 1$ $P = >.95$
*Estimates based on probability samples.

disability limiting the kind or the amount of work they could do. White prisoners of all ages reported this kind of disability slightly more frequently than black prisoners of all ages.

Table 6-22 summarizes the same thing for parolees by race. Black parolees of all ages reported this kind of disability slightly more frequently than white parolees of all ages.

Table 6-23 summarizes the same thing for probationers by race. Black probationers of all ages reported this kind of disability more frequently than white probationers of all ages.

The proportions of prisoners, parolees, and probationers who reported a disability limiting the kind or the amount of work they could do may be compared by comparing Tables 6-18 through 6-23. Prisoners of both races and all ages reported this kind of disability slightly more frequently than either parolees or probationers, who reported this at about the same frequency. This remained true for both races combined at all age intervals, except the 35 to 44 year old age group, where prisoners reported this kind of disability twice as frequently as parolees or probationers. Prisoners of both races reported this kind

Table 6-22
Percent Distribution of Reported* Work-Limiting Disability: Adult Male Parolees, according to Race

Race	Disability Limiting Work (Percent Distribution By Row)			
	No	Yes	Total	N
White	88.2	11.8	100.0	204
Black	86.8	13.2	100.0	159

$X^2 = 0.06$ $DF = 1$ $P = >.80$
*Estimates based on probability samples.

Table 6-23
Percent Distribution of Reported* Work-Limiting Disability: Adult Male Probationers, according to Race

Race	Disability Limiting Work (Percent Distribution By Row)			
	No	Yes	Total	N
White	88.7	11.3	100.0	203
Black	82.7	17.3	100.0	52

$X^2 = 0.86$ $DF = 1$ $P = >.70$
*Estimates based on probability samples.

of disability more frequently than parolees. While prisoners of both races reported this kind of disability more frequently than white probationers, black probationers reported this kind of disability more frequently than prisoners of either race. White parolees reported this kind of disability at about the same frequency as white probationers, but black probationers reported it more frequently than black parolees.

2. Limited in Kind or Amount of Other Activities

A person is limited in the kind or the amount of his activities other than work if he is unable on account of his health to participate in the type of activities or the amount of activities other than work that ordinary people do routinely. Such activities may include, but are not limited to, sports, games, or hobbies. A person may be limited in the kind but not the amount of activities he can do, or in the amount but not the kind of activities he can do. Here, however, both of these activity limitations are grouped together.

Among prisoners of both races and all ages, 10.8 percent reported this kind of disability. Among prisoners of both races combined, those over 45 years old reported this kind of disability most frequently (35.0 percent), and those between 35 and 44 years of age reported this kind of disability least frequently (2.7 percent); next were those between 25 and 34 years of age (3.4 percent) and those under 25 years old (10.0 percent). Among parolees of both races and all ages, 10.9 percent reported this kind of disability. Among parolees of both races combined, those over 45 years old reported this kind of disability most frequently (42.9 percent), and those between 35 and 44 years of age reported this kind of disability least frequently (4.2 percent), followed by those under 25 years old (7.9 percent) and those between 25 and 34 years of age (9.3 percent).

Among probationers of both races and all ages, 10.4 percent reported this kind of disability. Among probationers of both races combined, those over 45 years old reported this kind of disability most frequently (52.9 percent), and those between 35 and 44 years of age reported this kind of disability least frequently (4.3 percent), followed closely by those between 25 and 34 years of age (4.5 percent) and by those under 25 years old (9.1 percent). White prisoners of all ages reported a disability limiting the kind or amount of work they could do more frequently than did black prisoners of all ages. This trend remained true for parolees and probationers.

Prisoners, parolees, and probationers of both races and all ages reported disability limiting the kind or amount of work they could do at about the same overall frequency. Among offenders of both races combined under 25 years old, prisoners and probationers reported this kind of disability at about the same rate, but parolees reported it slightly less frequently. Among offenders of both races combined between 25 and 34 years of age, again prisoners and probationers reported this kind of disability at about the same rate, but parolees reported it twice as frequently. Among offenders between 35 and 44 years of age, parolees and probationers reported this kind of disability at about the same rate, but prisoners reported it only half as frequently. Among offenders over 45 years old, probationers reported this kind of disability about 25.0 percent more frequently than parolees, who in turn reported it about 25.0 percent more frequently than prisoners. This kind of disability did not vary significantly by race for prisoners, parolees, or probationers.

3. Long-Term Bed Disability

Long-term bed disability may be measured according to the proportion of members of a population who have been confined to bed for more than three months during any given period, a year for example. Since long-term bed disability may be caused by either a chronic physical condition or a chronic mental condition, in measuring these two causes should be distinguished.

Table 6-24 summarizes, by age within race, for the population of prisoners spending six months or longer at Tennessee State Penitentiary during 1972; the number per 1,000 persons of chronic, bed-disability cases having physical causes; of those having mental causes; and the ratio between the two kinds. Among prisoners of both races and all ages, the rate of reported chronic bed disability from physical causes was 26.5 per 1,000 persons, and the rate of reported chronic bed disability from mental causes was 60.8 per 1,000 persons. The ratio of bed disability from physical causes to bed disability from mental causes was 0.436. Thus, the majority of prisoners of both races and all ages who were reported as confined to bed for more than three months were so on account of a mental condition.

Among prisoners of both races combined, those between 35 and 44 years of age reported the highest rate of chronic bed disability from physical causes, followed by those between 25 and 34 years of age, over 45 years old, and under 25 years old. Among prisoners of both races combined, those under 25 years old reported the highest rate of chronic bed disability from mental causes, followed by those between 35 and 44 years of age, and those between 25 and 34 years of age. Prisoners over 45 years old reported the lowest rate of chronic bed disability from mental causes. Prisoners of both races combined over 45 years old reported an equal proportion of chronic bed disabilities from physical and mental conditions. Prisoners of both races under 45 years old reported substantially more chronic bed disabilities from mental conditions than from physical conditions. This was more true of the age group under 25 years old (ratio 0.200) than of the other age brackets, and more true of the 35 to 44 year old age group (ratio 0.428) than of the 25 to 34 year old age group (ratio 0.561).

Table 6-24
Chronic Bed Disability Reported,* from Physical Causes–from Mental Causes: Adult Male Prisoners, by Age within Race

Age and Race	Ratio of Bed Disability Patients			
	Bed-Disability Patients from Physical Causes per 1,000 Persons	Bed-Disability Patients from Mental Causes per 1,000 Persons	Prisoners Sampled	Ratio
Both Races				
17 years and over	26.5	60.8	2040	.436
17-24 years	22.5	112.5	400	.200
25-34 years	26.4	47.1	870	.561
35-44 years	32.4	75.7	370	.428
45 years and over	25.0	25.0	400	1.000
White				
17 years and over	35.0	53.0	1170	.660
17-24 years	47.1	94.1	170	.501
25-34 years	39.6	33.3	480	1.189
35-44 years	37.5	91.7	240	.409
45 years and over	17.9	28.6	280	.626
Black				
17 years and over	14.9	71.3	870	.209
17-24 years	4.3	126.1	230	.034
25-34 years	10.3	64.1	390	.161
35-44 years	23.1	46.2	130	.500
45 years and over	41.7	16.7	120	2.497

*Estimates based on validated prison records.

Among prisoners of all ages, white prisoners reported a rate of chronic bed disability from physical causes higher than that of black prisoners, but black prisoners reported a rate of chronic bed disability from mental causes higher than that of white prisoners. While both white and black prisoners of all ages reported more chronic bed disabilities from mental causes than from physical causes, the ratio of physical to mental causes was higher for white prisoners (0.660) than for black prisoners (0.209). Among white prisoners those under 25 years old reported the highest rate of chronic bed disabilities from physical causes, followed by those between 25 and 34 years of age, and those between 35 and 44 years of age. Among white prisoners those over 45 years old reported the lowest rate of chronic bed disabilities from physical causes. Among white prisoners those under 25 years old reported the highest rate of chronic bed disabilities from mental causes, followed by those between 35 and 44 years of age. Among white prisoners those over 45 years old reported the lowest rate of chronic bed disabilities from mental causes, followed by those between 25 and 34 years of age. White prisoners between 25 and 34 years of age reported more chronic bed disabilities from physical conditions than from mental conditions (ratio 1.189). White prisoners under 25 and over 35 years old reported more chronic bed disabilities from mental conditions than from physical conditions. This was more true of the 35 to 44 year old age group (ratio 0.409) than of other age groups, and more true of the age group under 25 years old (ratio 0.501) than of the age group over 45 years old (0.626).

Among black prisoners those over 45 years old reported the highest rate of chronic bed disabilities from physical causes, followed by those between 35 and 44 years of age. Among black prisoners those under 25 years old reported the lowest rate of chronic bed disabilities from physical causes, followed by those between 25 and 34 years of age. Among black prisoners those under 25 years old reported the highest rate of bed disabilities from mental causes, followed by those between 25 and 34 years of age, and those between 35 and 44 years of age. Among black prisoners those over 45 years old reported the lowest rate of chronic bed disabilities from mental causes. Black prisoners over 45 years old reported more chronic bed disabilities from physical conditions than from mental conditions (ratio 2.497). Black prisoners under 45 years old reported more chronic bed disabilities from mental conditions than from physical conditions. This was more true for the age group under 25 years old (ratio 0.034) than for other age groups, and was more true for the 25 to 34 year old age group (ratio 0.161) than for the 35 to 44 year old age group (ratio 0.500).

Two parolees and four probationers reported more than three months of bed disability during the period studied, and all were from physical causes. Both of these parolees and all four of the probationers were white. Two of the probationers and one of the parolees were under 25 years old. Two of the probationers were between 25 and 34 years of age. The second parolee was between 35 and 44 years of age. Thus, no black parolees or black probationers reported chronic bed disability during that period, nor did anyone of either race over 45 years.

4. Long-Term Hospitalization

Only two prisoners confined at Tennessee State Penitentiary during 1972 reported having spent over three months at an outside hospital. One of these prisoners, black, over 45 years old, and suffering from leukemia, spent 112 days at an outside hospital in 1972 before he died. The other prisoner, white, between 25 and 34 years of age, and suffering from chronic asthma, spent 147 days at an outside hospital during 1972. Similarly, one parolee and one probationer from among those sampled reported spending more than three months at a hospital between 1 July 1972 and 30 June 1973. The parolee reported suffering from a chronic back ailment, the probationer, from a mental condition; both were under 25 years old and white.

D. Comparison Statistics

The only available statistics relating to disability for the general adult-male United States population in 1972 were hospital discharge rates per 100 persons, and hospital days per person with one hospital episode or more. The general adult-male United States population in 1972 had the following estimated rates of hospital discharges per 100 persons of all races: 8.0 for those between 17 and 24 years old; 8.3 for those between 25 and 34 years old; 10.7 for those between 35 and 44 years old; 15.7 for those between 45 and 64 years old; and 28.4 for those over 65 years old.[18] The general adult-male United States population in 1972 had the following estimated rates of hospital days per person with one hospital episode or more: 8.1 for those between 17 and 24 years old; 10.1 for those between 25 and 34 years old; 11.3 for those between 35 and 44 years old; 14.4 for those between 45 and 64 years old; and 18.5 for those over 65 years old.[19]

On the basis of this data, prisoners spending six months or longer at Tennessee State Penitentiary during 1972 who were between 17 and 24 years of age had a reported hospital-discharge rate that was 16.3 percent higher than that of the general adult-male United States population in the same age bracket in 1972. Those prisoners between 25 and 34 years of age had a rate that was 47.0 percent higher; and those between 35 and 44 years of age had a rate that was 26.2 percent higher than the rate of the general adult-male population in this age bracket. Parolees between 17 and 44 years of age had a reported hospital-discharge rate that was 14.6 percent lower than the 1972 rate for the general adult-male United States population in this wide age bracket (8.9 per 100).[k] Probationers between 17 and 44 years of age had a reported hospital-discharge rate that was 10.1 percent higher than the rate for the general adult-male population in this age bracket. (See Tables 6-10, 6-11, and 6-12.)

On the basis of this data, also, 17 to 24 year-old prisoners, spending six months or longer at Tennessee State Penitentiary during 1972 had 9.9 percent fewer reported hospital days per person with one hospital episode or more than the general adult-male United States population in this age bracket in 1972. But in the 25 to 34 year-old age group, prisoners reported 31.7 percent more hospital days per person; and in the 35 to 44 year-old age group about the same rate. Parolees between 17 and 44 years of age had 38.7 percent more reported

[k]Do parolees under 45 have a lower than average hospitalization rate as a result of: differentially greater treatment received in prison? the less active life there? Or are they less able to afford hospitalization? or are they unwelcome in the community or in medical centers?

hospital days per person (and for slightly longer stays) than did the general adult-male-United States population in this wide age bracket (7.5 per person). Probationers between 17 and 44 years of age had twice as many reported hospital days per person as the general adult-male population in this age bracket.

7 Medical Consultations

A. Terms Relating to Medical Consultation

Medical consultations include visits with a physician, a dentist, or any other medical specialist. The term "physician" includes all medical doctors and osteopathic physicians, whether they are engaged in a general or a limited, specialized practice. The term "dentist" includes all doctors of dental medicine or dental surgery, whether they are engaged in a general or a limited practice. The term "other medical specialist" includes physicians and dentists who are engaged in a limited (specialized) rather than a general practice, and includes but is not limited to ophthalmologists, neurologists, and psychiatrists. Here also optometrists are included with ophthalmologists as eye specialists, even though an optometrist is not a medical doctor.

A consultation with a physician, a dentist, or any other medical specialist is considered to be a visit if the purpose of the consultation was for examination, diagnosis, treatment, or advice.[1] A visit may include the services of the practitioner himself, or the services of a nurse or another para-professional acting under the direct supervision of the practitioner.[2] A consultation with a physician, a dentist, or another medical specialist by telephone is considered to be a visit if the purpose of the call is to ask advice rather than to schedule or cancel an appointment.[3] A visit may be made by a patient to the practitioner's office or clinic, or it may be made by the practitioner to a patient's home or to any location other than a hospital. Consultations between physicians, dentists, or other medical specialists and hospital inpatients are not considered visits.[4]

Services performed on a mass basis are not included in the tabulation of consultations or visits. A service received on a mass basis is defined as any service involving only a single test, for instance, a test for diabetes, or a single procedure, for example, a smallpox vaccination, when the identical service was administered to all persons present for this purpose at a given location on the same day.[5] Hence, obtaining a chest x-ray in a tuberculosis chest x-ray trailer is not counted as a physician visit, but a chest x-ray given in a physician's office or in an outpatient clinic by appointment is counted as a physician visit.[6]

B. Physician Visits

Consultations with a physician are tabulated separately here for each of the three criminal-offender populations (prisoners, parolees, probationers). As to visits no special considerations need be directed to those made by parolees or probationers. A brief notation is warranted on the physician visits of prisoners. Inmates at Tennessee State Penitentiary visit as a rule with a physician at the prison hospital. Even so, these visits are tabulated here as consultations with a physician by an outpatient: as long as the prisoner was in fact an outpatient at the time he arrived for the visit, and whether or not he was admitted to the prison hospital as an inpatient as a result of the visit. Visits of physician to in-hospital patients are not so tabulated.

By reason of the volume of daily complaints and the existence of several circumstances to be expected as concomitants of the condition of imprisonment (attempts to avoid work or to seek drugs, for example), diagnostic procedures are more systematic inside prison than in a noninstitutionalized setting. Most medical complaints of prisoners are screened by medical technical assistants; (MTAs; at Tennessee State Penitentiary civilian employees, usually with experience as medics or orderlies) before the prisoner-patient is referred to a physician for further consultation. The role of the MTA does not exist in a noninstitutionalized setting; the only similar role in the outside community is that of the visiting nurse or the Community Health Medic. Unfortunately, not one parolee or probationer sampled reported having received the services of a visiting para-professional during the period in question.

1. Physician Visit Rates

Table 7-1 summarizes the ratio between morbidity complaints to MTAs by prisoners and their consultations with a physician. The average prisoner of both races and all ages made 2.13 complaints about his health to an MTA for each physician visit he received. This ratio remained fairly constant for prisoners of both races in most age brackets. The most noticeable variation was between white prisoners in the 35 to 44 year old age bracket, who made 3.18 complaints to an MTA per physician visit, and black prisoners in this age bracket, who made only 0.90 complaints per visit. Another noticeable variation was between black prisoners under 25 years old, who made 3.65 complaints per physician visit, and white prisoners in this age bracket, who made 2.39 complaints per visit.

Presumably, complaints made by prisoners to MTAs that did not result in a visit with a physician were unfounded (such as nuisance complaints made in an effort to avoid work) or trivial, requiring minimal diagnosis or treatment (such as a bandaid for a sore finger). The unfounded complaints are not germane to this study except to support the inference that complaints that were not screened out but referred to a physician merited the physician's time in the opinion of someone other than the complaining prisoner, such as the MTA.

Physician visits are measured according to rates per person per year. The data is summarized by demographic variables including age, race, marital status, and education.

Table 7-1
Morbidity Complaints Reported* to MTAs per Physician Consultations (Year): Adult Male Prisoners, by Age within Race

Age and Race of Complainant	Sample of Morbidity Complaints	Sample of Physician Visits	Complaints per Physician Visit per Year
Both Races			
17 years and over	1880	882	2.13
17-24 years	528	175	3.02
25-34 years	788	391	2.02
35-44 years	242	119	2.03
45 years and over	322	197	1.63
White			
17 years and over	1032	474	2.18
17-24 years	210	88	2.39
25-34 years	366	180	2.03
35-44 years	188	59	3.18
45 years and over	268	147	1.82
Black			
17 years and over	848	408	2.07
17-24 years	318	87	3.65
25-34 years	422	211	2.00
35-44 years	54	60	0.90
45 years and over	54	50	1.08

*Estimates based on probability samples.

As Table 7-2 reflects, prisoners of both races and all ages reported an average of 4.3 consultations with a physician during the twelve month period beginning on 1 July 1972 and ending on 30 June 1973. Black prisoners of all ages reported more visits than white prisoners of all ages. Among prisoners of both races, those over 45 years reported consultations at the highest rate, and those between 35 and 44 years of age reported consultations at the lowest rate. Among white prisoners, those 45 years of age or over reported consultations at the highest rate, followed closely by those under 25 years old. Among black prisoners, those between 25 and 34 years of age reported consultations at the highest rate. Among white prisoners, those between 35 and 44 years of age reported consultations at the lowest rate; but among black prisoners, those under 25 years old reported consultations at the lowest rate.

As Table 7-3 shows, parolees of both races and all ages reported an average of 0.9 consultations per person with a physician during the same period. White parolees of all ages reported more consultations than did black parolees. Among parolees of both races, those under 45 years of age reported about half as many physician visits per person as did those over 45 years old.

Table 7-2
Physician Visits and Physician Visits per Person per Year Reported:* Adult Male Prisoners, by Age within Race

Age and Race	Number and Rate of Physician Visits		
	Physician Visits	Persons Sampled	Number of Physician Visits per Person per Year
Both Races			
17 years and over	882	204	4.3
17-24 years	175	40	4.4
25-34 years	391	87	4.5
35-44 years	119	37	3.2
45 years and over	197	40	4.9
White			
17 years and over	474	117	4.1
17-24 years	88	17	5.2
25-34 years	180	48	3.8
35-44 years	59	24	2.5
45 years and over	147	28	5.3
Black			
17 years and over	408	87	4.7
17-24 years	87	23	3.8
25-34 years	211	39	5.4
35-44 years	60	13	4.6
45 years and over	50	12	4.2

*Estimates based on probability samples.

As Table 7-4 illustrates, probationers of both races and all ages reported an average of 2.5 consultations with a physician during this period. Black probationers of all ages reported 2.2 times more physician visits than white probationers of all ages. Among probationers of both races, those under 45 years of age reported fewer physician vists per person than those over 45 years old. Among white probationers, those under 45 years old reported far fewer physicial visits per person than those over 45 years old; while among black probationers, those under 45 years old reported far more physician visits than those over 45 years old.

Table 7-5 contains ratios of reported physician visit rates for prisoners and for parolees, compared by age within race with probationers. From comparing prisoners with probationers, a ratio of 1.72 was observed for offenders of both races and all ages. Thus, prisoners of both races and all ages reported physician visits at a higher rate than did probationers of both races and all ages. A higher ratio (ratio: 2.05) was observed for white offenders of all ages than for black

Table 7-3
Physician Visits and Physician Visits per Person per Year Reported:* Adult Male Parolees, by Age within Race

Age and Race	Number and Rate of Physician Visits		
	Physician Visits	Persons Sampled	Physician Visits per Person per Year
Both Races			
17 years and over	322	360	0.9
17-44 years	259	315	0.8
45 years and over	63	45	1.4
White			
17 years and over	199	207	1.0
17-44 years	157	180	0.9
45 years and over	42	27	1.6
Black			
17 years and over	123	153	0.8
17-44 years	102	135	0.8
45 years and over	21	18	1.2

*Estimates based on probability samples.

offenders of all ages (ratio: 1.07). White offenders over 45 years old had a ratio (ratio: 1.13) that was similar to the ratio for black offenders under 45 years old (ratio: 0.98). White offenders under 45 years old had a higher ratio (ratio: 2.06), and black offenders over 45 years old had a much higher ratio (ratio: 7.00). From comparing parolees with probationers, a ratio of 0.36 was observed for offenders of both races and all ages. Parolees of both races and all ages reported physician visits at a lower rate than probationers of both races and all ages. A higher ratio (ratio: 0.50) was observed for white offenders of all ages than for black offenders of all ages (ratio: 0.18). Black offenders over 45 years old had a higher ratio (ratio: 2.00).

Prisoners who were separated reported the most physician visits (6.3 per person), followed by those who were single (4.7 per person) and those who were married (4.3 per person). Sample prisoners who were widowed or divorced had only 3.1 reported visits per person. Among parolees those who were married reported the fewest physician visits (0.6 per person), while those who were widowed reported the most (1.7 per person), followed by those who were divorced (1.2 per person), separated (1.1 per person), and single (1.0 per person). Among probationers those who were married reported the most physician visits (3.5 per person), followed by those who were divorced (2.5 per

Table 7-4
Physician Visits and Physician Visits per Person per Year Reported:* Adult Male Probationers, by Age within Race

Age and Race	Number and Rate of Physician Visits		
	Physician Visits	Persons Sampled	Physician Visits per Person per Year
Both Races			
17 years and over	635	254	2.5
17-44 years	561	234	2.4
45 years and over	74	20	3.7
White			
17 years and over	404	202	2.0
17-44 years	333	187	1.8
45 years and over	71	15	4.7
Black			
17 years and over	231	52	4.4
17-44 years	228	47	4.9
45 years and over	3	5	0.6

*Estimates based on probability samples.

person). Among probationers those who were single reported the fewest physician visits (1.0 per person), followed by those who were separated (1.2 per person). The rate for probationers who were widowed would have been difficult to obtain, since only two probationers were widowers.

Table 7-6 contains ratios of reported physician visit rates for prisoners and for parolees compared by marital status with probationers. In the comparison of prisoners with probationers, separated offenders had the highest ratio (ratio: 5.25) followed by single offenders (ratio: 4.70). Married and divorced offenders had lower ratios (ratios: 1.23 and 1.24 respectively). In the comparison of parolees with probationers, single offenders had the highest ratio (ratio: 1.00) followed by separated offenders (ratio: 0.92). Married offenders had the lowest ratio (ratio: 0.17) followed by divorced offenders (ratio: 0.48).

Prisoners with 12 years or more of education reported the most physician visits (4.8 per person), followed by those with between 9 and 11 years (4.6 per person), and those with less than 7 years (4.5 per person). Among prisoners those with 7 or 8 years of education reported physician visits at the lowest rate (3.3 per person). Among parolees those with 12 years or more of education reported physician visits at the highest rate (1.6 per person). Among parolees those with 7 or 8 years of education reported physician visits at the lowest rate

Table 7-5
Physician-Visit Rates Reported:* Adult Male Prisoners and Parolees Compared with Adult Male Probationers, by Age within Race

Age and Race	Ratio: Rates for Prisoners/Probationers	Ratio: Rates for Parolees/Probationers
Both Races		
17 years and over	1.72	0.36
17-44 years	1.75	0.33
45 years and over	1.32	0.38
White		
17 years and over	2.05	0.50
17-44 years	2.06	0.50
45 years and over	1.13	0.34
Black		
17 years and over	1.07	0.18
17-44 years	0.98	0.16
45 years and over	7.00	2.00

*Estimates based on probability samples.

Table 7-6
Physician-Visit Rates Reported:* Adult Male Prisoners and Parolees Compared with Adult Male Probationers, by Marital Status

Marital Status	Ratio: Rates for Prisoners/Probationers	Ratio: Rates for Parolees/Probationers
Single	4.70	1.00
Married	1.23	0.17
Widowed		
Separated	5.25	0.92
Divorced	1.24	0.48

*Estimates based on probability samples.

(0.5 per person), followed by those with less than 7 years of education (0.6 per person), and those with between 9 and 11 years of education (0.7 per person). Among probationers those with less than 7 years of education reported physician visits at the highest rate (4.1 per person), followed by those with 7 or 8 years (3.7 per person), and those with 12 years or more of education (3.4 per person). Among probationers those with between 9 and 11 years of education reported physician visits at the lowest rate (0.9 visits per person).

Table 7-7 contains ratios of reported physician visit rates for prisoners and for parolees compared by education with probationers. In the comparison of prisoners with probationers, offenders with between 9 and 11 years of education had the highest ratio (ratio: 5.11), while those with 7 or 8 years had the lowest (ratio: 0.89), followed by those with less than 7 years (ratio: 1.10) and those with 12 years or more of education (ratio: 1.41). In the comparison of parolees with probationers, offenders with between 9 and 11 years of education had the highest ratio (ratio: 0.78), followed by those with 12 years or more of education (ratio: 0.47). Offenders with less than 7 years of education or with 7 or 8 years had lower ratios (ratios: 0.15 and 0.14 respectively).

2. Physician Visit Rates per Morbidity Condition

Table 7-8 summarizes the ratio between reported physician visits and reported morbidity conditions for sampled prisoners by age within race. Among prisoners of both races and all ages, the average prisoner reported 0.82 physician visits per morbidity condition. Exactly the same ratio remained true for black and white prisoners of all ages. Prisoners under 25 years old of both races combined reported fewer physician visits (0.57) per condition than other prisoners, and this was more true for black prisoners in this age bracket (0.48 visits per condition). Among all prisoners, only black prisoners between 35 and 44 years of age and over 45 years old reported more than an average of one physician visit per condition (1.15 and 1.04 visits per condition respectively).

Table 7-9 summarizes the ratio between reported physician visits and reported morbidity conditions for parolees by age within race. Among parolees of both races and all ages, the average parolee reported 1.18 physician visits per morbidity condition. Parolees of both races combined under 45 years old reported 1.11 visits per condition, and those over 45 years old reported 1.62

Table 7-7
Physician-Visit Rates Reported:* Adult Male Prisoners and Parolees Compared with Adult Male Probationers, by Education

Years of School Completed	Ratio: Rates for Prisoners/Probationers	Ratio: Rates for Parolees/Probationers
0-6	1.10	0.15
7-8	0.89	0.14
9-11	5.11	0.78
12 or over	1.41	0.47

*Estimates based on probability samples.

Table 7-8
Physician Consultations per Morbidity Condition Reported:* Adult Male Prisoners, by Age within Race

Age and Race of Patient	Physician Visits	Morbidity Conditions	Physician Visits per Morbidity Condition per Year
Both Races			
17 years and over	882	1072	.82
17-24 years	175	306	.57
25-34 years	391	432	.91
35-44 years	119	130	.92
45 years and over	197	204	.97
White			
17 years and over	474	576	.82
17-24 years	88	126	.70
25-34 years	180	216	.83
35-44 years	59	78	.76
45 years and over	147	156	.94
Black			
17 years and over	408	496	.82
17-24 years	87	180	.48
25-34 years	211	216	.98
35-44 years	60	52	1.15
45 years and over	50	48	1.04

*Estimates based on probability samples.

visits per condition. White parolees of all ages reported 1.28 physician visits per morbidity condition, and black parolees of all ages reported 1.06 visits per condition. White parolees under 45 years old reported 1.17 visits per condition, while those over 45 years old reported 1.91 visits per condition. Black parolees under 45 years old reported 1.03 visits per condition, while those over 45 years old reported 1.24 visits per condition.

Table 7-10 summarizes the ratio between reported physician visits and reported morbidity conditions for probationers by age within race. Among probationers of both races and all ages, the average probationer reported 3.27 physician visits per morbidity condition. Probationers of both races combined under 45 years old reported 3.26 visits per condition, and those over 45 years old reported 3.36 visits per condition. White probationers of all ages reported 2.59 physician visits per morbidity condition, and black probationers of all ages reported 6.08 visits per condition. White probationers under 45 years old reported 2.41 visits per condition, while those over 45 years old reported 3.94 visits per condition. Black probationers under 45 years old reported 6.71 visits

Table 7-9
Physician Consultations per Morbidity Condition Reported:* Adult Male Parolees, by Age within Race

Age and Race of Patient	Physician Visits	Morbidity Conditions	Physician Visits per Morbidity Condition per Year
Both Races			
17 years and over	322	272	1.18
17-44 years	259	233	1.11
45 years and over	63	39	1.62
White			
17 years and over	199	156	1.28
17-44 years	157	134	1.17
45 years and over	42	22	1.91
Black			
17 years and over	123	116	1.06
17-44 years	102	99	1.03
45 years and over	21	17	1.24

*Estimates based on probability samples.

per condition, while those over 45 years old reported only 0.75 physician visits per condition.

The ratios between physician visits and morbidity conditions may be compared for prisoners, parolees, and probationers by comparing Tables 7-8, 7-9, and 7-10. Among offenders of both races and all ages, probationers reported 2.8 times more physician visits per morbidity condition than parolees, and 4.0 times more than prisoners. Parolees reported 43.9 percent more visits per condition than prisoners. Among offenders under 45 years old, probationers reported 2.9 times more visits per condition than parolees, and 4.1 times more than prisoners. Parolees reported 40.5 percent more visits per condition than prisoners. Among offenders over 45 years old, probationers reported 2.1 times more visits per condition than parolees, and 3.5 times more than prisoners. Parolees reported 67.0 percent more visits per condition than prisoners. These comparisons remained virtually the same for white offenders of each age bracket, but differed substantially for black offenders. Among black offenders of all ages, probationers reported 5.7 times more physician visits per morbidity condition than parolees, and 7.4 times more than prisoners. Black parolees reported 29.3 percent more visits per condition than black prisoners. Among black offenders under 45 years old, probationers reported 6.5 times more visits per condition than parolees, and 8.4 times more visits per condition than

Table 7-10
Physician Consultations per Morbidity Condition Reported:* Adult Male Probationers, by Age within Race

Age and Race of Patient	Physician Visits	Morbidity Conditions	Physician Visits per Morbidity Condition per Year
Both Races			
17 years and over	635	194	3.27
17-44 years	561	172	3.26
45 years and over	74	22	3.36
White			
17 years and over	404	156	2.59
17-44 years	333	138	2.41
45 years and over	71	18	3.94
Black			
17 years and over	231	38	6.08
17-44 years	228	34	6.71
45 years and over	3	4	0.75

*Estimates based on probability samples.

prisoners. Black parolees reported 28.8 percent more visits per condition than prisoners. Among black offenders over 45 years old, however, parolees reported 65.3 percent more physician visits per morbidity condition than probationers, and 19.2 percent more than prisoners. Black prisoners reported 38.7 percent more visits per condition than probationers.

C. Clinical Tests

In addition to physician consultations, this research examined the outcome of eight clinical tests which are of use to buttress a physician's personal diagnosis. These tests included:

1. biopsies for malignant neoplasms
2. sputum test for active tuberculosis
3. Heaf patch test for tubercular exposure
4. Wassermann reaction test for syphilis
5. Australian antigen test for hepatitis
6. urine screening tests for drug abuse
7. electrocardiograms for cardiac irregularities
8. x-rays

Space in this report does not permit detailed analysis of these testing outcomes.[a]

[a]Clinical tests were monitored in 1972 only for approximately 1,000 prisoners who had spent six months at Tennessee State Penitentiary at the time of testing, unless otherwise indicated, with results as follows:

1. *Biopsies.* 34 prisoners reported the excision of tissue for a biopsy, three of which yielded signs of malignancy. Prisoners of both races received biopsies at about the same rate. Black prisoners under 25 and white prisoners between 35 and 44 years old reported biopsies least frequently. Three sampled probationers and one sampled parolee reported having a biopsy during the study period, one of which yielded signs of a malignancy.
2. *Sputum test.* 12 prisoners gave a positive result on a sputum test sometime during 1972, but only 5 of these continued to give a positive result at year's end. An estimated 216 sputum tests were performed periodically on these 12 prisoners and 3 others who had given positive sputums prior to 1972. Of these 16 prisoners, 12 are white and 4 are black; 7 were between 35 and 44 years old.
3. *Heaf patch test.* All 204 sampled prisoners were studied for Heaf reactions. No sampled prisoner of either race under 35 years old reacted positively to this test upon or since commitment. Out of 37 sample white prisoners between 35 and 44 years old, 7 reacted positively at intake as did 4 out of 13 black prisoners sampled in this age bracket. Out of 40 sample white prisoners over 45 years old, 13 reacted positively at intake, as did 4 out of 12 black prisoners in this bracket. None of these prisoners reacted positively to a Heaf test administered following the first year of commitment.
4. *Wassermann reaction test.* All 204 sampled prisoners were studied for Wassermann reactions, 8 of whom were determined to have had syphilis (3 in its tertiary stage and 5 in its secondary stage) upon intake. Of 360 sampled parolees, 6 reported some stage of syphilis during the study period. Of 254 sampled probationers, none reported any stage of syphilis during this period.
5. *Australian antigen test.* Hepatitis was diagnosed for 7 prisoners, one of whom contracted the disease prior to commitment. No sample parolee but 3 sample probationers reported contracting this disease during the study period.
6. *Urine screening tests.* Urine specimens were obtained weekly for 32 prisoners who were known to be drug users. These prisoners received tokens each week when a urine test was negative, but lost tokens when a test was positive. Out of 856 tests, 198 showed signs of drug abuse for 19 different prisoners at one or more times.
7. *Electrocardiograms.* Twice as many white prisoners (62 out of 610 studied) as black prisoners (20 out of 390 studied) received electrocardiograms. White prisoners over 45 and black prisoners between 35 and 44 years old received these tests most frequently. A disproportionately high proportion (11 percent) of white prisoners under 25 received EKGs, but none of 40 black prisoners over 45 years old received an EKG, however. Of prisoners who received one EKG, 16 whites and 5 blacks received two or more such tests during 1972, and 11 of these were over 45. Of 254 probationers and 360 parolees sampled, 5 probationers and 6 parolees reported receiving an EKG during the study period.
8. *X-rays.* Diagnostic (rather than therapeutic) x-rays were received by prisoners of both races and all ages at the rate of 1.5 per person during 1972, with very slight variation by age or race except for whites over 45 years old (1.95 per person). Out of 1,462 x-rays, 427 revealed abnormality. X-rays were provided in the following percentages, by type:

upper extremities	26
lower extremities	25
chest	12
spine	11
gastrointestinal	8
skull	6
skull	6
kidney (I.V.P.)	6
K.U.B.	2
cholecystogram	2
other	2

D. Dental Visits

As with physician visits, dental visits may be measured according to rates per person per year. Table 7-11 summarizes by age the number and rate of reported dental visits per person per year for prisoners. Prisoners of both races and all ages reported an average of 0.7 dental visits per person per year. Among prisoners of both races combined, those under 35 years old reported dental visits most frequently, followed by those over 45 years old, and those between 35 and 44 years of age.

Table 7-12 summarizes by age the number and rate of reported dental visits per person per year for parolees. Parolees of both races and all ages reported an average of 0.6 dental visits per person per year. Among parolees of both races combined, those under 25 years old reported dental visits most frequently,

Table 7-11
Dental Visits and Dental Visits per Person Reported:* Adult Male Prisoners, by Age

Age	Number and Rate of Dental Visits		
	Dental Visits	Persons Sampled	Dental Visits per Person Per Year
17 years and over	141	204	0.7
17-24 years	31	40	0.8
25-34 years	67	87	0.8
35-44 years	19	37	0.5
45 years and over	24	40	0.6

*Estimates based on probability samples.

Table 7-12
Dental Visits and Dental Visits per Person Reported:* Adult Male Parolees, by Age

Age	Number and Rate of Dental Visits		
	Dental Visits	Persons Sampled	Dental Visits per Person per Year
17 years and over	226	354	0.6
17-24 years	104	111	0.9
25-34 years	82	129	0.6
35-44 years	20	72	0.3
45 years and over	21	42	0.5

*Estimates based on probability samples.

followed by those between 25 and 34 years of age, those over 45 years old, and those between 35 and 44 years of age.

Table 7-13 summarizes by age the number and rate of reported dental visits per person per year for probationers. Probationers of both races and all ages reported an average of 0.5 dental visits per person per year. Among probationers of both races combined, those under 25 years old reported dental visits most frequently, followed by those between 25 and 35 years of age, and those over 35 years old.

White prisoners of all ages reported dental visits more frequently during this study (0.8 per person) than black prisoners of all ages (0.5 per person). White parolees reported dental visits at a slightly higher rate (0.7 per person) than black parolees of all ages (0.6 per person). Black and white probationers reported dental visits at about the same rate (0.5 per person).

Table 7-14 contains ratios of reported dental visit rates for prisoners and for parolees by age and by race, compared with probationers. In comparing prisoners with probationers, a ratio of 1.40 was observed for offenders of both races and all ages. Thus, prisoners of both races and all ages reported dental visits at a higher rate than did probationers of both races and all ages. Offenders of both races combined between 25 and 34 years of age and those over 45 years old had higher ratios (ratios: 1.60 and 1.50 respectively) than did offenders under 25 years and those between 35 and 44 years old (ratios: 1.33 and 1.25 respectively). White offenders had a higher ratio (ratio: 1.60) than did black offenders of all ages (ratio: 1.00). In comparing parolees with probationers, a ratio of 1.20 was observed for offenders of both races and all ages. Thus, parolees of both races reported dental visits at a slightly higher rate than probationers of both races and all ages. Offenders of both races combined under 25 years old had the highest ratio (ratio: 1.50), followed by those over 45 years

Table 7-13
Dental Visits and Dental Visits per Person Reported:* Adult Male Probationers, by Age

Age	Number and Rate of Dental Visits		
	Dental Visits	Persons Sampled	Dental Visits per Person per Year
17 years and over	133	254	0.5
17-24 years	84	145	0.6
25-34 years	31	66	0.5
35-44 years	10	23	0.4
45 years and over	8	20	0.4

*Estimates based on probability samples.

Table 7-14
Dental-Visit Rates Reported:* Adult Male Prisoners and Parolees Compared with Adult Male Probationers, by Age and Race

Age then Race	Ratio: Rates for Prisoners/Probationers	Ratio: Rates for Parolees/Probationers
17 years and over	1.40	1.20
17-24 years	1.33	1.50
25-34 years	1.60	1.20
35-44 years	1.25	0.75
45 years and over	1.50	1.25
White	1.60	1.40
Black	1.00	1.20

*Estimates based on probability samples.

old, and those between 25 and 34 years of age (ratios: 1.25 and 1.20 respectively). Offenders between 35 and 44 years of age had the lowest ratio (ratio: 0.75). White offenders had a slightly higher ratio (ratio: 1.40) than black offenders of all ages (ratio: 1.20).

E. Eye Examinations

As with physician and dental visits, eye examinations may be measured according to rates per person per year. Prisoners of both races and all ages reported an average of 0.5 eye examinations per person per year. Among prisoners of both races combined, those over 45 years old reported an average of 0.8 eye examinations per person, while those under 45 years old reported an average of 0.5 eye examinations per person. Parolees of both races and all ages reported an average of 0.5 eye examinations per person per year. Among parolees of both races combined, those between 25 and 34 years of age reported an average of 0.6 examinations per person; those under 25 years old an average of 0.5 per person; those over 45 years old an average of 0.3 per person; and those between 35 and 44 years of age an average of 0.2 per person. Probationers of both races and all ages reported an average of 0.3 eye examinations per person per year. Among probationers of both races combined, those under 25 years old reported an average of 0.4 examinations per person; those between 25 and 44 years of age an average of 0.3 per person; and those over 45 years old an average of 0.2 per person. Black prisoners reported eye examinations at a higher rate (0.7 per person) than white prisoners of all ages (0.4 per person). White parolees reported eye examinations at a slightly higher rate (0.5 per person) than black parolees (0.4 per person). Black and white probationers reported eye examinations at the same rate (0.3 per person).

Table 7-15 contains ratios of reported eye examination rates for prisoners and for parolees by age and race, compared with probationers. In the comparison of prisoners with probationers, a ratio of 1.67 was observed for offenders of both races and all ages. Thus, prisoners reported eye examinations at a slightly higher rate than probationers of both races and all ages. Offenders of both races combined over 45 years old had the highest ratio (ratio: 4.00), while offenders under 25 years old had the lowest ratio (ratio: 1.25), followed by those between 25 and 44 years of age (ratio: 1.67). Black offenders had a higher ratio (ratio: 2.33) than white offenders of all ages (ratio: 1.33). In comparing parolees with probationers, a ratio of 1.67 also was observed for offenders of both races and all ages. Thus, parolees reported eye examinations at a slightly higher rate than probationers of both races and all ages. Offenders of both races combined between 25 and 34 years of age had the highest ratio (ratio: 2.00), followed by those over 45 years old (ratio: 1.50), and those under 25 years old (ratio: 1.25). Offenders between 35 and 44 years of age had the lowest ratio (ratio: 0.67). White offenders had a slightly higher ratio (ratio: 1.67) than black offenders of all ages (ratio: 1.33).

F. Other Medical Specialist Visits

A number of prisoners received consultations with medical specialists other than physicians, dentists, ophthalmologists or optometrists in general practice. These other medical specialists included orthopedists, radiologists, urologists and cardiologists; a few prisoners visited a psychiatrist or a neurologist. Table 7-16 summarizes the proportion of prisoners spending 6 months or longer during 1972 at Tennessee State Penitentiary and reporting consultations with one or

Table 7-15
Eye-Examination Rates Reported:* Adult Male Prisoners and Parolees Compared with Adult Male Probationers, by Age and Race

Age then Race	Ratio: Rates for Prisoners/Probationers	Ratio: Rates for Parolees/Probationers
17 years and over	1.67	1.67
17-24 years	1.25	1.25
25-34 years	1.67	2.00
35-44 years	1.67	0.67
45 years and over	4.00	1.50
White	1.33	1.67
Black	2.33	1.33

*Estimates based on probability samples.

Table 7-16
Consultations with Other Medical Specialists Reported:* Adult Male Prisoners, by Age within Race

Age and Race	Percentage Receiving Specialist Consultation		
	Prisoners Who Visited Specialists	Population of Prisoners	Percentage Receiving at Least One Consultation
Both Races			
17 years and over	63	1000	6.3
17-24 years	7	150	4.7
25-34 years	25	500	5.0
35-44 years	20	200	10.0
45 years and over	11	150	7.3
White			
17 years and over	47	610	7.7
17-24 years	4	80	5.0
25-34 years	17	250	6.8
35-44 years	18	170	10.6
45 years and over	8	110	7.3
Black			
17 years and over	16	390	4.1
17-24 years	3	70	4.3
25-34 years	8	250	3.2
35-44 years	2	30	6.7
45 years and over	3	40	7.5

*Estimates based on verified prison records.

more of these medical specialists. Among such prisoners of both races and all ages, 6.3 percent reported having consulted with one medical specialist or more in that period. Among prisoners of both races combined, those between 35 and 44 years of age were most likely to have consulted with a medical specialist, followed by those over 45 years old, those between 25 and 34 years of age, and those under 25 years old. White prisoners of all ages were more likely than black prisoners of all ages to have consulted with one or more medical specialists.

The following is a list combining the proportion of prisoners spending six months or longer at Tennessee State Penitentiary who reported having visited a medical specialist, and the percent of these prisoners who reported having visited each type of specialist in relation to all medical specialists:

	N	%
Orthopedist - Hand Specialist	20	32

	N	%
Radiologist	15	24
Urologist	13	21
Psychiatrist - Neurologist	8	13
Cardiologist	5	8
Other Medical Specialist	2	3
Total Medical Specialists	63	101

Out of 315 parolees reporting such information, 36 (12.0 percent) indicated they had consulted with a psychiatrist or a neurologist during the period of this study, as did 24 (11.0 percent) of the 227 probationers who reported. Half of these parolees were white and half black, while 17 of these probationers were white and 7 black. Among parolees who reported consulting with a psychiatrist or a neurologist, 28 were under 35 years old and 16 were under 25 years old. All such probationers except one were under 35 years old, and 19 were under 25 years old. Very few parolees or probationers reported having consulted with medical specialists other than psychiatrists or neurologists (in addition to ophthalmologists), however. Eight nonincarcerated offenders (parolees and probationers) reported having consulted with an orthopedist or a hand specialist; three reported having consulted with a urologist; two consulted with a radiologist; and two reported having consulted with an ear-nose-throat (ENT) specialist.

G. Comparison Statistics

The only statistics available in 1972 relating to medical consultations by the general adult-male United States population were: rates of physician visits, and rates of dental visits. The general adult-male United States population in 1972 had the following estimated rates of physician visits per person per year: 3.4 for those between 17 and 24 years of age; 3.7 for those between 25 and 44 years of age; 4.9 for those between 45 and 64 years of age; 5.8 for those between 65 and 74 years of age; and 7.3 for those over 75 years old. The general adult-male United States population in 1972 had the following estimated rates of dental visits per person per year: 1.5 for those between 17 and 24 years old; 1.3 for those between 25 and 44 years old; 1.4 for those between 45 and 64 years old; and 0.9 for those over 65 years old.[7]

On the basis of this data, prisoners between 17 and 24 years of age reported 29.4 percent more physician visits per person than the general adult-male United States population in this age bracket in 1972; prisoners between 25 and 44 years old reported 10.8 percent more physician visits than the general adult-male population in this age bracket. Parolees between 17 and 44 years old reported 77.8 percent fewer physician visits per person than the general adult-male United States population in this wide age bracket (3.6 per person). Probationers between 17 and 44 years old reported 33.3 percent fewer physician visits than the general adult-male population in this age bracket. (See Table 7-2, 7-3, and 7-4.) Also on the basis of this data, prisoners between 17 and 24 years old reported 40.0 percent fewer dental visits per person than the general adult-male United States population in this age bracket; prisoners between 25 and 34 years old reported 46.2 percent fewer dental visits than the general adult-male population in this age bracket. Parolees between 17 and 44 years old reported 42.9 percent fewer dental visits per person than the general adult-male United States population in this age bracket (1.4 per person). Probationers between 17 and 24 years old reported 64.3 percent fewer dental visits than the general adult-male population in this age bracket.[8]

8 Medical Treatment

A. Components of Medical Treatment

A medical treatment is any service or procedure performed either to prevent or to cure a morbidity condition. Medical treatment is divided into two classes; surgical and nonsurgical, each of which may be subdivided in turn. The consideration here is limited to surgical treatments.

A surgical operation includes any cutting or piercing of the skin or other tissue; stitching of cuts or wounds; setting of fractures and dislocations; the introduction of tubes for drainage; "tapping"; and terms with the suffix "-scopy," for example, cystoscopy.[1] Routine circumcisions are not considered surgery,[2] but will be discussed here in conjunction with surgery.

For present purposes, surgery may be subdivided into three types: major surgery, minor surgery, and plastic surgery.[3] Surgery is major if inpatient hospitalization is required. Thus, an appendectomy or a ligation and stripping of veins is always a major surgical operation. A tonsilectomy is usually a major operation, especially if performed on an adult. Surgery is minor if inpatient hospitalization is not required. The routine excision of warts or ingrown nails as a rule is minor surgery. Plastic surgery may be either major or minor, depending on the technique used (for example, on the amount of skin-grafting involved), but more often than not is major surgery.

Plastic surgery is discussed here separately from either major or minor non-plastic surgery. This is done because most plastic surgery operations performed on prisoners at Tennessee State Penitentiary are cosmetic rather than essential to the health or survival of the patient. No probationer sampled reported receiving any plastic surgery during the course of this study, and only one sample parolee reported receiving plastic surgery. Therefore, plastic surgery is not a true basis for comparison of the major or minor surgery of prisoners with the major or minor surgery of parolees or probationers. Specific plastic surgery procedures will be defined and discussed here in section B.

B. Surgical Procedures

Surgical procedures are subdivided into three classes: major surgery, minor surgery, and plastic surgery; each discussed separately.

1. Major Surgery

Table 8-1 summarizes the number and rate of reported major surgical operations by age within race for the estimated total population of prisoners at Tennessee State Penitentiary in 1972 who had spent six months or longer in prison when hospitalized for surgery. Among these prisoners of both races and all ages, the rate of reported major surgery was 7.2 operations per 100 persons. Among these prisoners of both races combined, the rate of reported major surgery was highest for those under 25 years old and lowest for those between 35 and 44 years old, followed closely by those between 25 and 34 years old and those over 45 years old. White prisoners of all ages had a reported major surgery rate of 6.6 operations per 100 persons, while black prisoners had a reported rate of 8.8 operations per 100 persons. Among white prisoners those under 25 years old had the highest reported major surgery rate, followed by those between 25 and 34 years of age and those over 45 years old. Among white prisoners between 35 and 44 years of age had the lowest reported major surgery rate. Among black

Table 8-1
Major Surgical Operations Reported:* Adult Male Prisoners, by Age within Race

Age and Race	Number and Rate of Major Surgical Operations		
	Surgical Operations	Prisoners	Major Operations per 100 Persons per Year
Both Races			
17 years and over	72	1000	7.2
17-24 years	19	150	12.7
25-34 years	32	500	6.4
35-44 years	11	200	5.5
45 years and over	10	150	6.7
White			
17 years and over	40	610	6.6
17-24 years	10	80	12.5
25-34 years	17	250	6.8
35-44 years	6	170	3.5
45 years and over	7	110	6.4
Black			
17 years and over	32	390	8.2
17-24 years	9	70	12.9
25-34 years	15	250	6.0
35-44 years	5	30	16.7
45 years and over	3	40	7.5

*Estimates based on probability samples.

prisoners those between 35 and 44 years of age had the highest reported rate, followed closely by those under 25 years old. Among black prisoners between 25 and 34 years of age had the lowest reported major surgery rate, followed by those over 45 years old.

Table 8-2 summarizes the number and rate of reported major surgical operations by age within race for parolees during the period between 1 July 1972 and 30 June 1973. Among parolees of both races and all ages, the rate of reported major surgical operations was 5.6 per 100 persons. Among parolees of both races combined, those over 45 had a higher rate of reported operations than those under 45 years old. Black parolees of all ages reported a higher major-surgery rate than did white parolees of all ages.

Table 8-3 summarizes the number and rate of reported major surgical operations by age within race for probationers, during the period between 1 July 1972 and 30 June 1973. Among probationers of both races and all ages, the rate of reported major surgery was 3.5 operations per 100 persons. Among probationers of both races combined, those over 45 years old had a higher rate of reported major surgery than those under 45 years old. White probationers of all ages had a rate of 4.5 reported operations per 100 persons. No sample black probationers in any age bracket reported having a major surgical operation during the same period.

Table 8-2
Major Surgical Operations Reported:* Adult Male Parolees, by Age within Race

Age and Race	Number and Rate of Major Surgical Operations		
	Surgical Operations	Persons Sampled	Major Operations per 100 Persons per Year
Both Races			
17 years and over	20	360	5.6
17-44 years	17	315	5.4
45 years and over	3	45	6.7
White			
17 years and over	7	207	3.4
17-44 years	7	180	3.9
45 years and over	0	27	–
Black			
17 years and over	13	153	8.5
17-44 years	10	135	7.4
45 years and over	3	18	16.7

*Estimates based on probability samples.

Table 8-3
Major Surgical Operations Reported:* Adult Male Probationers, by Age within Race

Age and Race	Number and Rate of Major Surgical Operations		
	Surgical Operations	Persons Sampled	Major Operations per 100 Persons per Year
Both Races			
17 years and over	9	254	3.5
17-44 years	7	234	3.0
45 years and over	2	20	10.0
White			
17 years and over	9	202	4.5
17-44 years	7	187	3.7
45 years and over	2	15	13.3
Black[a]			

[a]No sample Black probationers in any age bracket reported a major surgical operation.
*Estimates based on probability samples.

Table 8-4 contains ratios of reported major surgery rates for prisoners and for parolees compared by age within race with probationers. In the comparison of prisoners with probationers, a ratio of 2.06 was observed for offenders of both races and all ages. Thus, prisoners of both races and all ages reported major surgery at a higher rate than probationers of both races and all ages. Offenders of both races combined under 45 years old had a higher ratio (ratio: 2.43) than those over 45 years old (ratio: 0.67). No ratios could be computed for black offenders, since no black probationers reported any major surgery during the period in question. In the comparison of parolees with probationers, a ratio of 1.60 was observed for offenders of both races and all ages. Thus, parolees of both races and all ages reported major surgery at a slightly higher rate than probationers of both races and all ages. Offenders of both races combined under 45 years old had a higher ratio (ratio: 1.80) than offenders of both races combined over 45 years old (ratio: 0.67). Again, no ratios could be computed for black offenders, since no black probationers reported any major surgery.

It is of interest to note the most frequent types of major surgical operations reported by prisoners at Tennessee State Penitentiary during 1972. The percent distribution of reported major surgical operations is summarized by type of operation in Table 8-5. The most frequently reported major surgical operations were the truncal vagotomy and/or the antrectomy, for the correction of either a duodenal or a peptic ulcer, or both. Nine of the sixteen ulcers that required surgery during the patient's imprisonment were reported to have been incurred

Table 8-4
Major Surgery Rates Reported:* Adult Male Prisoners and Parolees Compared with Adult Male Probationers

Age and Race	Ratio: Rates for Prisoners/Probationers	Ratio: Rates for Parolees/Probationers
Both Races		
17 years and over	2.06	1.60
17-44 years	2.43	1.80
45 years and over	0.67	0.67
White		
17 years and over	1.47	0.76
17-44 years	1.78	1.05
45 years and over	0.48	–
Black[a]		

[a]No sample Black probationers reported any major surgery.
*Estimates based on probability samples.

prior to imprisonment. The other seven ulcers were reported to have been first noticed during imprisonment. The second most frequently reported major surgical procedures involved the suture of severe lacerations caused by external injuries. Five of these twelve sutures of lacerations were performed in the treatment of severe stab wounds, while another five were performed in the treatment of serious self-inflicted wounds; the rest were performed in the treatment of accidents. Each of these lacerations was first incurred during imprisonment. This data reflects the most basic meaning of health risk during imprisonment—exposure to external dangers such as assault or industrial accidents.

Eight of the reported major operations were performed on these prisoners to remove tumors; six to correct a hernia; and five to remove bullets or pellets that had caused injury to the patient prior to imprisonment, except in one case, an assassination attempt on an inmate. Five appendectomy operations were performed, four tonsilectomies, four operations for the removal of a gallbladder, three to correct poor vision caused by illness or injury, and three in the treatment of burns (one from an accident, two from torture by others). Six other major surgery operations were reported for these prisoners.[a]

It is also of interest to note the most frequent types of reported major surgical operations on parolees and probationers during the same period. The major surgical operations reported for nonincarcerated offenders totalled 29,

[a]Since a total rather than a sample population is being measured, surgical operations are not itemized when performed only on one prisoner, to ensure privacy.

Table 8-5
Major Surgical Operations Reported* and Percent Distribution: Prisoners with at Least Six Months of Confinement, by Type of Operation

Type of Operation	Percent Distribution by Column	
	Number	Percent
Truncal vagotomy/antrectomy	16	22
For duodenal ulcer	(10)	(14)
For peptic ulcer	(6)	(8)
Suture of severe lacerations	12	17
For stab wounds	(5)	(7)
For self-inflicted wounds	(5)	(7)
For accidents	(2)	(3)
Excision of neoplasms (tumors)	8	11
Correction of herniae	6	8
Excision of bullets/pellets	5	7
Appendectomy	5	7
Excision of gallbladder	4	6
Tonsilectomy	4	6
Correction of vision	3	4
Treatment of burns	3	4
Other major surgery	6	8
Total major surgery	72	100

*Reports based on verified prison records.

and are summarized by type of operation, the number of each type, and the percentage of each type in relation to the total, as follows (percentage distribution by column):

	N	%
Suture of lacerations or setting of fractures	12	41
of lower limbs	(7)	(24)
of upper limbs	(5)	(17)
Correction of herniae	5	17
Correction of spine or disc	2	7
Excision of bullet/pellet	2	7
Appendectomy	2	7
Tonsilectomy	2	7
Excision of part of lung	1	3
Excision of part of bladder	1	3
Slicing of gums	1	3
Total major surgery	29	95

The comparison of major surgery reported for parolees and probationers with that reported for prisoners provides several noteworthy observations. Lacerations and fractures were reported more frequently for the nonincarcerated offenders than for prisoners. The lacerations and fractures that parolees or probationers reported as requiring major surgery were all incurred by accident, while most lacerations that prisoners reported as requiring major surgery were caused by stabbings or were self-inflicted. Major hernia operations were reported by parolees and probationers more frequently than by prisoners. The balance of major-surgery operations reported by nonincarcerated offenders were less serious (and less expensive)[b] than the balance of major surgery operations reported for prisoners.

2. Minor Surgery and Circumcisions

Table 8-6 summarizes by age the number and rate of reported minor surgical procedures and circumcisions performed on prisoners during 1972 who had spent six months or longer at Tennessee State Penitentiary at the time of the procedure. Among these prisoners of both races and all ages, 7.0 minor surgical procedures and 1.8 circumcisions per 100 persons were reported. Among these prisoners of both races combined, those between 35 and 44 years of age had the highest reported minor surgery rate, while those under 25 years old had the highest reported circumcision rate. Among these prisoners of both races combined, those over 45 years old had the lowest reported minor surgery rate.

Table 8-6
Minor Surgical Procedures Reported:* Adult Male Prisoners, by Age

Age in Years	Number and Rate of Procedures and Circumcisions				
	Minor Surgical Procedures		Circumcisions		Population
	Number	Rate	Number	Rate	
17 and over	70	7.0	18	1.8	1,000
17-24	13	8.7	8	5.3	150
25-34	28	5.6	8	1.6	500
35-44	22	11.0	0	0.0	200
45 and over	7	4.7	2	1.3	150

*Estimates based on validated prison records.

[b]Since a significant proportion of both probationers and parolees may be expected to become prisoners at a subsequent time, the fact that they receive less serious and less expensive operations outside of prison tends to suggest that some of the serious and expensive operations which are performed upon prisoners are necessitated by conditions that pre-existed commitment.

No prisoners between 35 and 44 years of age reported having been circumcized in 1972. The reported minor-surgery rate was slightly higher for white prisoners of all ages (7.2 procedures per 100 persons) than for black prisoners of all ages (6.7 .per 100). The reported circumcision rate was slightly higher for black prisoners of all ages (2.6 per 100) than for white prisoners of all ages (1.3 per 100).

It is of interest to note the types of reported minor surgery that prisoners received during 1972. These procedures consisted mainly of the excision of cysts, warts, hemorrhoids, and ingrown fingernails or toenails. The minor surgical procedures reported by prisoners at Tennessee State Penitentiary during 1972 who had spent six months or longer in prison at the time of the procedure are summarized by type of procedure, the number of each type, and the percentage of each type in relation to the total, as follows (percentage distribution by column):

	N	%
Excision of cyst	25	36
Excision of wart	12	17
Hemorrhoidectomy	12	17
Excision of nail	8	11
Total procedures	70	101

Two probationers reported having a hemorrhoidectomy during the same period; apart from this, no parolees or probationers reported any minor surgery.

3. Plastic Surgery

Table 8-7 summarizes by age the number and rate of plastic surgical procedures reported by prisoners during 1972 who had spent six months or longer at Tennessee State Penitentiary at the time of the procedure. Among these prisoners of both races and all ages, the rate of reported plastic surgery was 7.4 procedures per 100 persons. Among these prisoners of both races combined, those under 25 years old had the highest reported plastic surgery rate, followed by those between 25 and 34 years of age. Among these prisoners of both races combined, those over 45 years old had the lowest reported plastic surgery rate, followed in turn by those between 35 and 44 years of age. The rate of reported plastic surgery was nearly twice as high for white prisoners of all ages (9.0 per 100 persons) as for black prisoners of all ages (4.9 per 100 persons).

It seems important to note the types of plastic surgery that prisoners reported receiving during 1972. The plastic surgical procedures in 1972 reported for prisoners who had spent six months or longer in prison at the time of the surgery are summarized by type of procedure, the number of each type, and the

Table 8-7
Plastic Surgery Reported:* Adult Male Prisoners, by Age

Age in Years	Number and Rate of Plastic Surgery Operations		
	Surgical Operations	Prisoners	Plastic Surgeries per 100 Persons per Year
17 and over	74	1,000	7.4
17-24	15	150	10.0
25-34	44	500	8.8
35-44	11	200	5.5
45 and over	4	150	2.7

*Estimates based on validated prison records.

percentage of each type in relation to the total, as follows (percentage distribution by column):

	N	*%*
Rhinoplasty	20	27
Tattoo revision	18	24
W- or Z-plasty	16	22
Facelift	8	11
Blepharoplasty	5	7
Autoplasty	3	4
Otoplasty	2	3
Pyeloplasty	1	1
Thoracoplasty	1	1
Total plasty	74	100

Both pyeloplasty (revision of the kidneys) and thoracoplasty (revision of the chest cavity to compress the lungs) are major surgical procedures, not cosmetic, but vital to the health of the patients. These two procedures were included here in the tabulation of major surgery. The rest of the reported plastic surgery procedures are considered more major than minor, and for this reason were excluded. They were excluded from the tabulation of major surgery as well, because of their primarily cosmetic purpose. Moreover, only one sample parolee reported receiving any form of plastic surgery (for revision of a facial scar) during the period in question; and no sample probationers reported receiving any kind of plastic surgery. Thus, to include plastic surgery in measuring the major surgery of prisoners in comparison to that of parolees and probationers would seem to lead to a distortion that would unrealistically portray prisoners as requiring major surgery much more often than they did.

Trends in Mortality and Aggravated Assault

A. Cause-of-death Rates

Inmates at the Tennessee State Penitentiary died of a variety of reported, separate causes during both calendar year 1972 and fiscal year 1972-73. By far, homicide was the largest single reported cause of death during both periods of crime, followed by cardiac diseases and malignant neoplasms (cancer). During calendar year 1972, at least six inmates were reported killed by other persons, presumably by other inmates. Another inmate either fell, was pushed or jumped from the gallery of his cellblock, and was reported to have died of a fractured spine. Five inmates were reported to have died of cardiac-related causes, and two of malignant neoplasms. In addition, one inmate was reported to have died following an epileptic seizure; another, at work, from burns suffered when gasoline exploded; and a third inmate was reported to have drowned while trying to escape prison by swimming the Cumberland River. During fiscal year 1972-73, at least five inmates were reported killed by other persons, presumably by inmates. Three inmates died of mysterious causes, which suggested suicide. Of these inmates, one was found to have ingested "magic-shave," and his death was listed as a suicide; one was found hanging in his cell;[a] and one other inmate was alleged to have hanged himself in his cell while recovering from severe burns he received a year previously when guards had allegedly sprayed Mace or a similar substance into his cell while he (and/or someone else) was smoking.[b] An inmate died of bullet wounds, reportedly sustained when he was recaptured following an escape. During 1972 and the first half of 1973, at least eight inmates of the Tennessee State Penitentiary were the victims of criminal homicide. This is a minimal estimate, based on official records and not adjusted to account for hearsay evidence.[c] Therefore, in-depth attention will be directed toward the prison's homicide rates for this eighteen-month period.

[a]This death was originally ruled a homicide, and the "victim's" cell mate was charged. Subsequent investigation tended to reveal that this prisoner died, either accidently or by suicide, from a drug overdose.

[b]This death was ruled a suicide, as indeed it may have been. However, death came to this prisoner shortly after he began to litigate a Federal civil rights suit against prison administrators based on the incendiary MACE incident.

[c]Therefore, only deaths attributable to causes which were not open to question at the time of this study were tabulated. Deaths listed in this paragraph have been omitted from cause-of-death rates. Thus, cause-of-death rates (but not crude death rates) should be considered to reflect minimum, but not maximum data. These rates, if not accurate, could be expected to be higher rather than lower. The fact that they are rather high as tabulated should reinforce their significance.

Only two of the inmates who died during the eighteen-month period in question had spent less than one year in prison for their current sentence prior to death. One of these prisoners was stabbed to death during the first half of 1972, and the other prisoner reportedly committed suicide by ingesting "magic shave" during the first half of 1973. Since most of the inmates who died in prison during this period had spent one year or longer in confinement prior to death, their death rate should be measured in ratio to the number of prisoners who had been confined at Tennessee State Penitentiary for one year or longer during calendar year 1972 (CY 72) or fiscal year 1972-73 (FY 72-73). As the number of prisoners confined at this prison for one year or longer during 1972 or the first half of 1973 could be expected to be different for each age group of each race, specific death rates are constructed according to age within race.[d] Following this method, specific cause-of-death rates were obtained both for total deaths and for homicides.

1. Total Deaths

As Table 9-1 evidences, total death rates from all causes are similar for black and white inmates during CY 72, until they are broken down by age intervals within each race. Then the death rate for black inmates between 17 and 24 years of age is shown to be nearly twice as high as the death rate for white inmates in the same age bracket. This marked difference was caused by a series of reported homicides in which young black inmates were the principal victims. The highest death rate for white inmates during CY 72 was that of prisoners who had reached their 45th birthday. Presumably, this may be explained by the relatively advanced age of these prisoners. The highest death rate for black inmates during this period was that of prisoners between 35 and 44 years of age. However, the significance of this is reduced since only one black inmate in this age bracket died during CY 72, and only fifteen black inmates in this age bracket were estimated to have spent all of CY 72 at Tennessee State Penitentiary. Death rates for white inmates between 25 and 34 years old and over 45 years old exceed death rates for black inmates of comparable ages for CY 72. The lowest death rate for black inmates during CY 72 was that of prisoners between 25 and 34 years of age. The lowest death rate for white inmates during this period was that of prisoners between 35 and 44 years of age, followed by prisoners between 25 and 34 years of age.

Are prisoners of both races most likely to survive imprisonment when they are neither youths nor middle-aged? If so, why? Specific cause-of-death rates for non-homicide causes and homicides may illuminate possible answers to these

[d]However, items of data were not tabulated for all possible causes of death by age within race, since the sample populations were not large enough to permit this. Instead, items of data were categorized according to homicides and non-homicide causes.

Table 9-1
Deaths Reported* CY 72 from All Sources: Adult Male Prisoners, Confined at Least One Year, by Age within Race

Race and Age of Decedents	Deaths	Average Daily Count by Age within Race	Death Rate per 1,000
Both Races			
Ages 17 and over	16	810	19.75
17-24	5	127	39.37
25-34	2	291	6.87
35-44	1	149	6.71
Ages 45 and over	8	143	55.95
White			
Ages 17 and over	10	500	20.00
17-24	2	69	28.99
25-34	1	88	11.36
Ages 45 and over	7	109	64.22
Black			
Ages 17 and over	6	310	19.35
17-24	3	58	51.72
25-34	1	203	4.93
35-44	1	15	66.67
Ages 45 and over	1	34	29.41

*Estimates based on verified prison records.

questions. Reference to Table 9-2 shows that death rates from all reported causes are still similar for white and for black inmates during FY 72-73, until broken down by age intervals within each race. During FY 72-73 unlike CY 72, the death rate for white inmates between 17 and 24 years of age is higher than the death rate for black inmates in this age bracket. This may be explained by a reduction of homicides in which young black inmates were the principal victims. In FY 72-73 as in CY 72, no white inmate between 35 and 44 years of age is reported to have died in prison, and inmates of both races between 25 and 34 years old had relatively low death rates. White inmates of all age brackets except the 35 to 44 year old group had higher death rates than did black inmates of comparable ages. The highest death rates for inmates of both races during this period was that of those who had reached their 45th birthday.

2. Homicides

As Table 9-3 shows, the homicide rate for black inmates is more than six times as high as the homicide rate for white inmates who had been confined at

Table 9-2
Deaths Reported* FY 72-73 from All Sources: Adult Male Prisoners, Confined at Least One Year, by Age within Race

Race and Age of Decedents	Deaths	Average Daily Count by Age within Race	Death Rate per 1,000
Both Races			
Ages 17 and over	20	905	22.10
17-24	6	173	34.68
25-34	5	378	13.23
35-44	1	156	6.41
Ages 45 and over	8	195	41.03
White			
Ages 17 and over	12	510	23.53
17-24	3	68	44.12
25-34	3	203	14.78
Ages 45 and over	6	135	44.44
Black			
Ages 17 and over	8	395	20.25
17-24	3	105	28.57
25-34	2	175	11.43
35-44	1	55	18.18
Ages 45 and over	2	60	33.33

*Estimates based on verified prison records.

Tennessee State Penitentiary for one year or longer during CY 72. Three of the four black prisoners who were the victims of a reported homicide at this prison during CY 72 were between 17 and 24 years of age, and one was between 25 and 34 years of age. The only white prisoner who was the victim of a reported homicide at this prison during this period was between 25 and 34 years of age. The homicide rates for prisoners between 25 and 34 years of age are similar for white and black inmates. The homicide rate for black inmates between 17 and 24 years of age during CY 72 is astonishingly high.

As Table 9-4 shows, during FY 72-73, the homicide rate for black inmates was reduced by 41.1 percent over CY 72, but still is almost twice as high as the same rate for white inmates then at Tennessee State Penitentiary. The homicide rate for white inmates at this prison increased by 96.1 percent in FY 72-73 over CY 72. During FY 72-73, two of the three black inmates who were the victims of homicide were between 17 and 24 years of age, and the third black victim was between 25 and 34 years of age. The two white inmates who were the victims of homicide during this period were both between 25 and 34 years of age. The homicide rate for white inmates between 25 and 34 years of age in this period was 72.4 percent higher than the homicide rate for black inmates in the same age bracket.

Table 9-3
Homicides Reported* CY 72: Adult Male Prisoners, Confined at Least One Year, by Age within Victim's Race

Race and Age of Victim	Homicides	Daily Count by Age within Race	Homicide Rate per 100,000
Both Races			
Ages 17 and over	5	810	617.28
17-24 years	4	127	314.96
25-34 years	1	391	255.75
White			
Ages 17 and over	1	500	200.0
25-34 years	1	188	531.91
Black			
Ages 17 and over	4	310	1,290.32
17-24 years	3	58	5,172.41
25-34 years	1	203	492.61

*Estimates based on verified prison records.

In FY 72-73 compared with CY 72, the homicide rates remained virtually the same for black inmates between 25 and 34 years of age; increased by 85.2 percent for white inmates between 25 and 34 years of age; and decreased by 63.2 percent for black inmates between 17 and 24 years old. No white inmate under 25 years of age who had spent one year or more at Tennessee State Penitentiary during 1972 or the first half of 1973 was the victim of homicide during that period. No inmate of either race 35 years of age or older was the victim of homicide at this prison during the same eighteen-month period.

If inmates who are in their early maturity are the least likely to die of sickness or accidental injury, they are not the least likely to become victims of homicide. However, the most frequent homicide victim at Tennessee State Penitentiary during 1972 and the first half of 1973 was black and under 25 years old. Most of these young black homicide victims had been commited to the Tennessee State Penitentiary from Shelby County, which includes Memphis. According to reports by prison officials and inmates alike, they were the victims of contract murder ordered by the Memphis "Black Mafia," a group allegedly in control of prison gambling and smuggling operations.

B. Comparison Statistics

During this study an attempt was made at a correlation between the homicide victims and their alleged killers according to such demographic characteristics as race, age, county of commitment, and according to motive. Where homosexual reprisal was the murder motive, the sexual victim turned homicide offender was

Table 9-4
Homicides Reported* FY 72-73: Adult Male Prisoners, Confined at Least One Year, by Age within Victim's Race

Race and Age of Victim	Homicides	Daily Count by Age within Race	Homicide Rate per 100,000
Both Races			
Ages 17 and over	5	905	552.48
17-24 years	2	173	1,156.06
25-34 years	3	378	793.65
White			
Ages 17 and over	2	510	392.15
25-34 years	2	203	985.22
Black			
Ages 17 and over	3	395	759.49
17-24 years	2	105	1,904.76
25-34 years	1	175	571.42

*Estimates based on verified prison records.

generally white and younger than his black homicide victim. No correlation between offender and victim was observed according to other demographic characteristics when sex was the homicide motive. Where a contract was the homicide motive, identifying the killers became an insurmountable difficulty, mainly because the prison administration was unwilling (and in some cases unable) to disclose the identity of the killers. Inmates chose to follow their own code of *omertà*. In one or more instances, the prison administration asked this researcher not to pursue these correlations even though the names of some alleged contract killers were learned. In general, the administration seemed to fear that prosecution of these offenders might be impeded or barred as a result of premature disclosures of offender identities. Indeed, the prison administration was unsure in several instances whether the inmate suspected of murder was aware that he was a suspect.[e]

The effort at a correlation between homicide victims and their alleged killers was abandoned summarily in the interests both of justice and of research. Because some prisoners began to limit their cooperation with the research and because the prison administration threatened to terminate support for it out of a professed fear for the researcher's security, no further attempts were made to gather data relating to the killers of inmates. The objectives of this project, it

[e]In prison homicide cases, suspects may not be prosecuted until a long time has elapsed after the act, or they may never be prosecuted, due to evidentiary and testimonial difficulties, and for security reasons.

will be remembered, relate to incidence of harm and not to incidence of blame.

Some attention should be devoted toward drawing comparisons between the homicide rates for prisoners of both races and different ages, and the same rates for Tennessee residents not in prison at about the same time period.[f] During 1971, there were 496 deaths by homicide across Tennessee, with a rate of 12.4 per 100,000 population.[1] The homicide rate for white persons of both sexes and all ages was 8.0 per 100,000 population, while the homicide rate for nonwhite persons of both sexes and all ages was 33.9 per 100,000 population.[2] In general, therefore, the homicide rate for nonwhite persons across Tennessee in 1971 was four times higher than the homicide rate for white persons across Tennessee during the same period.

Age-specific homicide rates for persons of both sexes and all races across Tennessee in 1971 were highest (26.4 per 100,000 persons) for persons between 25 and 34 years of age; fairly high (20.3 per 100,000) for persons between 35 and 44 years of age; and fairly low (13.5 per 100,000) for persons between 15 and 24 years of age. Age-specific homicide rates were very low during this period in Tennessee for persons in all other age brackets.[3]

Homicide rates for persons across Tennessee are not available by age within race, or by age within race within sex. Traditionally, homicide rates have been higher for persons who live in urban areas of Tennessee than for persons who live in the rural areas of the state. In 1972, the homicide rates were estimated as being 18.6 per 100,000 for Memphis; 17.4 per 100,000 for Chattanooga; 13.9 per 100,000 for Nashville; and 9.7 per 100,000 for Knoxville.[4] The 1972 homicide rate for the State of Tennessee was estimated to be 11.3 per 100,000 persons.[5] Homicide rates for adult male prisoners of both races under 35 years of age and confined for one year or longer at Tennessee State Penitentiary during 1972 or the first half of 1973 are many times higher than the homicide rates recorded in 1971 or 1972 for Tennesseans living outside prison. Neither age- nor race-specific homicide rates are available for the general adult-male population of Tennessee for 1971, 1972 or 1973. For this reason, homicide rates for prisoners cannot be compared with homicide rates for nonprisoners in Tennessee by age within race.

Crude death rates are available for the general adult-male population of Tennessee in 1972, and these death rates are specific by age within race. As seen in Table 9-5, age-specific death rates for the general adult-male population of Tennessee in 1972 were higher for nonwhites than for whites in all age brackets between 15 and 75 years. In addition, age-specific death rates for the general adult-male population of Tennessee in 1972 increased significantly with each 10 year interval beginning with the twentieth birthday for nonwhites and the thirty-fifth birthday for whites. (See Table 9-5.)

[f]Data for the general population may be subject to underreporting, which is a common criticism of the Uniform Crime Reports system. However, it is acknowledged generally that underreporting is less of a problem for homicides than for most other serious crimes.

Table 9-5
Death Rates 1972 from All Sources: Adult Male, Tennessee Residents, by Age and Race

Age	Death Rates for Males per 1,000 Population (By Race)	
	White	Non-White
15-19 years	2.0	2.1
20-24 years	2.3	4.9
25-29 years	2.2	5.3
30-34 years	2.2	6.7
35-44 years	4.0	8.1
45-54 years	9.7	16.8
55-64 years	22.5	33.8
65-74 years	48.1	58.7
75 years and over	117.3	107.6

Source: State of Tennessee, Department of Public Health, *Annual Bulletin of Vital Statistics for the Year 1972.*

Several observations are suggested by a comparison of Table 9-5 with Tables 9-1 and 9-2. Death rates from all causes were substantially higher for prisoners in most age brackets spending one year or longer at Tennessee State Penitentiary during 1972 and the first half of 1973, than for the general adult-male Tennessee population in comparable age brackets of each race. White prisoners between 25 and 34 years of age and spending one year or longer in prison had a death rate 5.2 times higher in CY 72 and 6.7 times higher in FY 72-73 than the 1972 death rate of the general, white, adult-male Tennessee population in this age bracket. Black prisoners between 25 and 34 years of age and spending one year or longer in prison had a death rate in CY 72 only slightly higher than the 1972 death rate of the general, black, adult-male Tennessee population in this age bracket. In FY 72-73, however, black prisoners between 25 and 34 years of age and spending one year or longer in prison had a death rate about twice as high as the 1972 death rate of the general, black, adult-male Tennessee population in this age bracket.

For white prisoners between 35 and 44 years of age and spending one year or longer in prison no deaths were reported during imprisonment in either CY 72 or FY 72-73. Black prisoners between 35 and 44 years of age and spending one year or longer in prison had a death rate 8.2 times higher in CY 72 and 2.2 times higher in FY 72-73 than the 1972 death rate of the general, black, adult-male Tennessee population in this age bracket.

Comparisons between prisoners and the general adult-male Tennessee population are more difficult for ages under 25 and over 45 years of both races. Most prisoners under 25 years old and spending one year or longer in prison during CY 72 or FY 72-73 were between 20 and 24 years of age. With this in mind, an estimate may be made of the relationship between death rates of prisoners under 25 years old and the 1972 death rates of the general adult-male Tennessee population between 20 and 24 years of age. Using this method of comparison, white prisoners under 25 years old and spending one year or longer in prison had a death rate 12.6 times higher in CY 72 and 19.2 times higher in FY 72-73 than the 1972 death rate of the general, white, adult-male Tennessee population between 20 and 24 years of age. Again according to this method, black prisoners under 25 years old and spending one year or longer in prison had a death rate 10.6 times higher in CY 72 and 5.8 times higher in FY 72-73 than the 1972 death rate of the general, black, adult-male Tennessee population between 20 and 24 years of age.

Death rates for the general adult-male Tennessee population are not consolidated for persons who were 45 years old or older in 1972. These rates are available for each ten-year interval up to 75 years for white and non-white males. A comparison may be made in the case of white but not of black prisoners over 45 years old,[g] since most white prisoners spending one year or longer in prison who died during imprisonment in CY 72 or FY 72-73 were between 55 and 64 years of age. The death rates for white prisoners between 55 and 64 years of age and spending one year or longer in prison are estimated at 83.3 per 1,000 for CY 72 and 52.6 per 1,000 for FY 72-73. According to these estimates, death rates for white prisoners between 55 and 64 years of age and spending one year or longer in prison were 3.7 times higher in CY 72 and 2.3 times higher in FY 72-73 than the 1972 death rate of the general, white, adult-male population in this age bracket.

Further comparisons than those made would not be sufficiently reliable, in most instances because of the fewness or absence of prisoners in a given age bracket. For similar reasons, no comparison can be attempted between prisoners and the general adult-male population of Tennessee for cause-of-death rates based on causes of death other than homicide. Death rates were not measured for probationers or parolees during this study, because very few probationers or parolees remained on probation or parole for one year or longer during 1972 or the first half of 1973, and no deaths were reported among those who did.

C. Aggravated Assaults

Another part of the research concerned violence among inmates, whether lethal or not. Most of this violence involved stabbings and homosexual rapes. The

[g]Among black prisoners who died at the age of 45 years or older, not enough fell within a specific five or ten year age bracket.

information derived shed relatively little light on stabbings, but did illuminate a number of factors relating to homosexual rape.

1. Homosexual Rapes

Sampled prisoners were asked to estimate the number of forcible homosexual rapes that take place per year at the Tennessee State Penitentiary; these estimates were, in fact, the only source of knowledge encountered on this subject. The prison administrators averred continuously that they did not possess any records relating to homosexual rapes. For the questioning of respondents, the definition of forcible rape was clarified. They were clearly informed that they were to omit from their estimates any reference to consensual homosexuals relations, even where there appeared to be uneven bargaining power between the insertor (active partner) and the insertee (passive partner).[h] Instead, they were urged to recollect their knowledge (including hearsay knowledge) of homosexual relations (including oral but more likely anal) that had been accomplished by physical force or by threat of it.

As Table 9-6 indicates, among all respondents of both races, 97.8 percent stated that they recalled at least one instance of homosexual rape during the year preceding the interview; 73.9 percent recalled at least one episode per month; 37.0 percent recalled at least one episode per week; and 30.4 percent recalled that such acts occur more frequently than once per week. These estimates varied only slightly according to the respondent's race: none of the black respondents were of the opinion that rapes occurred at least four times a week, whereas 16.4 percent of the white respondents estimated that rapes did occur at this rate.

To verify these estimates, which were based upon a one year recall period, respondents were asked to specify how long before the interview it had been since they had last heard about an inmate being raped. As indicated in Table 9-7, among all respondents of both races, 85.0 percent could recall a rape having taken place within six months; 63.5 percent could recall a rape within two months; and 46.3 percent could recall a rape within one month. Indeed, 18.3 percent could recall a rape having occurred within one week. This information would seem to indicate the continuous commission of homosexual rapes at the Tennessee State Penitentiary.

The respondents were also asked to estimate the proportion of homosexual rapes that are reported to the prison administration. As shown in Table 9-8

[h]In a prison environment, more sophisticated prisoners sometimes "purchase" homosexual relations from naive and younger prisoners by providing the latter with status, protection, or money. This type of activity involves what is known as a "daddy-kid" or a "man-boy" relationship; in the researcher's opinion this is a form of rape based on coercion. However, the coercion is not physical, and this distinction was emphasized in the interviews.

Table 9-6
Estimates by Adult Male Prisoners, according to Respondent's Race, of the Number of Homosexual Rapes per Year

Rapes per Year	Agreement by Race of Respondent (Percent Distribution by Column)			
	White ($N = 55$)	Black ($N = 37$)	Both Races ($N = 92$)	Both Races Cumulative Responses
208-365 (At least four times per week and as often as each day)	16.4	0.0	9.7	9.7
104-207 (At least twice per week but not four times per week)	12.7	32.4	20.4	30.4
52-103 (At least once per week but not twice per week)	10.9	0.0	6.5	37.0
12-51 (At least once per month but not once per week)	36.4	37.8	36.6	73.9
1-11 (At least once per year but not once per month)	21.8	27.0	23.7	97.8
None–Never Occur	1.8	2.7	2.2	100.0
Total responses	100.0	99.9	100.1	

$X^2 = 14.59$ $DF = 5$ $P = <.02$
$\gamma = .15$
Based on probability sample.

among all respondents of both races, 72.8 percent stated that at least one-tenth are reported; 35.7 percent stated that at least one-third are reported; and 8.6 percent thought that three-fourths or more of the rapes were reported. On the contrary, 27.1 percent indicated that, in their opinion, less than 10 percent of the rapes committed in prison are ever reported. These estimates varied widely among respondents of both races. Some of the respondents seemed more naive than others about these gory aspects of prison life. Older white respondents seemed especially out of touch with this reality. For instance, 13.0 percent of the white respondents thought that three-fourths or more of the rapes were reported, but none of the black respondents considered that rapes were reported at this frequency.

The respondents were also asked to indicate approximately the time of day and the part of the week when they thought most rapes occur. Table 9-9 shows

Table 9-7
Recollection by Adult Male Prisoners, according to Respondent's Race, of Latest Occurrence of Homosexual Rape

Length of Time	Affirmative Response by Race (Percent Distribution by Column)			
	White (N = 51)	Black (N = 42)	Both Races (N = 93)	Both Races Cumulative Responses
Less than 1 week	7.8	31.0	18.3	18.3
More than 1 week but less than 1 month	31.4	23.8	28.0	46.3
4 to 8 weeks	11.8	23.8	17.2	63.5
3 to 6 months	21.6	21.4	21.5	85.0
Over 6 months	27.5	0.0	15.1	100.1
Total responses	100.1	100.0	100.1	

$X^2 = 27.03$ $DF = 4$ $P = <.001$
$\gamma = -.71$
Based on probability sample.

Table 9-8
Estimates by Adult Male Prisoners, according to Respondent's Race, of the Proportion of Homosexual Rapes Reported to the Prison Administration

Proportion of Rapes Reported	Agreement by Race of Respondent (Percent Distribution by Column)			
	White (N = 46)	Black (N = 24)	Both Races (N = 70)	Both Races Cumulative Responses
Three-fourths or over ("all," "most," etc.)	13.0	0.0	8.6	8.6
One-third or over ("half," "many," etc.)	17.4	45.8	27.1	35.7
One-tenth or over ("few," "sometimes," etc.)	41.3	29.2	37.1	72.8
Less than one-tenth ("almost never," "seldom," etc.)	28.3	25.0	27.1	99.9
Total responses	100.0	100.0	99.9	

$X^2 = 8.52$ $DF = 3$ $P = <.05$
$\gamma = -.10$
Based on probability sample.

Table 9-9
Perception by Adult Male Prisoners according to Respondent's Race, of Time of Day and of Week when Most Homosexual Rapes Occur

Time	Affirmative Response by Race (Percent Distribution by Column)		
	Both Races (N = 84)	White (N = 48)	Black (N = 36)
Weekday evenings	38.1	37.5	38.9
Weekend mornings and afternoons	22.6	14.6	33.3
Weekday afternoons	15.5	14.6	16.7
Weekday mornings	9.5	12.5	5.6
Other	14.3	20.8	5.6
Total responses	100.0	100.0	100.1

$X^2 = 7.67$ $DF = 4$ $P = >.10$
$\gamma = -.20$
Based on probability sample.

that the largest number of both black and white respondents thought that rapes take place most frequently on weekday evenings. One-third of the black respondents thought that rapes occur most frequently on weekend mornings and afternoons. In either event, the incidence of rape seems to be closely linked to those times of the week and the day when the majority of prisoners are idle.

Respondents were also asked to indicate approximately the area of the prison where they thought most rapes took place. Table 9-10 shows that a large majority of black respondents felt that rapes took place most frequently in the cellblocks, although only one-third of the white respondents supported this view. Another one-third of the white respondents felt that rapes took place most often in the main dining hall,[i] but only a few of the black respondents joined in this opinion. (See Table 9-10.) A smaller segment of both black and white respondents believed that most rapes took place in the prison auditorium, which also serves as the prison chapel and as the prison movie theatre. Among this last set of respondents, most indicated that rapes took place most often in the auditorium when it was used to show movies late at night.

In addition, respondents were asked to estimate per occurrence the number of different insertors who participated in raping the average insertee. Table 9-11 indicates that the majority of both black and white respondents thought that three or four insertors generally participated on one insertee. Thus, the gang-rape

[i]These repondents pointed to the main dining hall as the scene of rapes during hours of the morning or evening when the facility was supposed to be closed, or when it was closed to all except such persons as dining-hall orderlies or cooks.

Table 9-10
Perception by Sample Adult Male Prisoners, according to Respondent's Race, of the Prison Area where Most Homosexual Rapes Occur

Area	Affirmative Response by Race (Percent Distribution by Column)		
	Both Races (N = 85)	White (N = 48)	Black (N = 37)
Cellblocks	52.9	33.3	78.4
Main dining hall	25.9	33.3	16.2
Auditorium	12.9	18.8	5.4
Other	8.2	14.6	0.0
Total responses	99.9	100.0	100.0

$X^2 = 18.64$ $DF = 3$ $P = <.001$
$\gamma = -.73$
Based on probability sample.

Table 9-11
Estimates by Adult Male Prisoners, according to Respondent's Race, of Number of Insertors during Average Homosexual Rape

Insertors	Agreement by Race of Respondent (Percent Distribution by Column)		
	Both Races (N = 82)	White (N = 45)	Black (N = 37)
One or two	19.5	11.1	29.7
Three or four	67.1	75.6	56.8
Five or more	13.4	13.3	13.5

$X^2 = 4.68$ $DF = 2$ $P = <.10$
$\gamma = -.31$
Based on probability sample.

modus operandi seems to be the most prevalent among prison rapists. Other estimates ranged from one insertor per insertee to five or more insertors per insertee.

Finally, respondents were asked to state their opinion on the average racial match-up between the rapist and the raped in homosexual rapes in prison. Table 9-12 shows that the overwhelming majority of white respondents felt that the rapists are seldom, if ever, of the same race as those raped. The majority of black respondents felt that the rapists were sometimes but not always of the same race

Table 9-12
Perception by Adult Male Prisoners according to Respondent's Race, of Consistency of Race between Offender and Victim in Homosexual Rapes

Response Option	Affirmative Response by Race (Percent Distribution by Column)		
	Both Races (N = 85)	White (N = 45)	Black (N = 40)
Offender and victim usually of the same race	2.4	0.0	5.0
Offender and victim sometimes but not always of the same race	44.7	8.9	85.0
Offender and victim seldom of the same race	52.9	91.1	10.0
Total responses	100.0	100.0	100.0

$X^2 = 56.01$ $DF = 2$ $P = <.001$
$\gamma = -.98$
Based on probability sample.

as those raped. Table 9-13 suggests that the difference in perception based on the race of the respondents is explained by the fact that most of the white respondents were persuaded that homosexual rapes in prison were perpetrated by black inmates against whites. However, the majority of black respondents felt that this was not always true.

None of the black respondents was able or willing to recall a single incidence of a white raping a black. Most of these respondents strongly asserted the doubtful claim that no white would be strong enough to do this. Most of these black respondents indicated that both blacks and whites raped white insertees frequently, and that blacks raped blacks on occasion. White respondents admitted that when white inmates retaliated against blacks for having raped a white inmate, the white avengers usually stabbed or burned their victims instead of raping them. These respondents noted further that when the victim himself retaliated against his sexual aggressors, he customarily tried to stab them; but when vigilantes interceded on the victim's behalf, they burned or threatened or attempted to burn the aggressors. Similarly, nearly all black respondents thought that homosexual rapists perpetrated these offenses for sexual release. A substantial majority of white respondents thought that black homosexual rapists perpetrated these offenses primarily to weaken or to emasculate the white victims out of hatred. The remainder of the white respondents felt that rapists perpetrated the offense for a combination of the above reasons.

Table 9-13
Perception by Adult Male Prisoners, according to Respondent's Race, of Insertor's Race Compared with Insertee's Race in Homosexual Rapes

Race of Insertor	Race of Insertee	Affirmative Response by Race (Percent Distribution by Column)		
		Both Races (N = 79)	White (N = 41)	Black (N = 38)
Black	White	50.6	92.7	5.3
White	Black	1.3	0.0	2.6
Black	Black	3.8	0.0	7.9
White	White	1.3	0.0	2.6
Varies	Varies	43.0	7.3	81.6
Total responses		100.0	100.0	100.0

$X^2 = 60.43$ $DF = 4$ $P = <.001$
$\gamma = .97$
Based on probability sample.

2. *Stabbings*

According to Tennessee State Penitentiary records, nineteen inmates were stabbed by other inmates at the prison between 1 January 1972 and 30 June 1973. Presumably, any inaccuracy in these records would be understatement rather than overstatement. Therefore, part of the research was devoted to identifying the inmates' understanding of this problem, including its magnitude and its explanation.

A sample of inmates was asked to assess the seriousness of the problem of stabbings at the Tennessee State Penitentiary. Table 9-14 shows that the majority of white respondents (84.0 percent) and half of the black respondents considered stabbings to be a very serious problem. The overwhelming majority of both white and black respondents considered stabbings to be either a very serious or a fairly serious problem.

Each respondent was asked for causes why some inmates were stabbed by other inmates during imprisonment. Several major reasons were offered by a significant proportion of respondents. Table 9-15 indicates that of the respondents of both races, 21.2 percent believed that most stabbing victims had borne (true or false) witness against another criminal offender prior to coming to prison. In prison jargon, an inmate who tells any free-world person about the criminal behavior of another inmate is known as a "snitch." The practice of "snitching" is perceived by the largest number of respondents as the most frequent cause of inmate stabbings. The largest number of black respondents

Table 9-14
Perception by Adult Male Prisoners according to Respondent's Race, of the Seriousness of Stabbings as a Problem

Response Option	Affirmative Response by Race (Percent Distribution by Column)		
	Both Races (N = 90)	White (N = 50)	Black (N = 40)
Very serious	68.9	84.0	50.0
Fairly serious	23.3	10.0	40.0
Not very serious	2.2	4.0	0.0
Not serious at all	5.6	2.0	10.0
Total responses	100.0	100.0	100.0

$X^2 = 16.46$ $DF = 3$ $P = <.001$
$\gamma = .61$
Based on probability sample.

thought that the average stabbing victim had been either a "snitch" or had failed to pay a monetary debt when it became due and payable. Gambling is rampant in this and many other prisons. In addition, money may be borrowed by inmates from other inmates at will, at the usurious interest rate of 25 percent every two weeks. This amounts to 650 percent per annum (25 x 26). Respondents of both races indicated that a stabbing victim may be "stuck" by the person to whom he owes money (or on whom he "snitched"), or by an independent contractor, the latter having been hired for money or for release from his own debt.

The largest number of white respondents thought that the average stabbing victim had become involved in either a homosexual entanglement or a petty argument over trivia. These respondents noted particularly that a stabbing may take place between inmates who are rivals for another inmate's homosexual favors, or as a reprisal for a forcible homosexual rape. A number of respondents of both races suggested additional or other reasons that are summarized in Table 9-15.

All respondents were asked to reflect upon whether they felt the chances were likely that they could become the next victim of a stabbing. The answers to this question are curious. Table 9-16 shows that a majority of black respondents and over one-fourth of white respondents answered categorically that they were not likely to become a stabbing victim. Most of these respondents were quick to point out that they were not "snitches"; and/or that they did not gamble more than they could afford to pay if they lost; and/or that they did not engage in homosexual relations other than as the patrons of a homosexual prostitute.

The majority of white respondents and nearly a majority of the black

Table 9-15
Perception by Adult Male Prisoners, according to Respondent's Race, of Major Reasons Why some Inmates are Stabbed by Others

Stated Reason	Affirmative Response by Race (Percentage of Sample Responding)[a]		
	Both Races (N = 104)	White (N = 59)	Black (N = 45)
Outside snitch[b]	21.2	16.9	26.7
Homosexual[c]	15.4	23.7	4.4
Small argument	13.5	23.7	0.0
Monetary debt	12.5	1.7	26.7
Theft[d]	7.7	10.2	4.4
Other reason[e]	26.9	20.3	35.6

$X^2 = 33.95$ $DF = 5$ $P = <.001$
$\gamma = .19$

[a]Total may be less than 100.0 because of lack of explanation by some respondents.

[b]Includes both testimony and out of court declarations.

[c]Includes both rivalry and reprisal for assault.

[d]Includes larceny, robbery, and burglary.

[e]Includes assorted responses ranging from intoxication on either julip or drugs; turned down for parole; "all (mixed) up."

Based on probability sample.

Table 9-16
Perception by Adult Male Prisoners, according to Respondent's Race, of whether They Themselves Could Become the Next Victim of a Stabbing

Response Option	Affirmative Response by Race (Percent Distribution by Column)		
	Both Races (N = 87)	White (N = 47)	Black (N = 40)
Not likely	39.1	27.7	52.5
Likely that I could[a]	34.5	34.0	35.0
Likely anyone could[b]	26.4	38.3	12.5
Total responses	100.0	100.0	100.0

$X^2 = 8.86$ $DF = 2$ $P = <.02$
$\gamma = -.49$

[a]But unlikely that everyone could.

[b]Therefore likely that I could.

Based on probability sample.

respondents were more paranoid about the possibility of being stabbed themselves. These responses tended to be divisible into two categories: those who felt that they had become vulnerable to stabbings because of some aspect of their own behavior; and those who felt that anyone, including themselves could be stabbed, because of the capriciousness of the inmates who commit stabbings. Many of the respondents in the second category observed that they would be most likely to be stabbed during the course of being robbed. During one of the final days of data gathering at the Tennessee State Penitentiary, this researcher shared the awesome opportunity of witnessing the immediate aftermath of a stabbing that resulted from an attempted robbery.[j] The victim's res-gestae conversation yielded every reason to believe (as he stated that he did) that he could not have foreseen or prevented his predicament in any way.[k]

It is of interest to note that all of the respondents of both races agreed that the relationship between the offender and the victim of a stabbing cannot be predicted on the basis of race, except in the rape-retaliation situation.[l] Most of the respondents agreed that an inmate who stabs another inmate intends to kill, not merely to wound his victim. Between 1 January 1972 and 30 June 1973, four of the nineteen stabbing victims were dead on arrival at the prison hospital, and a fifth was dead on arrival at a hospital outside the prison. The reasons why most stabbing victims survive, notwithstanding the intent of their attackers seemed to be a mystery to many inmate respondents. Some thought that the cutlery weapons (most of which were improvised and rather dull) were insufficient for the job. A few respondents (all but one of whom admitted familiarity with Marvin Wolfgang's theory)[m] keenly observed that most stabbings take place in or about the prison yard, which is situated in proximity to the prison hospital.

---

[j]Ths victim had been stabbed, apparently, near the shower stall of his cellblock on a weekend morning. He walked about 300 feet out of the cellblock and toward "Operations" (the barricaded headquarters of custodial security, near the main gate to the prison yard), where he began to stumble and was noticed by the Corporal of the Guard. The victim was interrogated but would not (he said he could not) identify his assailants. He stated that robbery was the motive, and then collapsed. A stretcher was obtained and the victim was dispatched to the prison hospital for transport to an outside hospital by ambulance. During the sequence of events, which lasted about ten minutes from attack to transport, the victim's abdomen became progressively more convulsive, and most of his clothing became saturated with blood.

[k]This victim's statements tended to indicate that he had not voluntarily interacted with his assailant(s) in any way, but that he had been surprised by the assailant(s) who lay in wait for him. The victim had not entered an area in which he could have predicted that trouble might result. If he precipitated the event, the precipitation could be only rumors that he had money in his possession.

[l]At this prison, most homicides that have been attributed to a retaliation for a concurrent or previous rape have included interracial participants, the nonsexual aggressor (rape victim or victim's champion, turned aggressor) is white and the stabbing victim is black. Most similar stabbings that have not resulted in death followed this pattern, according to respondents. Except for the rape-prevention or rape-vengeance motive, race is not a predictive factor in stabbings, most respondents reported.

[m]These respondents suggested that homicide was the motive for most stabbings, and that when death failed to result, this could be attributable to the proximity of immediate

medical attention. See M. Wolfgang, "A Sociological Analysis of Criminal Homicide," *Federal Probation* 23 (1961): 48-55. Interestingly enough, most respondents detected substantial victim precipitation in fatal and non-fatal stabbings that occur in prison, although all but one of the respondents professed knowledge of Wolfgang's theory of victim precipitated criminal homicide, M. Wolfgang, "Victim-Precipitated Criminal Homicide," *Journal of Criminal Law, Criminology and Police Science* 48 (1957): 1-11. Perhaps some of those respondents had the occasion to read Wolfgang's anthology, *Studies in Homicide* (New York, 1967), in which the above two articles are reprinted.

10 Implications

The present study has generated many descriptive statistics and some test statistics, as an outline of how prisoners at Tennessee State Penitentiary compare with adult male parolees and probationers in Tennessee in terms of morbidity conditions and in terms of medical consultation, diagnosis, and treatment. Given these descriptive statistics, some interpretive analysis is to be expected.

A. Overview of Implications

Perhaps the single most important contribution of this study is its testament that prison medical records may be studied by an ethical researcher without compromising the privacy of inmates. At the same time, it has shown that significant use can be made of the material contained within prison medical records; that in turn emphasizes the need for prisons to maintain complete and accurate medical records on all inmates. The study has made clear the long-existing overlap of criminology and public health by demonstrating the close relationship of medical sociology as a field to the administration of justice. It has uncovered the dearth of health-care services available to non-incarcerated offenders in Tennessee, and urged the need to evaluate both morbidity conditions and health care delivery services as they affect criminal offenders both inside and outside prison.

Beyond this general overview, specific implications based on the descriptive data obtained should be advanced only with extreme caution for several fundamental reasons. First, the research was conducted in a single state during an eighteen-month period, and the descriptive data might have differed significantly had offenders from some other state been sampled and studied, or had the sample Tennessee offenders been studied over a longer period of time. Secondly, in many ways this was a pilot study, since it was conducted without benefit of the guidance of prior related research. Thirdly, it was conducted by a single researcher, which limited necessarily the size of the sample populations and the parameters of the inquiry, and which resulted also in a delay in data analysis. Finally, by the time the descriptive statistics and the interpretive analysis of those statistics become internalized by persons other than the researcher, much of the data will be several years old.

B. Specific Interpretations

The research does show that prisoners at Tennessee State Penitentiary reported most varieties of morbidity conditions during the period studied at much higher rates than did the Tennessee probationers and parolees; these in turn reported most such conditions at fairly similar rates. On the basis of this evidence, one conclusion is that the condition of imprisonment does have an effect on the quantity and type of morbidity conditions reported by prisoners.

A derivative question immediately emerges for consideration. Does imprisonment cause prisoners to suffer from manifest morbidity conditions at a higher rate than they would suffer from the same conditions outside prison during the same period of time; or does imprisonment inspire prisoners simply to report unfounded morbidity conditions at a higher rate than they would report such conditions outside of prison? This question relates to whether the majority of morbidity conditions that sample prisoners reported represent an actual departure from a state of physical or mental well-being, or whether they represent a widespread trend toward hypochondriasis. Even if the latter were true, many medical practitioners would still argue that an actual departure from a state of mental well-being is present to some extent when a patient complains of an imaginary departure from a state of physical well-being.[1]

Many kinds of morbidity conditions about which a patient complains cannot be proven or disproven. In the final analysis, a departure from a state of well-being is not much more than a patient's perception that such a departure has occurred. To minimize planned deception on the part of the prisoners sampled, several safeguards were maintained. First, responses by prisoners to the health questionnaire items were cross-referenced against prison medical records. A high level of accuracy was observed in the recollections of most prisoner respondents. Secondly, only the first two digits of the three-digit ICDA codes[a] were used to classify morbidity conditions for the purpose of tabulating gross acute condition rates in Chapter Six.[b] In this way, the diagnoses of interrelated subconditions stemming from a single principal condition were not recorded. Such additional diagnoses could be a function of the precision of the professional medical examination; this in turn could distort the prisoner complaint rates, since prisoners reported consulting with physicians at a considerably higher rate than did probationers or parolees. Thirdly, recurring sequelae of the same initial symptomatology were not recorded unless three or more months intervened between complaints for the same condition. This was done in an effort to minimize the effect that the differential cost of treatment (free for the prisoners) could be expected to have upon colic (recurrent) complaints about the same original morbidity condition.

[a]Digits 00 through 99 were used. (For ICDA see Chapter Two, n. 2.)

[b]The third digit was considered for the purpose of tabulation of specific-condition rates in Chapter Seven; digits 001 through 999 were used here.

A further derivative question emerges for consideration. Do criminal offenders report morbidity conditions at a higher rate during imprisonment rather than before or after imprisonment simply because as prisoners they become more concerned with their own bodies–more anatomically egocentric–than do nonincarcerated offenders (probationers or parolees)? This question relates to the actual time when inmates noticed most of these conditions for the first time. Did they notice these conditions at some time prior to imprisonment, and then forget about the conditions only to "rediscover" them later during imprisonment? Few inmates admitted to having known about their present morbidity conditions prior to commitment, and those inmates who did report conditions preexisting imprisonment were referring largely to chronic, not to acute conditions.

This question relates also to the etiology of morbidity conditions that inmates report while in prison. Are most of these conditions new, having accrued since the inmate was committed to prison? Or, are some of these conditions old, having preexisted the inmate's commitment to prison? In the present study, only prisoners who had spent six months or longer continuously in prison were sampled and studied. Presumably, conditions that had existed prior to an inmate's commitment would have been discovered during the first three months of imprisonment. If discovered during that period, acute conditions would have subsided prior to the end of the first six months of imprisonment. Conditions that did not subside during that period would have been labeled as chronic, as are all morbidity conditions lasting for more than three months at a time.

Based upon the data obtained from probability samples of offenders, a second conclusion of the present study is that acute morbidity conditions did accrue among prisoners at Tennessee State Penitentiary at a substantially higher rate than among adult male probationers or parolees in Tennessee during the period in question. This conclusion relates to acute conditions only and not to chronic morbidity conditions, since chronic conditions are measured according to their prevalence at any given time rather than according to the point of their original incidence. Some further study might be devoted to a scrutiny of both acute and chronic conditions reported by prisoners prior to imprisonment; its basis would be the medical records of private medical practitioners with whom inmates might have consulted before being committed to prison.

The rate at which sample prisoners reported acute physical conditions varied inversely according to age for both black and white prisoners under 45 years old. Black prisoners over 45 years old reported acute physical conditions at the same rate as did black prisoners between 35 and 44 years of age. White prisoners over 45 years old reported these conditions at a higher rate than did white prisoners between 25 and 44 years of age. Clearly, prisoners in the youngest and oldest age brackets tended to report acute morbidity conditions at substantially higher rates than other prisoners. There is significant evidence to suggest that imprisonment may have more adversely affected the health of prisoners in these age brackets than the health of other prisoners. Couple this with evidence that prisoners under 25 years old are most likely to become victims of homicide or homosexual rape, and the overall desirability of confining offenders under 25 years old to prison should be questioned on grounds both of health and economics.

Of the prisoners studied, those who had been confined in prison for the longest and the shortest periods of time (more than ten years or less than one year) reported acute physical conditions at substantially higher rates than other prisoners. Among prisoners who had been confined to prison for more than ten years, this was true particularly for those who had been considered for but denied parole. Couple this evidence with that set forth above relating to prisoners over 45 years old, and the overall desirability of confining offenders to prison for excessively long or for uncertain terms should be questioned on grounds both of health and of economics.

Prisoners of both races and all ages reported acute respiratory conditions at about the same rate as the general adult-male United States population in 1972. However, nonincarcerated offenders of both races and all ages reported acute respiratory conditions at less than half this rate. This could mean that criminal offenders outside prison are stronger and more resistant to acute respiratory conditions than the general population. On the other hand, it could mean instead that criminal offenders outside prison are less concerned with their health and fail to identify respiratory conditions when they do exist to the same extent as the general population. In either case, the evidence suggests that the prisoners sampled did not report acute respiratory conditions at a rate differentially higher than would be expected.

Prisoners of both races and all ages reported acute digestive system conditions at a rate about seven times higher than the rate for the general adult-male United States population in 1972. Nonincarcerated offenders of both races and all ages reported acute digestive system conditions at about the same rate as the general population. This seems to indicate that criminal offenders outside prison experience these acute conditions at an expected rate, but that imprisonment brings a dramatic rise in this rate. One reason for this wide rate differential could be the anxieties and life stresses commonly associated with prison condition. These anxieties and stresses may include daily fear for life or health, complications in the lives of family members on the outside, rising and falling expectations relating to parole, as well as many other situational disturbances.

Prisoners of both races and all ages reported acute injuries at a rate about two times higher than the rate at which the general adult-male United States population reported acute injuries during 1972; and they reported infectious and parasitic diseases at a rate about three times higher than the rate for the general population. Nonincarcerated offenders of both races and all ages reported acute injuries as well as infectious and parasitic diseases at about half the rate of the general population. The higher injury rate for prisoners may be explained by an increase in violence during imprisonment, possibly attributable to the closeness of confinement or to interactions among persons of whom an abnormally high number are prone to violence. The low injury rate for nonincarcerated offenders could be explained by their greater toughness and motor dexterity compared to the average person in the free world. The higher infectious and parasitic disease rate for prisoners could be explained by poor hygiene and poor sanitary conditions inside prison. The low infectious and parasitic disease rate for non-incarcerated offenders seems to be less readily explicable. Could this be due to their possessing stamina and disease resistance to a greater degree than the average person? Could this be due to underreporting caused in part by a lack of concern about their health and a failure to identify those infectious and parasitic diseases that do exist? The answers to these questions, if possible to obtain, would document the extent to which the unsanitary conditions within a prison affect inmates and their health.

Nonincarcerated offenders of both races and all ages reported chronic stomach or duodenal ulcers, upper gastrointestinal disorders, gastritis and duodenitis, frequent constipation at rates up to four times higher than the rates at which the general adult-male United States population reported comparable chronic conditions in 1968. In turn, prisoners of both races and all ages reported each of these chronic digestive conditions at rates that were several times higher than corresponding rates for the sample nonincarcerated offenders. This evidence tends to suggest that criminal offenders suffer from chronic digestive conditions to a greater extent than the average person, both inside and outside prison. If true, this could be attributable to an ongoing feeling of anxiety, fright, and instability caused at least in part by a life-style of stealth and dangers of apprehension. Parolees as well as probationers reported these chronic conditions at lower rates than prisoners. Thus, offenders seem to experience an aggravation of these chronic digestive conditions during imprisonment, followed by a regression of these conditions upon release. Some future research might be motivated by a desire to determine whether criminal offenders initially develop chronic digestive conditions as a result of their drive to perform criminal activities, and whether these conditions intensify during imprisonment.

Prisoners of both races and all ages reported both intestinal and stomach conditions (chronic and "not otherwise specified" or n.o.s.) at rates much higher than the rates at which the general adult-male United States population reported these conditions in 1968. Again, these rate differentials do not stem necessarily from imprisonment. For instance, nonincarcerated offenders reported stomach conditions (n.o.s.) at a higher rate than the general population, although prisoners reported intestinal conditions (n.o.s.) at a much higher rate than nonincarcerated offenders. At least a part of this symptomatology seems to be attributable to the criminal offender's life-style outside as well as inside prison, rather than to the condition of imprisonment alone.

At Tennessee State Penitentiary, 16.5 percent of the prisoners who spent the entire first half of 1973 in prison had been diagnosed as evidencing the symptomatology of at least one mental disorder. Many of them had been diagnosed as evidencing multiple psychiatric sequelae. Unquestionably, none of these prisoners should be incarcerated within a prison where no psychiatric therapy is available. Moreover, most of these prisoners (81.4 percent) received their first psychiatric diagnosis during their term of imprisonment, as a result of behavior suggesting that they might be dangerous to themselves or to others. If the diagnoses are to be accepted at face value (as they must be in the absence of contrary evidence), then these prisoners are not receiving either the restraint or the treatment that their personalities require. If in addition some of these prisoners represent a danger to their fellow inmates, then the entire prisoner population is not receiving a sufficient amount of protection.

Since such a high proportion of prisoners with diagnosed mental disorders received their first psychiatric evaluation while in prison, several derivative questions arise. What proportion of these prisoners before imprisonment suffered from psychiatric sequelae that could have been identified through a complete psychiatric evaluation? What proportion of the general prisoner population (those without a diagnosis of a mental disorder on record) would evidence mental disorder symptomatology if they were given a complete psychiatric evaluation? The answers to each of these questions might be startling. Although the data here presented cannot answer these questions, it does establish probable cause for the mandate that all inmates at this and every prison be given a thorough psychiatric evaluation at intake and at regular intervals thereafter.

Feelings of a desire to commit suicide were reported by prisoners much more frequently than by nonincarcerated offenders, and by probationers more frequently than by parolees. This tends to suggest that imprisonment fosters the contemplation of self-destruction, and that persons who have been released from prison consider self-destruction to a lesser extent than do criminal offenders who have never been imprisoned. Does this mean that parolees are so relieved to be out of prison that they become rejuvenated psychologically?

Feelings of a desire to commit suicide were reported by married prisoners at a higher rate than by other prisoners; but by divorced or separated probationers at a higher rate than by other probationers. This tends to suggest that a person whose family relationships have not disintegrated prior to imprisonment may adopt feelings during imprisonment resembling those of persons outside prison whose family relationships have disintegrated. Similarly, feelings of a desire to commit suicide were reported by prisoners with a ninth grade education or more at a higher rate than by other prisoners; but by probationers with less than a seventh grade education at a higher rate than by other probationers. This tends to suggest also that a prisoner during imprisonment adopts feelings resembling those of less educated persons outside prison.

Self-destructiveness among prisoners was divided into two varities based on the actor's principal objective: the "Mortality Type" or simply "Type One"; and the "Morbidity Type," or simply "Type Two." The Type One actor intends to cause his own death, while the Type Two actor intends only to cause injury or mutilation to his own body, and all the while scrupulously avoids death. Type One self-destructiveness, which is most common outside of prison, was found to be uncommon at Tennessee State Penitentiary. Type Two self-destructiveness, which is regarded as uncommon outside prison, was found to be common among at least twenty-two inmates of this prison during the period studied, and almost routine among eight of these prisoners. On the basis of the Type Two actor's apparent desire to injure himself in order to enjoy masochistically a protracted period of recovery, it seems that his self-mutilation bears a relationship to an affinity for ongoing hospital-medical care. Could this type of self-mutilator be a "hospital addict" who exhibits the rather uncommon "Munchausen Syndrome"?[2] If so, the Type Two actor would seem to present the characteristics of the "acute abdominal type" first identified by Asher;[3] or of the type, first identified by Enoch,[4] who ingests foreign objects repeatedly. Some of these self-mutilators had a history of addiction to alcohol; and most, a history of frequent surgery. These also are characteristics of the "Munchausen Syndrome."[5] An urgent medical study seems needed to determine whether these self-mutilators do in fact suffer from the "Munchausen Syndrome," since if they do, they should be transferred from prison to a therapeutical setting where they may become detoxified from their peculiar addiction.

Prisoners in all age brackets of both races reported selected symptoms of psychological distress (determined by omnibus scores) at much higher rates than probationers in the same age brackets of each race. Clearly, prisoners seem to be more emotionally upset than nonincarcerated criminal offenders. Additional research might well be directed toward uncovering the sources of this greater psychological distress. Prison violence, a concern for the welfare of family members on the outside, plus uncertainty surrounding the parole decision may be among many factors that increase psychological distress.

Curiously, widowed, divorced or separated prisoners reported psychological distress at rates higher than the single or married. Perhaps this could be explained by the fact that persons with disintegrated family relationships enjoy greater freedom outside prison than do persons with integrated family relationships, and therefore miss their freedom more. Prisoners who were in the lowest (less than 7 years) and the highest (12 years or more) education levels reported psychological distress at higher rates than other prisoners. Again, perhaps loss of freedom and adjustment to the routine of imprisonment may be factors. The prisoner with a below-average education may be accustomed to motor freedom, while the prisoner with an above-average education may be accustomed to conceptual freedom, both to a greater extent than the average prisoner.

Black prisoners over 35 years old and white prisoners under 35 years old reported selected symptoms of psychological distress at rates that surpassed greatly the rates at which black probationers reported distress. This may indicate that these prisoners suffer the greatest increase of psychological distress during imprisonment. There appears to be some correlation between these prisoners' age within race and their status as inmates. At Tennessee State Penitentiary as at most American state prisons, young black prisoners and older white prisoners play dominant roles and achieve the most powerful positions and consequent high status. For example, older white prisoners control high-paying jobs that are based on influence with the prison administration; young black inmates control most black-market services available to prisoners, such as gambling, prostitution, and narcotics. This tends to suggest that prisoners who enjoy less power and therefore less status than other prisoners may become the most psychologically distressed.

Married parolees and those with less than 7 years of education reported selected symptoms of psychological distress at rates surpassing greatly the rates at which other probationers reported distress. This indicates that these parolees suffer the greatest increase of psychological distress as a result of imprisonment. Married parolees have a double burden of reintegrating themselves with their families and of supporting their families. Parolees with the least education encounter the most obstacles in their efforts to obtain a stable job with decent pay.

Normally, both restricted activity and bed disability associated with acute conditions (short-term disabilities) would be expected to increase with advancing age among members of any given population. This expectation proved out in the present study for probationers, since those over 45 years old reported restricted activity and bed disability at higher rates than those under 45 years old. This expectation was partially proved out for prisoners, since those over 45 years old reported bed disability at a higher rate than those under 45 years old, although the reverse emerged for restricted activity. The expectation did not prove out for parolees, since those under 45 years old reported restricted activity and bed disability at higher rates than those over 45 years old. In addition, both prisoners and parolees under 45 years old reported restricted activity as well as bed disability at higher rates than probationers in this age bracket.

Perhaps younger prisoners report restricted activity at a higher rate than older prisoners simply to avoid work on some occasions, since the status of restricted activity is easier for a prisoner to obtain than bed disability. However, it could be that the prison situation exposes the younger prisoner to frequent minor acute conditions that necessitate restricted activity but not bed disability. Perhaps younger parolees report restricted activity and bed disability at higher rates than younger probationers as a result of a weakened body (increased proneness to acute morbidity conditions) caused by or at least during the mobility restrictions imposed by imprisonment. On the other hand, it could be that young probationers avoid the temptation to stay at home or in bed, even when they do not feel well, in an effort to retain a job which they need and which is in jeopardy on account of their conviction. In this case, it could be also the case that younger parolees succumb to the temptation to stay at home or in bed whenever this becomes convenient as a method of avoiding unpleasantness associated with searching for, being refused, or being terminated from a job.

Short-stay hospital discharges were reported by all offender populations at higher rates for those over 45 than for those under 45 years old. Overall hospital discharge rates did not vary much by race for prisoners or probationers; both reported hospital discharges at about the same rate, within corresponding age brackets. Black probationers under 45 years old reported no hospital discharges at all; this could be due to their better health, or to their lack of access to hospital facilities as a result of poverty or of social ostracism.

Prisoners consulted with a physician more often than parolees or probationers, except for black probationers under 45 years old; they visited a physician at about the same rate as prisoners. This could be explained on the basis of several factors. Prisoners are situated in a closer proximity to physicians than are most nonincarcerated offenders. Prisoners' visits with a physician are free, while many nonincarcerated offenders have to pay for a visit to a physician. However, prisoners consulted with a physician fewer times per separate morbidity condition than either parolees or probationers. The prisoners sampled seem to have been in poorer health than the nonincarcerated offenders.

Probationers visited physicians more than twice as often as parolees. Very likely, a differential access to community services may explain this difference. Most probationers have roots in their community that have not been broken, except possibly by military service, and even then only for two or three years. The probationers sampled had never been in prison as a rule. One who has roots in the community where he resides may enjoy the services of a family physician. If not, at least he may have occasion to become the steady patient of a particular physician as the years pass by. On the contrary following his release from prison, a parolee is more likely than a probationer to reside in a community that is strange and possibly new to him as well. A community may seem strange to a parolee even if he grew up there, because of the passage of time spent in prison. Many parolees are reintegrated into different communities from the ones where they grew up and lived prior to imprisonment. Parolees are more likely than probationers to have broken family ties, including ties with the family physician. A parolee is less likely than a probationer to have a job or savings that will provide him with enough money to afford a physician.

The prisoners studied reported more major surgery for ulcers than for any other causes. Nonincarcerated offenders reported more major surgery for herniae and fractures than for any other causes. This seems to show the possibility that various forms of psychological distress that occur or become aggravated during imprisonment may result in such chronic physical conditions as ulcers, which bear a relationship to emotional stress. Presumably, nonincarcerated offenders sustain less psychological distress and are more physically mobile than prisoners.

Outside prison, offenders may lift heavy objects and work more actively than prisoners at jobs requiring physical exertion.

C. The Meaning of Imprisonment as a Health Risk

The health risks of imprisonment as it has been studied at Tennessee State Penitentiary are not absolute but rather relative concepts. This prison does not appear to be a dangerous place for all prisoners to the same extent or in the same way. In this respect, Tennessee State Penitentiary and probably most American state prisons differ substantially from slave labor concentration camps. It would be difficult to imagine, for example, how the "bear pits" of Devil's Island could have been anything but dangerous to every prisoner confined in them. The kind and the degree of dangerousness at Tennessee State Penitentiary, however, seem to vary in relation to characteristics of each individual prisoner. The prison seems to be more dangerous for some classes of prisoners than for others. Its dangerousness seems to harm different classes of prisoners in different ways.

Prisoners of both races under 25 years old, plus white prisoners over 45 years old reported acute sicknesses at much higher rates than did other prisoners sampled. Those of both races under 25 years old also reported acute injuries at higher rates. Those of both races over 45 years old reported selected, chronic digestive conditions at much higher rates than did younger prisoners who were sampled. Single and married prisoners of both races and all ages reported acute physical sicknesses as well as selected symptoms of psychological distress at higher rates than other sample prisoners. Differential rates of medical consultation, diagnosis and treatment seem to validate the morbidity-condition rate differentials.

The present study establishes a general and ultimate conclusion: imprisonment penalizes the health of different classes of prisoners in separate ways and in various degrees. Such states as Illinois that have attempted to require all offenders to serve prison sentences of equal length in proportion to the seriousness of their crimes (mandatory minimum and/or maximum sentences) will not achieve uniformity of punishment. These "equal" sentences will cause the physical or the emotional health of some prisoners to deteriorate more than the health of other prisoners, no matter the seriousness of their crimes.

11 Specific Recommendations for Planned Change

A. Overview of Recommendations

His study completed, every researcher has the added onus of postulating specific recommendations for planned change, if his work has demonstrated the need for change, as this study has. Recommendations are subjective, and depend somewhat upon the implications a researcher has perceived, these in turn are subjective, also. No set of implications and no set of recommendations on a subject researched should be considered as final, but as simply the starting point for continuous re-evaluation.

This study stands as a pilot effort to compare in the same state the health and safety of prisoners with that of nonincarcerated, convicted offenders. In part by reason of its novelty, this study has general substantial evidence of the need for considerable future research on the present topic. If such research is to be meaningful, however, some additional data must be made available prior to its commencement. The research conducted here should be replicated as soon as possible in states other than Tennessee; and for females as well as for males, for juveniles as well as for adults. Further, the kind of research conducted here should be replicated in the same state at different points in time, in order to reflect changes, if any, in health and safety patterns.

B. Recommendations Pertaining to General Health

Specific recommendations are enumerated for emphasis and for convenience of identification and reference.

ITEM ONE. *No male under twenty-five (25) years old should be housed in any part of an institution of confinement (prison or jail) where he would interact routinely with inmates over twenty-five (25) years old.*

This recommendation is mandated by the testimony of prisoners of both races and all ages (see Chapter Nine), who related that males under 25 years old are most frequently the victims of homosexual rape. This recommendation is buttressed by the evidence showing that among prisoners of all ages those under 25 years old have the highest gross rates of both acute sicknesses and acute injuries (Chapter Two). Of interest should be subsequent research to determine whether gross, acute-condition rates for male prisoners under 25 years old decline following their segregation from older offenders. Research should be conducted to determine whether female prisoners under 25 years old have higher gross rates of acute conditions than older female prisoners, and should, therefore, also be segreated.

ITEM TWO. *All persons who are to be housed in an institution of confinement (prison or jail) should receive a mandatory and comprehensive physical examination from a licensed physician at the time of or prior to intake; and this examination should include the systematic use of such biological, chemical, and physical diagnostic evaluation techniques as laboratory tests and x-rays.*

This recommendation is mandated by the seeming confusion concerning the origin of both acute and chronic (but especially chronic) conditions that prisoners notice for the first time during imprisonment (see Chapter Three). This physical examination should be mandatory and not subject to waiver by the prisoner, since its purpose is twofold: to protect the prisoner by identifying hidden morbidity conditions; and to protect the prison administration by identifying specific conditions as having originated prior to the commencement of imprisonment. This examination should be conducted by a licensed physician, not only to insure a competent diagnosis, but also to provide the prison administration with an expert witness who can, if necessary, testify in a court of law to each prisoner's physical condition at the time of intake. This examination should include the systematic (rather than selective) utilization of biological (e.g. sputum test for tuberculosis), chemical (e.g. Wassermann Reaction test for syphilis), and physical (e.g., x-rays) diagnostic tests, in order to support the physician's personal evaluation.

ITEM THREE. *All persons who are to be housed in an institution of confinement (prison or jail) should receive a mandatory and comprehensive psychiatric evaluation from a licensed psychiatrist at the time of or prior to intake; and this evaluation should be summarized according to the classification of mental disorders which is set forth in the* International Classification of Diseases, adapted for use in the United States (8th edition), *as modified by the American Psychiatric Association in its* Diagnostic and Statistical Manual of Mental Disorders (2d edition).

This recommendation is warranted because of the seeming confusion concerning the origin of chronic mental disorders that seem to be noticed for the first time (or the first time on record) among prisoners during imprisonment. This examination should be mandatory and should be conducted by a licensed psychiatrist for the same reasons as were noted in Item Two. This evaluation should be summarized according to the classification of mental disorders set forth in ICDA as modified in DSM-II so that all psychiatric diagnoses will be standardized. This is essential if such diagnoses are to be understood by the social services staff and other prison administrative personnel.

ITEM FOUR. *All persons who are to be released from an institution of confinement (prison or jail) should receive both a mandatory and comprehensive physical examination from a licensed physician, and a mandatory and comprehensive psychiatric evaluation from a licensed psychiatrist; and each of these evaluations should be repeated in the same manner as they were conducted at the time of the prisoner's intake, no matter how long ago that was.*

This recommendation is warranted in view of the confusion that may develop in the minds of parolees and other released prisoners concerning the origin of acute and chronic conditions which they notice for the first time after imprisonment (see Chapter Three). These evaluations should be mandatory and should be conducted by licensed practitioners for the same reasons as were noted in Item Two. The physical examination should utilize clinical diagnostic tests, and the psychiatric evaluation should be summarized according to the classification of mental disorders as set forth in ICDA and modified in DSM-II, so that an accurate comparison may be made between a prisoner's physical and mental health upon release and his health upon arrival. These evaluations should be repeated upon each prisoner's release, whether he served twenty-four hours or twenty-five years, since a person's health or safety can be as easily jeopardized in a matter of seconds as over many years.

ITEM FIVE. *All persons who are housed in an institution of confinement (prison or jail) should be offered the opportunity to consult with (a) a licensed physician and (b) a licensed psychiatrist, both of his own choice, at intervals that are regular and reasonable, preferably at the institution, but privately; and prisoners who are legally indigent should have the cost of these consultations paid for by the state following the appointment of an assigned medical counsel (medical guardian for juveniles) by a court or by a medical society.*

This recommendation is set forth as a check on the willingness and the competence of prison medical personnel to provide all prisoners with needed medical attention. There seems to be a pervading risk that prison medical personnel may not be sufficiently specific in the diagnosis or treatment of morbidity conditions reported by prisoner patients. Any prisoner should have the opportunity to seek the professional opinion and/or advice of an outside physician, and this opportunity should not be denied on account of indigence. It is time medical practitioners become concerned with the medical rights of prisoners to the same extent as legal practitioners have become concerned with legal rights of the confined.

ITEM SIX. *A state's duty to supervise persons who have been convicted of criminal offenses, then released on parole or on probation should include a duty to monitor the health and safety of these nonincarcerated offenders, and to provide them with access to medical consultation, diagnosis, and treatment at the same frequency as this access is provided for the state's prisoners; and nonincarcerated offenders who are legally indigent should have the cost of this health care paid for by the state following the appointment of an assigned medical counsel (medical guardian for juveniles) by a court or by a medical society.*

This recommendation is necessitated from the information obtained through this study that in Tennessee nonincarcerated offenders received substantially less medical consultation, diagnosis, and treatment than prisoners. In the case of the parolee, to release him from an institutional setting into a community where he cannot obtain sufficient medical services seems to contribute to the many other difficulties that parolees encounter in the readjustment process. In the case of parolees and probationers, the chances are high that many of these presently nonincarcerated offenders will become prisoners at some future time. A state should begin as early as possible in the criminal-justice process to obtain comprehensive physical and psychiatric evaluations for all persons who have been convicted of most crimes. In this way, prison administrators would soon be able to facilitate better and more rapid classification of the "new" prisoner at intake; justify the segregation or quarantine of prisoners who can be shown to present a danger to other prisoners due to violence or disease; and document more fully the origin of morbidity conditions anteceding imprisonment.

C. Recommendations Pertaining to Medical Records

The following recommendations are ancillary to those proposed above. Although these recommendations may not relate to matters having a direct effect upon the general health of criminal offenders, they are intended to improve the ongoing process of monitoring the health of offenders.

ITEM SEVEN. *All records pertaining to morbidity conditions of persons housed at an institution of confinement (prison or jail) should be coded by the medical practitioner who diagnoses or treats the condition immediately following his diagnosis or the treatment, according to the three-digit categories standardized in the* International Classification of Diseases, Adapted for use in the United States (8th edition); *and coded medical records should be retained and made a part of the offender's permanent institutional record.*

The single most exacting task of the present study was the necessary coding of all the morbidity conditions noted in the medical records of sample prisoners, and of the conditions reported by sample prisoners, parolees, and probationers. If ongoing research in this area is to be encouraged, institutions should require that medical records of inmates be standardized. No person is in a better position to codify a patient's condition than the medical practitioner who diagnoses or treats the condition. The three-digit ICDA codes should be required, and identified in as particular and complete a manner as possible. Needless to say, the medical records of nonincarcerated offenders should be coded in the same way, in the event (which seems remote at present) that a state should begin to follow the recommendation in Item Six and compile medical records on nonincarcerated offenders.

ITEM EIGHT. *The medical records of all persons housed at an institution of confinement (prison or jail) should be made available periodically to the prisoner himself and to all medical or legal practitioners who represent him; and these records should be made available to independent researchers who are qualified by education, experience, and integrity to study confidential records without divulging the identity of any individual prisoner patient.*

The view that a confined person's medical records should be kept secret from him is a vestige of the *kein eingang* style of prison administration. There does not appear to be any compelling state interest or clear and present danger that would result from granting a prisoner, his representatives, and qualified researchers access to these records. These records do not contain names of informants or other privileged information relating to criminal prosecution, as might a presentence investigation report, for example. Suppression of these medical records may prevent a prisoner from litigating civil causes of action for damages resulting from injury caused by accident, assault, or malpractice. Suppression may prevent a prisoner from litigating civil causes of action for damages resulting from a reputation damaged by statements contained in the records that are defamatory but untrue. These do not seem to be valid reasons for limiting access to these records. Indeed, access to prison medical records by independent researchers would seem to serve as a check and balance against the mismanagement of these records by prison staff or the misuse of them by prisoners.

ITEM NINE. *Statutes that limit or curtail a confined person's right of access to his own medical records, or a qualified independent researcher's access to prison medical records, should be repealed; enabling legislation should be passed in each state to facilitate this access, which should not be left to the discretion of prison administrators; in the absence of prompt and diligent enabling legislation, a court of law should not hesitate to mandate this access in a proper case.*

Each state legislature should face up to a duty to correct archaic laws that impede access to medical records by qualified researchers, and impede a prisoner's access to his own medical records. When this matter is left to the discretion of prison administrators, access is either denied unilaterally or granted with partiality. On this issue each state should formulate a uniform policy, subject to review in the courts. In states that do not formulate such a policy by legislation, the matter should be decided by the initiative of the courts; it cannot remain undecided.

D. Recommendations Pertaining to Administration

ITEM TEN. *A state prison should provide both hospital and outpatient medical services to prisoners at all hours of the day and night, and on every day of the week; these services should include a registered nurse (not an inmate) present at the prison at all times; a licensed physician on call for the prison at all times; and a registered emergency vehicle available at the prison at all times for immediate and direct emergency transportation from the prison to the nearest outside hospital.*

The hospital-medical facilities of a prison should never be relegated to the supervision (including the night supervision) of a layman, and especially not of an inmate. A prison should employ a registered nurse to be on duty during each personnel shift around the clock. A licensed physician who is ready, willing, and able to respond to emergency calls at the prison should be retained on a contract basis. Perhaps most imperative of all, a prison should keep an emergency vehicle such as an ambulance or rescue wagon available at the prison at all times, except when it is in use. Since prisons are normally located outside metropolitan areas, the time it takes for an emergency vehicle to travel to the prison from the nearest hospital may well turn an aggravated assault into a homicide, or a self-inflicted injury into a suicide.

ITEM ELEVEN. *Prisoners should not be permitted to have access to the medical records of other prisoners; to administer, handle, or possess any pharmaceutical substances whether controlled by law or not, except non-harmful drugs that have been prescribed for their personal use; or to have or to exercise any authority or discretion over other prisoners' access to medical consultation, diagnosis, or treatment.*

It should be self-evident that the role of the prisoner orderly may become too powerful and dangerous to the welfare of any institution of confinement. Although prisoners may work out well in clerical or custodial positions at the hospital-medical facility, as soon as they are allowed to become surrogate medical technical assistants (MTA's), invariably they begin to smuggle medication as contraband, or to extort money from fellow inmates.

ITEM TWELVE. *No building, hallway, walkway, room, attic, or cellar located behind prison walls, and no open area inside prison walls should be accessible to any inmates without a prison staff member being in full view of the entire area, and at night without a custodial prison staff member being in full view of the entire area.*

Rapes continue to take place in areas of prisons that are not within the sight of staff members, as do some stabbings. Insufficient manpower should not be a legitimate excuse for failing to supervise areas of a prison that are open to inmates. If manpower is too scarce to supervise the entire inside area of a prison, all areas that must remain unsupervised should be sealed off from inmate access, and rigorously inspected to prevent the unlawful entry of inmates into these areas. Although noncustodial-prison staff members may be permitted to supervise prisoners at work or in therapy during the day, supervision at night should be the exclusive responsibility of custodial personnel.

ITEM THIRTEEN. *All persons without exception who enter a prison should be required to successfully pass a metal detection test; prisoners should be required to successfully pass a metal detection test when passing in either direction through a passageway that affords access to a cellblock, an industry, a hospital-medical facility, a shipping-receiving area, or a mess-hall; all prison staff personnel, including custodial personnel, should be required while on duty to wear clothing that has not been worn by them as they entered the prison for duty, and to submit to a complete search by custodial personnel, who have been selected at random and rotated each day, prior to entering the prison, but after exchanging their clothes.*

Contraband does not enter a prison magically, or by unidentifiable flying objects. It enters a prison through poor security precautions that facilitate the criminal activity of free-world persons, including prison staff members. The metal detection test is a basic requirement for prison security, but one metal detector at the main entrance is not sufficient for a large prison. A network of both stationary and portable metal detectors scattered throughout the area inside a prison should reduce the transportation of lethal weapons from one area to another. Contraband other than weapons is more difficult to regulate. The Federal mints appear to have contained the temptation to abscond with currency by requiring workers to exchange clothing at the time they report for work. Such a precaution, coupled with frequent body searches by other corrections officers selected at random and rotated daily, should reduce if not eliminate the inward flow of hard narcotics, firearms and other illegal commodities.

ITEM FOURTEEN. *Felony sentence patterns in most jurisdictions should be reconsidered in terms of structure and duration. As a general rule, these sentences should be made more definite and should reflect the seriousness of both the offense(s) on which present commitment is based and prior offenses for which the offender has been convicted, rather than concern for reform or rehabilitation of the offender. For most offenders, there should be a presumption of probation. When a prison sentence is imposed, however, it should continue for a definite period until the offender is released unconditionally. Parole should be abolished as unworkable and unnecessary.*

Emotional distress on the part of all criminal offenders (prisoners, probationers, parolees) studied seems to have some relationship to anxiety over indeterminate sentences of uncertain duration. There is no reason why sentences cannot be fixed and specified clearly at time of imposition. Probation sentences should be imposed for persons convicted of most crimes, unless the interests of justice such as community protection mandate imprisonment. However, the decision to commit a person should not be the subject of vacillation. Once committed, a person should remain imprisoned until released without parole conditions, which seem to create substantial anxiety not only during parole but during the last portion of imprisonment. Both probation and prison sentences should be for a time certain, not subject to reduction for vague and subjective reasons such as "good time" or rehabilitative progress.

ITEM FIFTEEN. *A prison sentence should be imposed upon only offenders who need to be incapacitated to protect the community from clear and present danger. Persistent violent offenders who cause physical danger to the community are examples of such persons. Since only the most dangerous offenders should be confined, when a prison sentence is imposed it should be for a definite period of at least five years. Long prison sentences should be served in functional but not fortified settings where surroundings are healthful. Toward this objective, dangerous offenders might be transported to remote geographical areas accessible primarily from the air, from which escape would be futile.*

Most inmates of state prisons at the moment do not need to be there for protection of the community. Nor is any hard evidence available to suggest that prisons deter persons from committing crimes. Since imprisonment is costly and dangerous in terms of the health of confined persons, only offenders for whom no other disposition would satisfy the interests of justice should be committed. This study has shown that the health of prisoners deteriorates the most at the beginning and at the end of confinement. Thus, the "taste of jail" concept is counterproductive and short sentences to prison are much worse than no imprisonment at all. When a dangerous felon is sentenced to prison, he should understand that his commitment for a specified time period without chance of early release is based exclusively upon the seriousness of his past criminal behavior. To minimize deterioration of health during confinement, long prison sentences might be served in remote geographical areas–such as Alaska–where inmates could be permitted ample freedom to enjoy fresh air and physical mobility, since security could be minimum.

Appendix A: Supplementary Tables on Sample, Adult-Male Prisoners in Tennessee State Penitentiary and Adult-Male Parolees and Probationers

Table A-1
Percent Distribution by Race According to Age: Adult-Male Prisoners

Age	White	Black	Total	*N*
17 years and over	57.4	42.6	100.0	204
17-24 years	42.5	57.5	100.0	40
25-34 years	55.2	44.8	100.0	87
35-44 years	64.9	35.1	100.0	37
45 years and over	70.0	30.0	100.0	40

Table A-2
Percent Distribution by Race according to Age: Adult-Male Probationers

Age	White	Black	Total	*N*
17 years and over	79.5	20.5	100.0	254
17-24 years	79.3	20.7	100.0	145
25-34 years	83.3	16.7	100.0	66
35-44 years	73.9	26.0	99.9	23
45 years and over	75.0	25.0	100.0	20

Table A-3
Percent Distribution by Race according to Age: Adult Male Parolees

Age	White	Black	Total	*N*
17 years and over	57.5	42.5	100.0	360
17-24 years	55.3	44.7	100.0	114
25-34 years	58.1	41.9	100.0	129
35-44 years	58.3	41.7	100.0	72
45 years and over	60.0	40.0	100.0	45

Table A-4
Percent Distribution by Marital Status according to Age: Adult-Male Prisoners

Age	Single	Married	Widowed	Separated	Divorced	Total	*N*
17 years and over	35.3	44.6	4.4	6.4	9.3	100.0	204
17-24 years	55.0	45.0	0.0	0.0	0.0	100.0	40
25-34 years	41.4	41.4	3.4	6.9	6.9	100.0	87
35-44 years	18.9	51.4	5.4	5.4	18.9	100.0	37
45 years and over	17.5	45.0	10.0	12.5	15.0	100.0	40

Table A-5
Percent Distribution by Marital Status according to Age: Adult-Male Probationers

Age	Single	Married	Widowed	Separated	Divorced	Total	*N*
17 years and over	34.5	47.2	0.8	5.6	11.9	100.0	252
17-24 years	54.5	33.8	0.0	4.8	6.9	100.0	145
25-34 years	10.9	64.1	0.0	3.1	21.9	100.0	64
35-44 years	4.3	65.2	0.0	17.4	13.0	99.9	23
45 years and over	0.0	70.0	10.0	5.0	15.0	100.0	20

Table A-6
Percent Distribution by Marital Status according to Age: Adult-Male Parolees

Age	Single	Married	Widowed	Separated	Divorced	Total	*N*
17 years and over	25.4	37.3	4.2	16.9	16.1	100.0	354
17-24 years	57.4	27.0	0.0	7.8	7.8	100.0	115
25-34 years	16.5	40.9	0.0	26.0	16.5	99.9	127
35-44 years	4.1	50.7	8.2	16.4	20.5	99.9	73
45 years and over	0.0	30.8	23.1	15.4	30.8	100.0	39

Table A-7
Percent Distribution by Education according to Race: Adult-Male Prisoners

Race	Education in Years of School Completed							
	0-6	7-8	9-11	12	13-15	16	Total	*N*
White	18.8	23.9	37.6	13.7	4.3	1.7	100.0	117
Black	14.9	16.1	44.8	9.2	9.2	5.7	99.9	87

Table A-8
Percent Distribution by Education according to Race: Adult-Male Probationers

Race	Education in Years of School Completed							
	0-6	7-8	9-11	12	13-15	16	Total	*N*
White	7.1	28.6	28.6	23.0	12.2	0.5	100.0	196
Black	6.1	8.2	49.0	28.6	6.1	2.0	100.0	49

Table A-9
Percent Distribution by Education according to Race: Adult-Male Parolees

Race	Education in Years of School Completed							
	0-6	7-8	9-11	12	13-15	16	Total	*N*
White	14.3	33.3	14.3	28.5	4.8	4.8	100.0	189
Black	10.2	12.2	42.9	28.6	6.1	0.0	100.0	147

Table A-10
Percent Distribution by Education according to Age: Adult-Male Prisoners

Age in Years	Education in Years of School Completed							
	0-6	7-8	9-11	12	13-15	16	Total	*N*
17 and over	17.2	20.6	40.7	11.8	6.4	3.4	100.1	204
17-24	2.5	15.0	62.5	5.0	7.5	7.5	100.0	40
25-34	10.3	19.5	46.0	14.9	6.9	2.3	99.9	87
35-44	18.9	29.7	37.8	8.1	5.4	0.0	99.9	37
45 and over	45.0	20.0	10.0	15.0	5.0	5.0	100.0	40

Table A-11
Percent Distribution by Education according to Age: Adult-Male Probationers

Age in Years	Education in Years of School Completed							
	0-6	7-8	9-11	12	13-15	16	Total	*N*
17 and over	5.3	23.2	33.3	25.6	11.4	1.2	100.0	246
17-24	2.9	21.4	40.0	24.3	10.7	0.7	99.9	140
25-34	6.2	23.4	18.8	34.4	17.2	0.0	100.0	64
35-44	15.0	35.0	35.0	10.0	0.0	5.0	100.0	20
45 and over	9.1	22.7	31.8	22.7	9.1	4.5	99.9	22

Table A-12
Percent Distribution by Education according to Age: Adult-Male Parolees

Age in Years	Education in Years of School Completed							
	0-6	7-8	9-11	12	13-15	16	Total	*N*
17 and over	13.0	24.5	26.3	28.2	4.4	2.7	100.1	339
17-24	0.0	18.2	33.3	42.4	3.0	3.0	99.9	99
25-34	16.7	21.0	23.2	32.6	4.3	2.2	100.0	138
35-44	9.5	28.6	33.3	14.3	9.5	4.8	100.0	63
45 and over	38.5	46.1	7.7	7.7	0.0	0.0	100.0	39

Table A-13
Percent Distribution by Type of Offense, according to Age within Race: Adult-Male Prisoners

Race and Age	Violent Crimes				Nonviolent Crimes			
	Homicide	Sexual	Robbery	Total Violent	Property	Total Nonviolent	Total	*N*
Both Races								
17 years and over	23.5	12.7	29.4	68.6	29.4	31.4	100.0	204
17-24 years	22.5	15.0	27.5	67.5	32.5	32.5	100.0	40
25-34 years	8.0	12.6	34.5	59.8	37.9	40.2	100.0	87
35-44 years	27.0	10.8	35.1	73.0	21.6	27.0	100.0	37
45 years and over	55.0	12.5	15.0	85.0	15.0	15.0	100.0	40
White								
17 years and over	23.1	12.0	23.9	61.5	35.0	38.5	100.0	117
17-24 years	5.9	23.5	17.6	47.1	52.9	52.9	100.0	17
25-34 years	6.3	8.3	31.3	52.1	43.8	47.9	100.0	48
35-44 years	29.2	12.5	29.2	70.8	20.8	29.2	100.0	24
45 years and over	57.1	10.7	10.7	78.6	21.4	21.4	100.0	28
Black								
17 years and over	24.1	13.8	36.8	78.2	21.8	21.8	100.0	87
17-24 years	34.8	8.7	34.8	73.9	26.1	26.1	100.0	23
25-34 years	10.3	17.9	38.5	69.2	30.8	30.8	100.0	39
35-44 years	23.1	7.7	46.2	76.9	23.1	23.1	100.0	13
45 years and over	50.0	16.7	25.0	100.0	0.0	0.0	100.0	12

Table A-14
Percent Distribution by Type of Offense, according to Age within Race: Adult-Male Probationers

Race and Age	Violent Crimes				Nonviolent Crimes			
	Homicide	Sexual	Robbery	Total Violent	Property	Total Nonviolent	Total	*N*
Both Races								
17 years and over	8.3	2.4	1.2	15.7	55.1	84.3	100.0	254
17-24 years	2.8	0.8	2.1	8.3	62.1	91.7	100.0	145
25-34 years	7.6	1.5	0.0	13.6	54.5	86.4	100.0	66
35-44 years	21.7	8.7	0.0	39.1	43.5	60.9	100.0	23
45 years and over	35.0	5.0	0.0	50.0	20.0	50.0	100.0	20
White								
17 years and over	7.9	2.5	1.0	14.9	55.4	85.1	100.0	202
17-24 years	2.6	0.9	1.7	7.0	62.6	93.0	100.0	115
25-34 years	7.3	1.8	0.0	12.7	54.5	87.3	100.0	55
35-44 years	17.6	11.8	0.0	41.2	35.3	58.8	100.0	17
45 years and over	40.0	6.7	0.0	53.3	26.7	46.7	100.0	15
Black								
17 years and over	9.6	1.9	1.9	19.2	53.8	80.8	100.0	52
17-24 years	3.3	3.3	3.3	13.3	60.0	86.7	100.0	30
25-34 years	9.1	0.0	0.0	18.2	54.5	81.8	100.0	11
35-44 years	33.3	0.0	0.0	33.3	66.7	66.7	100.0	6
45 years and over	20.0	0.0	0.0	40.0	0.0	60.0	100.0	5

Table A-15
Percent Distribution by Type of Offense, according to Age within Race: Adult-Male Parolees

Race and Age	Violent Crimes				Nonviolent Crimes			
	Homicide	Sexual	Robbery	Total Violent	Property	Total Nonviolent	Total	*N*
Both Races								
17 years and over	24.7	1.1	13.1	47.2	40.0	52.8	100.0	360
17-24 years	7.9	0.0	14.9	31.6	49.1	68.4	100.0	114
25-34 years	21.7	0.0	14.0	48.8	44.2	51.2	100.0	129
35-44 years	43.1	0.0	11.1	54.2	36.1	45.8	100.0	72
45 years and over	46.7	8.9	8.9	71.1	11.1	28.9	100.0	45
White								
17 years and over	25.1	1.9	9.2	40.1	47.3	59.9	100.0	207
17-24 years	6.3	0.0	11.1	17.5	47.6	82.5	100.0	63
25-34 years	25.3	0.0	5.3	41.3	58.7	58.7	100.0	75
35-44 years	35.7	0.0	19.0	54.8	45.2	45.2	100.0	42
45 years and over	51.9	14.8	0.0	66.7	18.5	33.3	100.0	27
Black								
17 years and over	24.2	0.0	18.3	56.9	30.1	43.1	100.0	153
17-24 years	9.8	0.0	19.6	49.0	51.0	51.0	100.0	51
25-34 years	16.7	0.0	25.9	59.3	24.1	40.7	100.0	54
35-44 years	53.3	0.0	0.0	53.3	23.3	46.7	100.0	30
45 years and over	38.9	0.0	22.2	77.8	0.0	22.2	100.0	18

Table A-16
Percent Distribution by Length of Time Imprisoned according to Race: Adult-Male Prisoners

Length of Time in Prison	White (N = 117)	Black (N = 87)	Both Races (N = 204)
10 years or over	7.7	8.0	7.8
5- 9 years	8.5	11.5	9.8
48-59 months	10.3	6.9	8.8
36-47 months	12.8	17.2	14.7
24-35 months	10.3	11.5	10.8
18-23 months	17.9	21.8	19.6
12-17 months	8.5	11.5	9.8
6-11 months	23.9	11.5	18.6
Total	99.9	99.9	99.9

Table A-17
Percent Distribution by Proportion of Sentence Completed, according to Race: Adult-Male Prisoners

Proportion of Sentence Completed	White (N = 117)	Black (N = 87)	Both Races (N = 204)
Decile			
1st	16.2	19.5	17.6
2nd	18.8	18.4	18.6
3rd	10.3	10.3	10.3
4th	12.0	8.0	10.3
5th	4.3	3.5	3.9
6th	15.4	6.9	11.8
7th	6.0	10.3	7.8
8th	9.4	12.6	10.8
9th	7.7	10.3	8.8
Total	100.1	99.8	99.9

Table A-18
Percent Distribution of Persons by Length of Time Remaining before Parole Eligibility: Adult-Male Prisoners

Length of Time Before Parole Eligibility	White ($N = 117$)	Black ($N = 87$)	Both Races ($N = 204$)
Time Arrived	2.6	3.4	2.9
1- 5 months	4.3	5.7	4.9
6-11 months	9.4	10.3	9.8
12-23 months	20.5	21.8	21.1
24-35 months	12.8	8.0	10.8
36-47 months	6.8	4.6	5.9
48-59 months	6.8	1.2	4.4
5- 9 years	10.3	18.4	13.7
10 years or over	26.5	26.4	26.5
Total	100.0	99.8	100.0

Notes

Notes

Chapter One
Introduction and Background to Health Problems of Prisoners

1. A. Solzhenitsyn, *The Gulag Archipelago, 1918-1956: An Experiment in Literary Investigation* (New York, 1973); J. Barron, *KGB and the Secret Work of Soviet Secret Agents* (Pleasantville, 1974).

2. See W. Lewis, *From Newgate to Dannemora* (Ithaca, 1965), p. 124.

3. Ibid., citing Herre, "A History of Auburn Prison from the Beginning to about 1867" (Ed.D. dissertation, Pennsylvania State University, 1950).

4. See, *inter alia*, P. Berrigan, *Prison Journals of a Priest Revolutionary* (New York, 1969); H. Griswold et al., *An Eye for An Eye* (New York, 1971); G. Jackson, *Blood in My Eye* (New York, 1972); idem, *Soledad Brother* (New York, 1970); E. Knight, *Black Voices from Prison* (New York, 1970); A. Macdonald, *Prison Secrets* (New York, 1969); E. Pell, ed., *Maximum Security: Letters from Prison* (New York, 1972); Prisoner "X," *Prison Confidential* (Los Angeles, 1969); B. Sands, *My Shadow Ran Fast* (Englewood Cliffs, 1964); A. Selp, *Prison Meditations* (New York, 1963). Historians: W. Lewis, *From Newgate to Dannemora* (Ithaca, 1965); B. McKelvey, *American Prisons* (Montclair, 1972); D. Rothman, *The Discovery of the Asylum: Social Order and Disorder in the New Republic* (Boston, 1971). Legal scholars: F. Cohen, *The Discovery of Prison Reform,* 21 *BUFF. L. REV.* 855 (1972); R. Goldfarb and L. Singer, *Redressing Prisoners' Grievances*, 39 G.W. L. REV. 175 (1970); D. Greenberg and F. Stender, *The Prison as a Lawless Agency*, 21 BUFF. L. REV. 799 (1972); P. Hirschkop and R. Millemann, *The Unconstitutionality of Prison Life*, 55 VA. L. REV. 795 (1969); Note, *Prisoners' Rights Under Section 1983*, 57 GEO. L.J. 1270 (1969); R. Singer, *Privacy, Autonomy, and Dignity in the Prison: A Preliminary Inquiry Concerning Const. Aspects of the Degradation Process in our Prisons*, 21 BUFF. L. REV. 669 (1972). See also, H. Badillo and M. Haynes, *A Bill of No Rights: Attica and the American Prison System* (New York, 1972). Sociologists and Journalists: B. Bagdikian, *The Shame of the Prisons* (New York, 1972); J. Bennett, *I Chose Prison* (New York, 1970); W. McGraw, *Assignment: Prison Riots* (New York, 1954); G. Sykes, *The Society of Captives* (New York, 1962). See also, E. Goffman, *Asylums* (Garden City, 1961); H. Hart, ed., *Punishment: For and Against* (New York, 1971); G. Shaw, *The Crime of Imprisonment* (New York, 1946); N. Walker, *Crime and Punishment in Britain* (Chicago, 1968). A few publications from prison administrators include: J. Bennett, *I Chose Prison* (New York, 1970); N. Carlson, *Attica: A Look at the Causes and the Future*, 7 CRIM. L. BULL. 817 (1971); Federal Bureau of Prisons, *Thirty Years of Progress* (Washington, 1967).

5. A Massachusetts statute provides: "No officer or employee of a state, county, or municipal agency shall: *** (c) improperly disclose confidential information acquired by him in the course of his official duties *** " 268A *Mass. Gen. Laws,* sec. 23.

A State of Washington, Division of Institutions, Department of Social Health and Services memorandum (Number 71-1 dated 1 February 1971) provides in part: "No employee of the Office of Adult Corrections or any adult correctional institution shall make available to any private person any of the records, files, or documents subject to this order, or any information pertaining to any resident confined within any adult correctional institution, and shall report directly to his immediate supervisor any request for such information, except those records required to be kept by statute. . . ." This memorandum reasoned that "all official files, documents, records, and information in the Office of Adult Corrections and in adult correctional institutions are to be regarded and handled as strictly confidential" 2 PRIS. L. RPTR. 385 (1973).

6. The same memorandum from the State of Washington provides also that: "Under circumstances approved by the Superintendent, designated staff members may permit visual inspection of institution records by representatives of public welfare agencies or institutions, by the assigned staff of the legal services program and by privately retained attorneys with written authorization of their resident clients when the scrutiny of institution records is pertinent to their work. These persons may be furnished copies of information they consider necessary in the preparation of their case. Under no circumstances shall a resident have access to or visually examine his file or its contents, copies furnished to the legal advisor excepted . . . " ibid. Why may a prisoner's legal advisor (not necessarily an attorney, apparently) have access to the prisoner's records which the prisoner himself may not have access to? If these records are so private, why then may the legal advisor show the prisoner photocopies of his record?

7. The Ninth Circuit has held that neither prisoners nor the press have a First Amendment right of access to prison records. Seattle-Tacoma Newspaper Guild v. Parker (No. 72-2330) (9th Cir. June 7, 1973). Contrast this with Olson v. Pope (No. 8361 Solano County, Calif. Superior Court, September 14, 1972). The Fifth Circuit has ruled that the government need not disclose to a defendant in an escape prosecution documents relating to the government's separate suit against Mississippi's Parchman Prison concerning prison conditions. The *ratio decidendi* is based on provisions of the Jencks Act, 18 U.S.C. 3500(a), under which such information is not subject to discovery. In its *obiter dictum*, the majority noted that this information would be irrelevant even if discoverable. U.S. v. Theriault, 474 F.2d 359 (5th Cir. 1973). How can information relating to conditions at a prison from which a prisoner has escaped be irrelevant to his prosecution for escape?

8. See, U.S. Bureau of Prisons, Policy Statements 1220.1A, published in 1 PRISON L. RPTR. 99 (1972).

9. Privileged *from* whom? Privileged *for* whom? Why? See, Morrissey v. Brewer, 408 U.S. 471, 487 (1972) (to protect informants and to ensure institutional security); Chronicle Pub. Co. v. Superior Ct., 54 Cal.2d 548, 568-570 (1972) (to encourage candor and complete disclosure of information concerning inmates from both public officials and private citizens); also, 3 PRIS. L. RPTR. 137, n. 5 (1974).

10. Ruffin v. Commonwealth, 62 Va. 21 Gratt. 790 (1871).

11. Coffin v. Reichard, 143 F.2d 443 (6th Cir. 1944), *cert. den.*, 325 U.S. 887 (1945).

12. Minimum standards: see, International Commission of Jurists, *Standard Minimum Rules for the Treatment of Prisoners*, Report Submitted to the Fourth United Nations Congress on the Prevention of Crime and the Treatment of Offenders, 17-26 August 1970, Kyoto, Japan; "A Model Act to Provide for Minimum Standards for the Protection of Rights of Prisoners," *Crime and Delinquency* (January, 1972), pp. 4-14; South Carolina Department of Corrections, *The Emerging Rights of the Confined* (Columbia, 1972). Model legislation: see, American Law Institute, *Model Penal Code* sec. 306.6 (Proposed Official Draft 1962); Commission on Uniform State Law, "The Uniform Act on the Status of Confined Persons," *Handbook of the National Conference of Commissioners on Uniform State Law* (Washington, 1964), p. 295; Advisory Commission on Intergovernmental Relations, "An Act to Establish a State Department of Correction," *State-Local Relations in the Criminal Justice System* (Washington, 1967); S. Krantz, et al., *Model Rules and Regulations on Prisoners' Rights and Responsibilities* (St. Paul, 1973).

13. National Advisory Commission on Criminal Justice Standards and Goals, *Report on Corrections* (Washington, 1973), p. 34.

14. Ibid., p. 31.

15. Ibid., p. 36.

16. These patterns include the exodus of blacks from the South to border and northern states, and from rural to urban areas; and the migration of whites from the North to border and southern states, and from urban to suburban areas. See, K. Davis, "The Urbanization of the Human Population," *Scientific American* (September, 1965), pp. 41-53; idem, "Urbanization—Changing Patterns of Living," in Simpson, ed., *The Changing American Population: A Report of the Arden House Conference* (New York, 1962), pp. 59-68; H. Sharp and L. Schnore, "The Changing Color Composition of Metropolitan Areas," *Land Economics* 38 (1962): 169-185.

17. U.S. Bureau of the Census, Census of Population: 1970, *General Social and Economic Characteristics, Tennessee* (Washington, 1972), pp. 44-162, 44-170.

18. Ibid., pp. 44-170.

19. For instance, the rapid growth of major cities—Tennessee had four Standard Metropolitan Statistical Areas (SMSA's) in 1970, and added a fifth, the Kingsport-Bristol area, in 1972—through migration has affected social relation-

ships. See, L. Wirth, "Urbanism as a Way of Life," *American J. Sociology* 44 (1938): 1-24; H. Gans, "Urbanism and Suburbanism as Ways of Life: A Re-evaluation of Definitions," in Rose, ed., *Human Behavior and Social Processes* (New York, 1962), pp. 306-323.

20. U.S. Bureau of Prisons, *National Prisoner Statistics: Prisoners in State and Federal Institutions for Adult Felons, 1970* (Washington, 1973).

21. State of Tennessee, Department of Correction, Division of Probation and Paroles, "Monthly Statistical Reports," month ending January (31), 1972 (unpublished internal department memorandum).

22. Ibid., months ending January (31) through November (30), 1972. Data for December, 1972 was not available.

23. Ibid., as adjusted.

24. State of Tennessee, Department of Correction, *Annual Report: 1972-1973* (Nashville, 1974), p. 17.

25. Ibid.

26. Ibid., p. 18.

27. Ibid., p. 58.

28. Ibid., pp. 57-58.

29. Ibid., p. 57.

30. Ibid., p. 58.

31. Ibid.

32. Ibid., p. 63.

33. Ibid., p. 58.

Chapter Two
Morbidity Trends: Acute Physical Conditions

1. U.S. Public Health Service, *Current Estimates from the Health Interview Survey, United States - 1972* (Washington, 1973), p. 48.

2. U.S. Public Health Service, *Eighth Revision International Classification of Diseases, Adapted for Use in the United States* (Washington, 1968).

3. Ibid., p. xxviii. Injury conditions are classified in the ICDA according to codes 800-999 (internal causation) and E800-E999 (external causation).

4. Ibid., illnesses are classified according to codes 000-796.

5. U.S. Public Health Service, *Current Estimates*, p. 50.

6. Ibid., p. 9.

7. Ibid.

8. Ibid. (as adjusted).

9. For regional variations, see U.S. Public Health Service, *Health Characteristics by Geographic Region, Large Metropolitan Areas, and Other Places of Residence, United States–1969-70* (Washington, 1974); these are too slight to

be included in the comparison between the present data and data available by 1974 on the 1972 general, adult-male population throughout the nation.

Chapter Three
Morbidity Trends: Specific Acute and Chronic Conditions

1. U.S. Public Health Service, *Prevalence of Selected Chronic Digestive Conditions, United States - July-December 1968* (Washington, 1973), p. 38 (hereafter, *Chronic Digestive Conditions*).

2. U.S. Public Health Service, *Eighth Revision International Classification of Diseases, Adapted for Use in the United States* (Washington, 1968).

3. See *Chronic Digestive Conditions*, p. 38.

4. See note 5.

5. The ICDA divides "Symptoms and Ill-Defined Conditions" into two subcategories: symptoms referable to systems or organs (780-789), and to senility and ill-defined diseases (790-796). The first subcategory includes symptoms referable to the nervous system, special senses, the cardiovascular and lymphatic system, the respiratory system, the upper gastrointestinal system, the lower gastrointestinal tract, the genitourinary system, limbs and joints. The second subcategory includes nervousness and debility, headache, uremia, and senility.

6. In the ICDA functional and symptomatic upper gastrointestinal disorders include anorexia (784.0); nausea and vomiting (784.1); pylorospasm (784.2); and heartburn (784.3); hematemesis (784.5); hiccough (784.6); and conditions relating to toothaches or to sore gums (520-529).

7. In the ICDA these conditions are labeled "refractive errors" (codes 370-379) and include myopia (370.0); hyperopia (370.1); presbyopia (370.2); astigmatism (370.3); and other unspecified refractive errors (370.9).

8. U.S. Public Health Service, *Current Estimates from the Health Interview Survey, United States - 1972* (Washington, 1973), p. 9.

9. See *Chronic Digestive Conditions*, p. 17.

Chapter Four
Chronic Mental Disorders

1. M. Kramer, "The History of the Efforts to Agree on an International Classification of Mental Disorders," in American Psychiatric Association, *Diagnostic and Statistical Manual of Mental Disorders*, 2d ed. (Washington, 1968), pp. xi-xviii.

2. Ibid., pp. xiv-xv.

3. Ibid., p. xvii.

4. From American Psychiatric Association, *Diagnostic and Statistical Manual of Mental Disorders*, 2d ed. (Washington, 1968), sec. 2, pp. 5-13; reprinted with permission.

5. Ibid., sec. 3, p. 14.

6. Ibid.

7. Ibid., pp. 22, 31-32.

8. Ibid., p. 22.

9. Ibid., pp. 24-31.

10. Ibid., pp. 31-32.

11. Ibid., p. 39.

12. Ibid., p. 41.

13. Ibid., p. 46.

14. Ibid., p. 48.

15. Ibid., pp. 51-52.

16. Ibid., p. 54.

17. Ibid.

18. See Chapter Eleven, Item 3.

19. On the widespread use of this definition see note 20.

20. See B. Ennis and L. Siegel, *The Rights of Mental Patients* (New York, 1973), passim.

21. Following J. Douglas, *The Social Meanings of Suicide* (Princeton, 1967), pp. 304-319 (hereafter, Douglas, *Suicide*), notification may be by suicidal action as a means of achieving sympathy ("fellow-feeling") or of getting revenge.

22. Émile Durkheim, *Suicide: A Study in Sociology* (New York, 1951).

23. See Douglas, *Suicide*, p. 273, on the assumption that suicidal actions have meaning, and that interpretation of intent may explain suicidal phenomena.

Chapter Five
Neurotic Conditions: Selected Symptoms of Psychological Distress

1. See American Psychiatric Association, *A Psychiatric Glossary,* 3d ed. (Washington, 1969), p. 63; also, L. Hinsie and R. Campbell, *Psychiatric Dictionary*, 4th ed. (New York, 1970), p. 501.

2. See American Psychiatric Association, *Diagnostic and Statistical Manual of Mental Disorders*, 2d ed. (Washington, 1968), p. 39.

3. See note 1.

4. See, *inter alia*, D. Crandell and B. Dohrenwend, "Some Relations Among Psychiatric Symptoms, Organic Illness, and Social Class," *American Journal of Psychiatry* 123 (1967): 1527-1538; H. Dupuy et al., *Selected Symptoms of Psychological Distress, United States* (Washington, 1970); T. Langner, "A

Twenty-two Item Screening Score of Psychiatric Symptoms Indicating Impairment," *Journal of Health and Human Behavior* 3-4 (1962-63); A. MacMillan, "The Health Opinion Survey: Technique for Estimating Prevalence of Psychoneurotic and Related Types of Disorder in Communities," *Psychological Reports* Monograph Supplement 7 (1957): 325-339; and S. Star, "The Screening of Psychoneurotics in the Army: Technical Development of Tests," in S. Stouffer et al., *Measurement and Prediction* (Princeton, 1950).

5. H. Dupuy et al., *Selected Symptoms of Psychological Distress, United States* (Washington, 1970), p. 1.

Chapter Six
Disability and Hospitalization

1. U.S. Public Health Service, *Current Estimates from the Health Interview Survey, United States - 1972* (Washington, 1973), p. 50 (hereafter, *Health Survey - 1972*).

2. U.S. Public Health Service, *Disability Components for an Index of Health* (Washington, 1971), p. 2. This definition was used by B. Wright, *Physical Disability–A Psychological Approach* (New York, 1960), p. 9.

3. Ibid. This definition was used by L. Haber, "Identifying the Disabled: Concepts and Methods in the Measurement of Disability," *Social Security Bulletin* (December, 1967).

4. *Health Survey - 1972*, p. 50.

5. Ibid., p. 51.

6. Ibid.

7. Ibid.

8. Ibid., p. 54.

9. Ibid.

10. Ibid., pp. 51-52.

11. Ibid., p. 52.

12. Ibid., p. 51.

13. U.S. Bureau of Prisons, Federal Prison Industries, Inc., *Board of Directors Annual Report, 1972* (Washington, 1973), pp. 8-9.

14. Ibid., p. 8.

15. *Health Survey - 1972*, p. 51.

16. See U.S. Public Health Survey, *Health Survey Procedure: Concepts, Questionnaire Development, and Definitions in the Health Interview Survey* (Washington, 1964), p. 45: disability means reduction of activity as a result of illness or injury; cosmetic plastic surgery is neither an illness or an injury.

17. See Chapter Eleven, Items Two and Three.

18. See *Health Survey - 1972*, p. 20.

19. Ibid., p. 22.

Chapter Seven
Medical Consultations

1. U.S. Public Health Service, *Current Estimates from the Health Interview Survey, United States - 1972* (Washington, 1973), p. 54. NOTE that services performed by MTA's to screen prisoner complaints prior to physician visits are *not* considered to be part of the physician visit unless a referral does result, in which case the MTA visit merges with the physician visit.
2. Ibid.
3. Ibid., p. 55.
4. Ibid.
5. Ibid.
6. Ibid.
7. Ibid.
8. Ibid. This data tends to diminish the hypothesis that imprisonment exerts a causal effect on the dental-visit rates of prisoners and parolees. See also, Chapter Six, footnote k.

Chapter Eight
Medical Treatment

1. U.S. Public Health Service, *Health Survey Procedure: Concepts, Questionnaire Development, and Definitions in the Health Interview Survey*, p. 50 (hereafter, *Health Survey Procedure*).
2. Ibid.
3. The U.S. Public Health Service does not tabulate surgical procedures as operations if they are not performed while the patient is a hospital inpatient (ibid.).

Chapter Nine
Trends in Mortality and Aggravated Assault

1. Federal Bureau of Investigation, *Crime in the United States: Uniform Crime Reports - 1971* (Washington, 1972), p. 76. This conflicts slightly with 486 homicides and a rate of 12.3 per 100,000 population reported by State of Tennessee, Department of Public Health, *Annual Bulletin of Vital Statistics for the Year 1971* (Nashville, 1973), p. 38.
2. State of Tennesee, Department of Public Health, *Annual Bulletin of Vital Statistics for the Year 1971* (Nashville, 1973), p. 38.
3. Ibid., p. 15.

4. Federal Bureau of Investigation, *Crime in the United States, Uniform Crime Reports - 1972* (Washington, 1973), pp. 78-94 and 218-220.

5. Ibid., p. 76.

Chapter Ten
Implications of the Study

1. See T. Langner and S. Michael, *Life Stress and Mental Health* (Glencoe, 1963); and G. Moss, *Illness, Immunity and Social Interaction: The Dynamics of Biosocial Resonation* (New York, 1973).

2. See M. Tyndel and J. Rutherdale, "The Hospital Addiction (Munchausen) Syndrome and Alcoholism," *International Journal of the Addictions* 8 (1973): 121-126.

3. R. Asher, "Manchausen's Syndrome," *Lancet* I (1951), p. 339.

4. M. Enoch, W. Trethowan, and J. Barker, *Some Uncommon Psychiatric Syndromes* (Bristol, 1967).

5. See note 2.

Bibliography

Bibliography

A. On Prisons

Adelson, L., Huntington, R., and Reay, D. "A Prisoner is Dead: A Survey of 91 Sudden and Unexpected Deaths which Occurred while Decedent was in either Police Custody or Penal Detention," *Police* 13 (1968): 49.

American Bar Association. *Minimum Standards for Criminal Justice: Sentencing Alternatives and Procedures.* Chicago: American Bar Association, 1968.

American Friends' Service Committee. *Struggle for Justice–A Report on Crime and Punishment in America.* New York: Hill and Hill, 1971.

American Law Institute. *Model Penal Code.* Philadelphia: American Law Institute, 1962.

Anzel, D. "Medical Care in Three Prisons in California," *American Journal of Corrections* 29 (1967): 13.

Attica: The Official Report of the New York State Special Commission on Attica. New York: Bantam, 1972.

Bakal, Yitzhak, ed. *Closing Correctional Institutions.* Boston: D.C. Heath, 1973.

Bagdikian, B. and Dash, L. *The Shame of the Prisons.* New York: Simon and Schuster, 1972.

Barbash, J. "An Investigation of the Predictability of Prison Adjustment," (Ph.D. dissertation, Temple University, 1956). Ann Arbor: University Microfilms, 1956.

Besharov, D. and Mueller, G. "The Demands of the Inmates of Attica State Prison and The United Nations Standard Minimum Rules for the Treatment of Prisoners–A Comparison," 21 BUFFALO L. REV. 839 (1972).

Blumberg, A., ed. *Current Perspectives on Criminal Behavior.* New York: Knopf, 1974.

_______. *The Scales of Justice.* New Brunswick: Transaction Books, 1973.

Carter, R., Glaser, D., and Wilkins, L. *Correctional Institutions.* New York: Lippincott, 1972.

Clemmer, D. *The Prison Community.* New York: Rinehart, 1958.

Cohen, F. "The Discovery of Prison Reform," 21 BUFFALO L. REV. 855 (1972).

Commission on Uniform State Law, "The Uniform Act on the Status of Convicted Persons," *Handbook of the National Conference of Commissioners on Uniform State Law.* Washington: Commission on Uniform State Law, 1964.

Cressy, D. "Limits on Organization of Treatment in the Modern Prison," in Cloward, *Theoretical Studies in the Social Organization of Prisons.* New York: Social Science Research Group, 1960.

"Crime and Punishment–A Prison Service Viewpoint," *Prison Officers' Magazine* 61 (1971): 305.

Cull, J. and Hardy. R. *Fundamentals of Criminal Behavior and Correctional Systems.* Springfield: Thomas, 1973.

Denzin, N. "Collective Behavior in Total Institutions: The Case of the Mental Hospital and the Prison," Revision of a paper presented to the 62d annual meeting of the American Sociological Association and the Society for the Study of Social Problems, San Francisco, August 27-31, 1967.

Eaton, J. *Prisons in Israel.* Pittsburgh: University of Pittsburgh Press, 1964.

Emery, F. *Freedom and Justice within Walls: The Bristol Prison Experiment.* London: Tavistock, 1970.

European Commission of Human Rights. *Human Rights in Prison.* Strasbourg: Council of Europe, 1970.

European Committee on Crime Problems. *The Effectiveness of Punishment and Other Methods of Treatment.* Strasbourg: Council of Europe, 1967.

Experimental Manpower Lab. for Correction, Rehabilitation Research Foundation. *A Manual for the Use of the Environmental Deprivation Scale (EDS) in Corrections: The Prediction of Criminal Behavior.* Elmore, Alabama: Draper Correctional Center, 1972.

Glaser, D. *The Effectiveness of a Prison and Parole System.* Indianapolis: Bobbs-Merrill, 1969.

Hirschkop, P. and Millemann, R. "The Unconstitutionality of Prison Life," 55 VA. L. REV. 795 (1969).

Hoffa, J. "Prison," *The Saturday Evening Post* (October, 1974): 45-46.

House of Representatives, Select Committee on Crime, "Reform of Our Correctional Systems," 93d Congress, 1st Session, House Report nos. 93-329. Washington: U.S. Government Printing Office, 1973.

International Commission of Jurists, *Standard Minimum Rules for the Treatment of Prisoners*, Report Submitted to the Fourth United Nations Conference on the Prevention of Crime and the Treatment of Offenders, 17-26 August 1970, Kyoto, Japan.

Kansas Association for Mental Health, Committee on Penal Reform. *A Citizens' Study of the Kansas Penal System.* Overland Park: Kansas Association for Mental Health, 1970.

Mathiesen, T. *The Defences of the Weak: A Sociological Study of a Norwegian Correctional Institution.* London: Tavistock, 1965.

_______. "The Sociology of Prisoners and Problems for Future Research," *British Journal of Sociology* 17 (1966): 360.

National Advisory Commission on Criminal Justice Standards and Goals. *A National Strategy to Reduce Crime.* Washington: U.S. Government Printing Office, 1973.

_______. *Report on Corrections.* Washington: U.S. Government Printing Office, 1973.

Ohm, A. *Personlich Keitswandlungen unter Freiheitsetzung. Ausklarungen von Strafen und Massnahmen.* Berlin: Walter de Gruyter, 1964.

Radzinowicz, L. and Wolfgang, M., eds. *Crime and Justice:* vol. 3: *The Criminal in Confinement.* New York: Basic Books, 1971.

Sellin, T. "Homicides and Assaults in American Prisons, 1964," *Acta criminologicae et medicinae legalis Japonica* 31 (1965): 1.

Sindwani, K. and Reckless, W. "Prisoners' Perceptions of the Impact of Institutional Stay," *Criminology* 10 (1973): 461-471.

Sutherland, E. and Sellin, T. *Prisons of Tomorrow.* Philadelphia: American Academy of Arts and Sciences, 1931.

Sykes, G. and Messinger, S. "The Inmate Social System," in Cloward, *Theoretical Studies in Social Organization of the Prison.* New York: Social Science Research Group, 1960.

Tappan, P. *Crime, Justice, and Correction.* New York: McGraw-Hill, 1960.

United States Department of Justice, Law Enforcement Assistance Administration. *New Environments for the Incarcerated.* Washington: U.S. Government Printing Office, 1972.

_______. *Prevention of Violence in Correctional Institutions.* Washington: U.S. Government Printing Office, 1973.

_______. *The Change Process in Criminal Justice.* (Report of the Fourth Symposium on Law Enforcement Science and Technology, May 1-3, 1972.) Washington: U.S. Government Printing Office, 1972.

Wilkins, L. *Social Deviance.* Englewood Cliffs: Prentice-Hall, 1965.

B. Historical

Abel, S. *The Hospitals: 1800-1948.* London: Heinemann, 1964.

Cohen, A. et al., eds. *The Sutherland Papers.* Bloomington: Indiana University Press, 1965.

Commission on Lunacy. *Report on Insanity and Idiocy in Massachusetts.* Boston: Wm. White Printer to the State, 1855.

Howard, J. *The State of the Prisons.* New York: Dutton, 1929.

Lewis, W. *From Newgate to Dannemora: The Rise of the Penitentiary in New York, 1791-1848.* Ithaca: Cornell University Press, 1965.

C. Epidemiological and Medicosociological

Abramson, J. et al. "Cornell Medical Index as a Health Measure in Epidemiological Studies: A Test of the Validity of a Health Questionnaire," *British Journal of Preventive and Social Medicine* 19 (1965): 103-110.

American Medical Association. *Proposal for a Program to Improve Medical Care and Health Services for the Inmates of the Nation's Jails and Prisons and Juvenile Detention Facilities.* Chicago: American Medical Association, 1973.

American Medical Association. *Medical Care in United States Jails: A 1972 A.M.A. Survey*. Chicago: American Medical Association, 1973.

Anderson, O. *The Uneasy Equilibrium: Private and Public Financing of Health Services in the United States, 1875-1965*. New Haven: College and University Press, 1968.

_______. "Patterns of Use of Health Services," in Freeman, et al., eds. *Handbook of Medical Sociology*. Englewood Cliffs: Prentice-Hall, 1972.

_______. "The Utilization of Health Services," in Freeman, et al., eds. *Handbook of Medical Sociology*. Englewood Cliffs, Prentice-Hall, 1972.

Anderson, O. and Seacat, M. *The Behavioral Scientists and Research in the Health Field: A Questionnaire Survey*. New York: Health Information Foundation, 1957.

Antonovsky, A. "Social Class and Illness: A Reconsideration," *Sociological Inquiry* 37 (1967): 311-322.

Baker, J. "Present Level of Medical Care for Prisoners–State and Local Systems," *Report of the 1973 National Medicolegal Symposium*. Chicago: American Bar Association, 1974.

Baker, T. "Problems in Measuring the Influence of Economic Levels of Morbidity," *American Journal of Public Health* 56 (1966): 499-507.

Barker, R. et al., "Adjustment to Physical Handicap and Illness: A Survey of the Social Psychology of Physique and Disability," *Social Science Research Council Bulletin*. (1953): 55.

Belknap, I. *Human Problems of a State Mental Hospital*. New York: McGraw-Hill, 1956.

Bierman, P. et al. "Health Services Research in Great Britain," *Milbank Memorial Fund Quarterly* 36 (1968): 9-102.

Bruhn, J. "Comparative Study of Attempted Suicides and Psychiatric Outpatients," *British Journal of Preventive and Social Medicine* 17 (1963): 197-201.

Burney, L. et al. "Implications for Comprehensive Health Care," *Milbank Memorial Fund Quarterly* 32 (1964): 45-56.

Calhoun, J. "Population Density and Social Pathology," *Scientific American* 206 (1962): 139-148.

Cartwright, A. *Human Relations and Hospital Care*. London: Routledge and Kegan Paul, 1964.

Davis, M. "Variations in Patients' Compliance with Doctors' Advice: An Empirical Analysis of Patterns of Communication," *American Journal of Public Health* (1968): 58.

Dorn, H. "Methods of Measuring Incidence and Prevalence of Disease," *American Journal of Public Health* 31 (1951): 271-278.

_______. "Mortality," in Hause and Duncan, eds. *The Study of Population*. Chicago: University of Chicago Press, 1959.

Dreitzal, H., ed. *The Social Organization of Health*. New York: MacMillan, 1971.

Dunne, J. "Legal Enforcement of Prisoners' Health Care Rights," *Report of the 1973 National Medicolegal Symposium.* Chicago: American Bar Association, 1974.

Elinson, J. "Methods of Sociomedical Research," in Freeman, et al., eds. *Handbook of Medical Sociology.* Englewood Cliffs: Prentice-Hall, 1972.

Epstein, L. "Validity of a Questionnaire for the Diagnosis of Peptic Ulcer in an Ethnically Heterogeneous Population," *Journal of Chronic Diseases* 22 (1969): 49-55.

Farr, W. *Vital Statistics.* London: H.M. Office of the Sanitary Institute, 1885.

Freeman, H., et al. *Handbook of Medical Sociology.* Englewood Cliffs: Prentice-Hall, 1972.

Graham, D. and Stevenson, I. "Disease as a Response to Life Stress: The Nature of the Evidence," in Lief, et al., eds. *The Psychological Basis of Medical Practice.* New York: Harper and Row, 1958.

Harrison, B. "A Plan to Improve Health Care in Our Jails," *Report of the 1973 Medicolegal Symposium.* Chicago: American Bar Association, 1974.

Kadushin, C. "Social Class and the Experience of Ill Health," *Social Inquiry* 34 (1964): 67-80.

Kahne, M. "Suicides in Mental Hospitals: A Study of the Effects of Personnel and Patient Turnover," *Journal of Health and Social Behavior* 9 (1968): 255-266.

Kelly, T. and Schieber, G. *Factors Affecting Medical Services Utilization: A Behavioral Approach.* Washington: The Urban Institute, 1972.

Little, A. "An 'Expectancy' Estimate of Hospitalization Rates for Mental Illness in England and Wales," *British Journal of Sociology* 16 (1965): 221-231.

Luck, G., et al. *Patients, Hospitals, and Operational Research.* London: Tavistock, 1971.

Mangus, A. "Medical Sociology: A Study of the Social Components of Illness and of Health," *Sociology and Social Research* 39 (1955): 158-164.

Marks, J., et al. "Ideology, Social Change, and Violence in a Mental Hospital," *Journal of Health and Human Behavior* 4 (1963): 258-266.

Marks, R. "Social Stress and Cardiovascular Disease: Factors Involving Social and Demographic Characteristics," *Milbank Memorial Fund Quarterly* 45 (1967): 51-108.

McNerney, W., et al. *Hospital and Medical Economics: A Study of Policies, Services, Costs, and Methods of Control.* Chicago: Hospital Research and Educational Trust, 1962.

Moriyama, I. "Vital and Health Statistics of the Future," *Milbank Memorial Fund Quarterly* 44 (1966): 318-327.

Roessler, R. and Greenfield, N., eds. *Physiological Correlates of Psychological Disorders.* Madison: University of Wisconsin Press, 1962.

Stein, L. "Morbidity in a London General Practice: Social and Demographic Data," *British Journal of Preventive and Social Medicine* 14 (1960): 9-15.

Steinfeld, J. "Present Level of Medical Care for Prisoners–Federal System," *Report of the 1973 National Medicolegal Symposium.* Chicago: American Bar Association, 1974.

Taylor, P. and Fairrie, A. "Chronic Disabilities and Capacity for Work. A Study of 3,299 Men Aged 16-64 in a General Practice and an Oil Refinery," *British Journal of Preventive and Social Medicine* 22 (1968): 86-93.

Webb, R. *Medical and Health Care in Jails, Prisons, and Other Correctional Facilities–A Compilation of Standards and Materials.* Washington: American Bar Association Resource Center on Correctional Law and Legal Services, 1973.

Weiss, J. "Psychological Factors in Stress and Disease," *Scientific American* 226 (1972): 104-113.

Witts, L., ed. *Medical Surveys and Clinical Trials.* London: Oxford University Press, 1959.

D. Psychiatric

Altman, I. and Haythorn, W. "Interpersonal Exchange in Isolation," *Sociometry* 28 (1965): 411-426.

American Psychiatric Association. *A Psychiatric Glossary.* Washington: American Psychiatric Association Publications Services, 1969.

_______. *Diagnostic and Statistical Manual of Mental Disorders*, 2d ed. Washington: American Psychiatric Association, 1968.

Bille, M. "The Influence of Distance on Admissions to Mental Hospitals," *Acta psychiatrica Scandinavia* 39 (1963): 226-233.

Hollingshed, A. and Redlich, R. *Social Class and Mental Illness.* New York: Wiley, 1958.

Leighton, D., et al. "The Character of Dangerous Psychiatric Symptoms in Selected Communities," in *The Sterling County Study of Psychiatric Disorder and Socio-Cultural Environment*, vol. 3. New York: Basic Books, 1963.

Menninger, K. *The Vital Balance: The Life Process in Mental Health and Illness.* New York: Viking Press, 1963.

Rappeport, J. *The Clinical Evaluation of the Dangerousness of the Mentally Ill.* Springfield: Thomas, 1967.

Srole, L., Langner, T., and Michael, S. *Mental Health in the Metropolis: The Midtown Manhattan Study*, vol. 1. New York: McGraw-Hill, 1962.

Szasz, T. *The Manufacture of Madness: A Comparative Study of the Inquisition and the Mental Health Movement.* New York: Harper and Row, 1970.

E. On Suicide

Dahlgren, K. *On suicide and Attempted Suicide.* Lund: Lindstadts, 1945.

Dublin, L. *Suicide: A Sociological and Statistical Study.* New York: Ronald Press, 1963.

Henry, A. and Short, J. *Suicide and Homicide.* Glencoe: The Free Press, 1954.

Johnson, E. *Correlates of Felon Self-Mutilations.* Carbondale: Center for the Study of Crime, Delinquency, and Corrections, Southern Illinois University, 1969.

"Self-Mutilation in a Prison Mental Hospital," *Journal of Social Therapy* 13 (1967): 133.

Toch, H. "Man in Isolation: Human Breakdowns in Prison." Chicago: 1975, Aldine-Atherton.

Tyndel, M. and Rutherdale, J. "The Hospital Addiction (Manchausen) Syndrome and Alcoholism," *International Journal of Addictions* 8 (1973): 121-126.

van Schumann, H. "Homosexualität und Selbstmord," *Kriminologische Schriftenrelhe aus der Deutschen kriminologischen Gesellschaft* 17 (1965).

Wolfgang, M. "An Analysis of Homicide-Suicide," *Journal of Clinical and Experimental Psychopathology and Quarterly Review of Psychiatry and Neurology* 19 (1958): 208-218.

_______. "Suicide by Means of Victim-Precipitated Homicide," *Journal of Clinical and Experimental Psychopathology and Quarterly Review of Psychiatry and Neurology* 20 (1959): 335-349.

F. On Vital and Health Statistics

State of Tennessee, Department of Correction. *Annual Report: 1970-1971.* Nashville: State Printing Office, 1972.

_______. Annual Report: 1972-1973. Nashville: State Printing Office, 1974.

State of Tennessee, Department of Labor. *Annual Report for the Fiscal Year Ending June 30, 1969.* Nashville: State Printing Office, 1970.

_______. *Annual Report of the Division of Workmen's Compensation for the Year Ending December 31, 1966.* Nashville: State Printing Office, 1967.

State of Tennessee, Department of Mental Health. *Annual Report: 1968-1969.* Nashville: State Printing Office, 1969.

State of Tennessee, Department of Public Health. *Annual Bulletin of Vital Statistics for the Year 1971.* Nashville: State Printing Office, 1972.

_______. *Annual Report of Hospitals and Related Facilities in Tennessee, 1970.* Nashville: State Printing Office, 1971.

_______. *Tennessee Morbidity Statistics, 1971.* Nashville: State Printing Office, 1972.

State of Tennessee, State Planning Commission. *Income and Employment in Tennessee.* Nashville: State Printing Office, 1970.

_______. *Tennessee 1960, 1970 Population, 1980 Projected Population, and Percent of Population Change for 1970-1980 by County.* Nashville: State Printing Office, 1972.

U.S. Bureau of Prisons, Federal Prison Industries. *Annual Report: 1972.* Washington: U.S. Government Printing Office, 1973.

U.S. Bureau of Prisons, Office of Research and Statistics. *National Prisoner*

Statistics: Prisoners in State and Federal Institutions for Adult Felons. Washington: U.S. Government Printing Office, 1972.

_______. *National Prisoner Statistics: State Prisoners: Admissions and Releases, 1970.* Washington: U.S. Government Printing Office, 1973.

_______. *Statistical Report: Fiscal Year, 1970.* Washington: U.S. Government Printing Office, 1971.

U.S. Department of Justice, Law Enforcement Assistance Administration. *Survey of Inmates in Local Jails 1972–Advance Report.* Washington: U.S. Government Printing Office, 1974.

U.S. Public Health Service. Publication no. 1,000, s. 1, no. 2. *Health Survey Procedure: Concepts, Questionnaire Development, and Definitions in the Health Interview Survey.* Washington: U.S. Government Printing Office, 1964.

_______. s. 10, no. 17. *Chronic Conditions and Activity Limitation, United States, July 1961-June 1963.* Washington: U.S. Government Printing Office, 1965.

_______. no. 57. *Types of Injuries, Incidence and Associated Disability, United States, July 1965-June 1967.* Washington: U.S. Government Printing Office, 1969.

_______. no. 72. *Current Estimates from the Health Interview Survey, United States–1970.* Washington: U.S. Government Printing Office, 1972.

_______. no. 74. *Health Characteristics of Low-Income Persons.* Washington: U.S. Government Printing Office, 1972.

_______. no. 77. *Acute Conditions, Incidence and Associated Disability, United States, July 1968-June 1970.* Washington: U.S. Government Printing Office, 1972.

_______. no. 79. *Current Estimates from the Health Interview Survey, United States–1971.* Washington: U.S. Government Printing Office, 1973.

_______. no. 80. *Limitation of Activity Due to Chronic Conditions, United States, 1969 and 1970.* Washington: U.S. Government Printing Office, 1973.

_______. no. 83. *Prevalence of Selected Chronic Digestive Conditions, United States, July-December 1968.* Washington, U.S. Government Printing Office, 1973.

_______. no. 84. *Prevalence of Selected Chronic Respiratory Conditions, United States, 1970.* Washington: U.S. Government Printing Office, 1973.

_______. no. 86. *Health Characteristics by Geographic Region, Large Metropolitan Areas, and Other Places of Residence, United States, 1969-70.* Washington: U.S. Government Printing Office, 1974.

_______. no. 89. *Edentulous Persons, United States–1971.* Washington: U.S. Government Printing Office, 1974.

_______. no. 92. *Prevalence of Chronic Skin and Musculoskeletal Conditions, United States–1969.* Washington: U.S. Government Printing Office, 1974.

_______. s. 11, no. 1. *Cycle I of the Health Examination Survey: Sample and*

Response, United States, 1960-1962. Washington: U.S. Government Printing Office, 1964.

______. no. 3. *Binocular Visual Acuity of Adults, United States, 1960-1962.* Washington: U.S. Government Printing Office, 1964.

______. no. 6. *Heart Disease in Adults, United States, 1960-1962.* Washington: U.S. Government Printing Office, 1964.

______. no. 7. *Selected Dental Findings in Adults, by Age, Race, and Sex, United States, 1960-1962.* Washington: U.S. Government Printing Office, 1965.

______. no. 12. *Periodontal Disease in Adults, United States, 1960-1962.* Washington: U.S. Government Printing Office, 1965.

______. no. 13. *Hypertention and Hypertensive Heart Disease in Adults, United States, 1960-1962.* Washington: U.S. Government Printing Office, 1966.

______. no. 15. *Prevalence of Osteoarthritis in Adults, by Age, Sex, Race, and Geographic Area, United States, 1960-1962.* Washington: U.S. Government Printing Office, 1966.

______. no. 16. *Oral Hygiene in Adults, United States, 1960-1962.* Washington: U.S. Government Printing Office, 1966.

______. no. 17. *Rheumatoid Arthritis in Adults, United States, 1960-1962.* Washington: U.S. Government Printing Office, 1966.

______. no. 23. *Decayed, Missing, and Filled Teeth in Adults, United States, 1960-1962.* Washington: U.S. Government Printing Office, 1967.

______. no. 25. *Binocular Visual Activity of Adults, by Region and Selected Demographic Characteristics, United States, 1960-1962.* Washington: U.S. Government Printing Office, 1967.

______. no. 28. *History and Examination Findings Related to Visual Acuity Among Adults, United States, 1960-1962.* Washington: U.S. Government Printing Office, 1968.

______. no. 33. *Selected Examination Findings Related to Periodontal Disease Among Adults, United States, 1960-1962.* Washington: U.S. Government Printing Office, 1969.

______. no. 37. *Selected Symptoms of Psychological Distress, United States.* Washington: U.S. Government Printing Office, 1970.

______. no. 38. *Parity and Hypertension.* Washington: U.S. Government Printing Office, 1972.

G. Methodology Bibliography

Blalock, H. *Social Statistics.* New York: McGraw-Hill, 1972.

Desmarez, J. ((Contribution a l'étude de la méthodologie medicolégale, médico-sociologique et criminologique)), *Revue de Droit Pénal et de Criminologie* 45 (1965): 887-932.

Edwards, A. *Statistical Methods.* New York: Holt and Winston, 1967.

"Epidemiological Methods in the Study of Chronic Diseases," *Report of World Health Organization (WHO) Expert Committee on Health Statistics.* WHO Technical Reports, s. 365 (1967): 1-31.

Fisher, R. and Yates, F. *Statistical Tables for Biological, Agricultural, and Medical Research.* Edinburgh: Oliver and Boyd, 1948.

Mannheim, H. and Wilkins, L. *Prediction Methods in Relation to Borstal Training.* London: H.M. Stationery Office, 1955.

Mueller, J., Schuessler, K., and Costner, H. *Statistical Reasoning in Sociology.* Boston: Houghton-Mifflin, 1970.

National Institute of Mental Health. *Crime and Delinquency Research in Selected European Countries.* Washington: U.S. Government Printing Office, 1971.

Pressat, R. *Demographic Analysis–Methods, Results, Applications.* Chicago: Aldine-Atherton, 1972.

State of Connecticut, Department of Correction. *Data Processing: IBM Application Brief.* New York: IBM World Trade Corporation, 1972.

Stockwell, E. "Use of Socioeconomic Status as a Demographic Variable," *Public Health Report* 81 (1966): 961-966.

Swaroop, S. *Introduction to Health Statistics.* Edinburgh: Livingstone, 1960.

Tull, D. and Albaum, G. *Survey Research–A Decisional Approach.* New York: Intext Educational Publishers, 1973.

Twain, D., Harlow, E., and Merwin, D. *Research and Human Services.* New York: Research and Development Center, 1970.

Tyler, L. *Tests and Measurements.* Englewood Cliffs: Prentice-Hall, 1971.

U.N. Handbook on Vital Statistics Methods. New York: Statistical Office of the United Nations, 1955.

U.S. Department of Justice, Law Enforcement Assistance Administration. *Correctional Records Information System of the District of Columbia Department of Corrections–System Description.* Washington: U.S. Government Printing Office, 1972.

U.S. Public Health Service. *Health Interview Survey Interviewer's Manual.* Washington: U.S. Government Printing Office, 1970.

_______. *Health Interview Survey Medical Coding Manual and The Short Index.* Washington: U.S. Government Printing Office, 1969.

_______. Publication no. 1,000, s. 2, no. 38. *Estimation and Sampling Variance in the Health Interview Survey.* Washington: U.S. Government Printing Office, 1970.

_______. no. 42. *Disability Components for an Index of Health.* Washington: U.S. Government Printing Office, 1971.

_______. no. 44. *Quality Control in a National Health Examination Survey.* Washington: U.S. Government Printing Office, 1972.

_______. no. 48. *Interviewing Methods in the Health Interview Survey.* Washington: U.S. Government Printing Office, 1972.

_______. no. 51. *Annotated Bibliography on Robustness Studies of Statistical Procedures.* Washington: U.S. Government Printing Office, 1972.

_______. no. 52. *Reliability of Estimates with Alternative Cluster Sizes in the National Health Survey.* Washington: U.S. Government Printing Office, 1973.

_______. no. 53. *Approximate Tests of Independence in Contingency Tables from Complex Stratified Cluster Samples.* Washington: U.S. Government Printing Office, 1973.

_______. no. 54. *Quality Control and Measurement of Nonsampling Error in the Health Interview Survey.* Washington: U.S. Government Printing Office, 1973.

_______. no. 54. *The Prediction Approach to Finite Population Sampling Theory: Application to the Hospital Discharge Survey.* Washington: U.S. Government Printing Office, 1973.

_______. no. 59. *Vision Test Validation Study for the Health Examination Survey among Youths 12-17 Years.* Washington: U.S. Government Printing Office, 1973.

_______. no. 61. *National Ambulatory Medical Care Survey: Background and Methodology.* Washington: U.S. Government Printing Office, 1974.

_______. no. 63. *The National Ambulatory Medical Care Survey: Symptom Classification.* Washington: U.S. Government Printing Office, 1974.

_______. s. C., no. 3. *1970 Census Data Used to Indicate Areas with Different Potentials for Mental Health and Related Problems: Methodology Reports.* Washington: U.S. Government Printing Office, 1972.

Wallace, H. and Dooley, V. "Availability and Usefulness of Selected Health and Socioeconomic Data for Community Planning," *American Journal of Public Health* 57 (1967): 762-771.

Welkowitz, J., et al. *Introductory Statistics for the Behavioral Sciences.* New York: Academic Press, 1971.

Wheeler, S. *On Record: Files and Dossiers in American Life.* New York: Russell Sage Foundation, 1969.

Wilkins, L. *Evaluation of Penal Measures.* New York: Random House, 1969.

_______. "Trends and Projections in Social Control Systems," *Annals of the American Academy of Political and Social Science* 381 (1969), 125.

_______. "Variety, Conformity, Control, and Research: Some Dilemmas of Social Defence," *International Review of Criminal Policy* 28 (1970): 18-23.

Wilkins, L. and MacNaughton, P. "New Prediction and Classification Methods in Criminology," *Journal of Research in Crime and Delinquency* 1 (1964): 19-32.

Wolfgang, M., ed. *Studies in Homicide.* New York: Harper and Row, 1967.

Woods, H. and Russell, W. *An Introduction to Medical Statistics.* London: Staples Press, 1936.

Index

About the Author

David A. Jones is a faculty member at the Institute of Criminal Law and Procedure, Georgetown University Law Center in Washington, D.C., where he is Deputy Director of the Project on Plea Bargaining in the United States. In addition, he is an Adjunct Professor at the Center for the Administration of Justice, The American University; and General Counsel for the National Justice Committee. Professor Jones is a member of the Bars of Massachusetts, New York, the District of Columbia, and the Supreme Court of the United States. He holds a Ph.D. from the School of Criminal Justice, State University of New York at Albany; a J.D. from Union University; and an A.B. from Clark University. Dr. Jones has taught at The University of Tennessee and at the State University of New York, and he has served as a legal consultant to the New Hampshire Governor's Commission on Crime and Delinquency.